Approaches to Teaching
Mann's *Death in Venice*
and Other Short Fiction

Approaches to Teaching World Literature

Joseph Gibaldi, series editor

For a complete listing of titles,
see the last pages of this book.

Approaches to Teaching Mann's

Death in Venice

and Other

Short Fiction

Edited by

Jeffrey B. Berlin

Consultant Editor
Richard H. Lawson

The Modern Language Association of America
New York   1992

©1992 by The Modern Language Association of America
All rights reserved. Printed in the United States of America
Second printing 2001

For information about obtaining permission to reprint material from
MLA book publications, send your request by mail (see address below),
e-mail (permissions@mla.org), or fax (646 458-0030).

Library of Congress Cataloging-in-Publication Data

Approaches to teaching Mann's Death in Venice and other short fiction
/ edited by Jeffrey B. Berlin, consultant editor, Richard H. Lawson.
    p.   cm. — (Approaches to teaching world literature ; 43)
Includes bibliographical references and index.
ISBN 0-87352-709-7 (cloth)   ISBN 0-87352-710-0 (pbk.)
1. Mann, Thomas, 1875–1955.   Tod in Venedig.   2. German
literature—Study and teaching. I. Berlin, Jeffrey B.   II. Lawson,
Richard H.   III. Series.
PT2625.A44T6416   1992
833'.912—dc20   92-16888

ISSN 1059-1133

Cover illustration of the paperback edition: *Nocturne*, by James Whistler.
Courtesy of Editorial Photocolor Archives. © Sotheby Parke-Bernet.

Set in Caledonia and Bodoni.

Published by The Modern Language Association of America
26 Broadway, New York, New York 10004-1789
www.mla.org

CONTENTS

PREFACE TO THE SERIES

In *The Art of Teaching* Gilbert Highet wrote, "Bad teaching wastes a great deal of effort, and spoils many lives which might have been full of energy and happiness." All too many teachers have failed in their work, Highet argued, simply "because they have not thought about it." We hope that the Approaches to Teaching World Literature series, sponsored by the Modern Language Association's Publications Committee, will not only improve the craft—as well as the art—of teaching but also encourage serious and continuing discussion of the aims and methods of teaching literature.

The principal objective of the series is to collect within each volume different points of view on teaching a specific literary work, a literary tradition, or a writer widely taught at the undergraduate level. The preparation of each volume begins with a wide-ranging survey of instructors, thus enabling us to include in the volume the philosophies and approaches, thoughts and methods of scores of experienced teachers. The result is a sourcebook of material, information, and ideas on teaching the subject of the volume to undergraduates.

The series is intended to serve nonspecialists as well as specialists, inexperienced as well as experienced teachers, graduate students who wish to learn effective ways of teaching as well as senior professors who wish to compare their own approaches with the approaches of colleagues in other schools. Of course, no volume in the series can ever substitute for erudition, intelligence, creativity, and sensitivity in teaching. We hope merely that each book will point readers in useful directions; at most each will offer only a first step in the long journey to successful teaching.

Joseph Gibaldi
Series Editor

PREFACE TO THE VOLUME

Readers are predictably fascinated by the work and world of Thomas Mann (1875–1955), the 1929 Nobel Prize laureate for literature. It is not surprising then that Mann's writings are continually and widely incorporated in undergraduate and graduate college and university courses for literature and nonliterature majors. What is surprising is that, despite the overwhelming number of critical studies on Thomas Mann, no pedagogically oriented volume about him has appeared in English.

This volume offers pedagogical essays written by experienced and successful instructors of Mann's short fiction. The essays focus primarily on Mann's *Tristan* (1903), *Tonio Kröger* (1903), and *Death in Venice* (*Der Tod in Venedig*, 1912). We chose these texts because, according to the survey that preceded preparation of this volume, they are Mann's most frequently taught short works. All are rewarding to teach.

This book is divided into two basic sections. The first discusses materials useful to the instructor and student of Mann's short fiction: editions and translations, reference works, background materials, general introductions and critical studies, and, finally, audiovisual materials. It is primarily based on information gathered from an international survey of instructors actively teaching Mann. The second part, "Approaches," contains fourteen essays, organized into two categories: "General Issues" and "Teaching Individual Texts." It is hoped that beginning and advanced students as well as instructors will find the essays not only illuminating but also pedagogically sound, providing clear explanations of effective ways to introduce, develop, and elucidate Mann's short fiction.

The majority of essays were written by instructors teaching at colleges or universities across the United States, but essays by teachers in Canada and England have also been included. Together with the "Materials" section, then, the "Approaches" section offers a broad, international perspective on how Mann is being taught.

Like the other volumes in the MLA series, this text is not intended to be the definitive prescription of how to teach its subject. A volume such as this cannot encompass the full oeuvre of a writer so productive and accomplished as Mann. *The Buddenbrooks* (1901), *The Magic Mountain* (1924), *Doctor Faustus* (1947), the *Joseph* novels (1933–43), and *Felix Krull* (1954) are all singular examples of his genius, enhanced by his other novels, short fiction, and essays. The writer's exile years are especially remarkable. Mann did not idly observe world events but was politically active as an astute and discerning commentator. His courageous lectures and broadcasts and his penetrating, effective essays were directed toward the betterment of humanity, in vehement opposition to National Socialism. The purpose and scope of this volume, however, do not permit more than tangential reference to these writings and activities.

As our survey reveals, Mann is widely studied in courses devoted to great books, general humanities, and modern literature in translation, in addition to the many courses for students of German literature. *Approaches to Teaching Mann's* Death in Venice *and Other Short Fiction* will benefit undergraduate and graduate students, but it is primarily designed for instructors teaching Mann in these various contexts. While instructors should encourage students to read Mann's works in the original German whenever possible, all quotations are given here in English. In this regard, parenthetical page numbers in the text refer to the Bantam edition, Death in Venice *and Other Stories,* translated by David Luke. Parenthetical page numbers given in the text with a volume number refer to Thomas Mann, *Gesammelte Werke in dreizehn Bänden.* Unless otherwise noted, all other translations are by the respective contributors. Mann's spelling of Lisaweta Iwanowna in *Tonio Kröger* is used throughout this volume.

A book such as this is, of course, the product of many minds. Invaluable information was provided by the survey of instructors teaching Mann. It is a pleasure to formally thank the people who took the time to respond. Additionally, I have profited from many conversations with all the contributors; their important essays here are of course appreciated. Numerous other individuals—not all of whom could be acknowledged, unfortunately—gave essential information and assistance.

I would especially like to thank Joseph Gibaldi, the series editor, for his exceptional encouragement, advice, and support, as well as the members of the MLA Publications Committee for their sponsorship. The comments of these members and of the anonymous consultant readers were of immense value, as was the counsel, at various stages of manuscript preparation, of the following: Manfred Dierks, Volkmar Hansen, Anthony Heilbut, Esther H. Lesér, David Luke, Harry Matter, and Georg Potempa. Similarly, I am particularly grateful to Elisabeth Mann Borgese, Hans Jörgen Gerlach, Gerald Gillespie, Ilsedore B. Jonas, Klaus W. Jonas, Donald A. Prater, Christa Sammons, Murray H. Sherman, and Harry Zohn. Alice von Kahler discussed with me on many occasions her husband's correspondence with Mann; her reminiscences and kindness have always been inspiring and much appreciated, as were my numerous visits with the late Mirjam Beer-Hofmann Lens, whose portrayal of the period and many courtesies I shall always treasure.

Recognition is due Bantam Books and its associate editor Linda Lowenthal for many favors. Others who have helped me include Knut Beck,

Wolfgang Mertz, and Gabriele Ullmann, all of S. Fischer Verlag; Beate Mnich of Kröner Verlag; William A. Koshland of Knopf Publishing Company; the Van Pelt Library at the University of Pennsylvania; and the staff of the Mann Collection at Princeton and of the Beinecke Rare Book and Manuscript Library at Yale.

It is an honor to acknowledge Golo Mann for his interest and support, as well as Hans Wysling and his staff at the Thomas-Mann-Archiv der Eidgenössischen Technischen Hochschule in Zurich.

I am grateful to the administration at the Philadelphia College of Textiles and Science for its long-standing support. I am also indebted to Barry Cohen, Wilfred Frisby, Stanley J. Gorski, Barbara W. Lowry, and J. Thomas Vogel, all of our library, whose continual assistance in obtaining interlibrary loan materials was most helpful. I acknowledge, as well, my gratitude to Evelyn Minick, director of our college library. For favors at various stages I express appreciation to my colleagues William R. Brown, Charles W. Dewees, Paul Kerstetter, and Matthew London. Christian B. Kulczytzky, who long ago awakened my interest in Thomas Mann, remains today a colleague and friend.

To the consultant editor, Richard H. Lawson, who admirably fulfilled his role, as well as to my former and current students, I am indeed grateful. I owe special thanks to my parents and parents-in-law.

To my wife, Anne, and our children, Rachel and Sam, my *Dreigestirn*, I happily dedicate this volume. In every way they enthusiastically, patiently, and willingly supported the making of this book and my others.

JBB

Part One

MATERIALS

Editions and Translations

Almost all the survey respondents who teach *Death in Venice* in German use T. J. Reed's edition *Der Tod in Venedig*, which provides invaluable documents and commentary. Equally helpful is his Oxford University Press edition, which includes the text in German with commentary in English, but it is currently out of print. In the past, some instructors have used the volume edited by A. W. Hornsey (also out of print), which contains the German text, a short but helpful introduction, notes in English, and a brief German-English vocabulary list. Another choice has been the George Boyd and Henry Rosenwald edition, which similarly contains the German text, a valuable introduction, notes, a selective bibliography, and a German-English glossary. Although the work is also out of print, both it and the Hornsey volume may still be used as library reference materials.

No equivalent of Reed's *Death in Venice* edition exists for Mann's other short fiction. Many respondents rely on Elizabeth Wilkinson's edition of *Tonio Kröger*, which includes the German text and a thoughtful introduction as well as brief notes in English. Some instructors have used the now out-of-print edition by John A. Kelly, which has a few introductory observations, selective notes, and an extensive vocabulary list. Several instructors have chosen the moderately expensive but in-print Manesse Verlag *Meistererzählungen* (*Der Tod in Venedig*, *Tristan*, *Tonio Kröger*, and *Mario und der Zauberer*). Otherwise, instructors use the convenient and inexpensive Fischer Taschenbuch texts for the narrative works and selected essays (for *Tristan*, the Reclam edition is popular and also inexpensive).

The methodology of the 1980 edition of Mann's *Gesammelte Werke* is delineated by Peter de Mendelssohn, its editor, in his essay "Die Frankfurter Ausgabe der Gesammelten Werke." There is general agreement, however, that the 1974 *Gesammelte Werke in dreizehn Bänden*, of which eleven thousand copies were originally printed and that soon went out of print, is better than the 1980 edition. Indeed, scholarly interest in the 1974 edition may be a prime reason that it was reprinted in 1990. Hermann Kurzke defines the basic differences between these editions in his article "Das Elend der Frankfurter Thomas-Mann-Ausgabe" (see also Hans R. Vaget's review of *Nachträge*, which represents the last volume of the 1974 edition of the *Gesammelte Werke*, and Hartmut Steinecke's instructive review of volume thirteen of that edition). As the survey showed, some classes enjoy discussing the history and variety of editions. In this regard, Hans Wisskirchen provides a good sketch of the major collected editions that have appeared since 1922 ("Thomas-Mann"). Such discussion is augmented by considering the points expressed in Erich Mater's still instructive "Möglichkeiten und Grenzen einer historisch-kritischen Edition der Werke Thomas Manns" (see also Wysling's "Fünfundzwanzig Jahre Arbeit im Thomas-Mann-Archiv").

A significant number of newly found Mann essays, not included in the 1974 or 1980 editions, were published in Harry Matter's Aufbau Verlag edition, *Aufsätze, Reden, Essays*, which strives for completeness (see K. W. Jonas's and Kurzke's positive reviews of this edition). Thus far three volumes have been published, covering the years 1893 to 1925, but all are out of print. However, the reunification of Germany now permits Fischer Verlag to publish these "East German" volumes, and plans are under way for them to appear within the near future. Among other good features of Matter's edition is the inclusion of text variants. Subsequent volumes for the years 1926 to 1955 are in preparation for publication by Fischer.

Concerning translations, Mann observed in the preface to the volume *Stories of Three Decades*, a collection of his selected but most important short fiction in Helen Tracy Lowe-Porter's translation:

> It was a good and gratifying idea of my American publisher to present to the English-reading public a single volume containing . . . the short stories which I have written. . . . [T]o the author this edition gives peculiar pleasure, presenting as it does a survey of his activities in this field for three decades, a whole generation, almost a whole life-span of artist and man—an autobiography, as it were, in the guise of a fable.   (v)

The Lowe-Porter translation is usually designated as the "official" English-language version of Mann's work, but despite Mann's stamp of approval (he once termed it "extraordinarily sensitive and accomplished" [Thirlwall 4]), it contains inaccuracies, as various critics have shown (e.g., Koch-Emmery; Lesér; Luke; Mendel; Probst; Spann; Vaget [rev. of *Death in Venice*]; Withon). With the exception of Kenneth Burke's translation of *Death in Venice*, which only a small portion of the survey respondents use, for many years the Lowe-Porter translations of Mann's works have monopolized the market, together with *Stories of Three Decades* or the more popular and less expensive Death in Venice *and Seven Other Stories*. For a comparison of the Lowe-Porter and Burke translations, James A. Hayes's extensive "Method of Determining the Reliability of Literary Translations" provides instructors with a sound basis for class discussion.

David Luke's translations of *Death in Venice, Tonio Kröger, Tristan, Gladius Dei, The Joker, The Road to the Churchyard*, and *Little Herr Friedemann* were published in an edition by Bantam Books in October 1988. Those teachers who used Luke's 1970 volume of the same works (long out of print and not including *Death in Venice*, then still protected by copyright) recall his accuracy and excellence, although, as Meno Spann points out, "there are no flawless translations" (110), and one can point to some (though few) inaccuracies in Luke, too (see Vaget's review). Some instructors profitably compare the Luke rendition with those of Lowe-Porter and Burke to initiate discussion about the art and problems inherent in translations. Finally, despite the criticism of Lowe-Porter's translations, some instructors maintain that, for classroom purposes, her renditions remain the choice. At the same time, the apparent dismissal of Lowe-Porter's contribution to Mann studies has made some teachers quite vocal; their resentment is perhaps epitomized by the views of Henry Hatfield:

> I would instance [Lowe-Porter's] skill in rendering both the rhapsodic and the sardonic styles in *Tristan*, and the whole battery of styles in *The Magic Mountain*. While Luke is remarkably accurate and Mrs. Lowe-Porter is less so, she does, it seems to me, come closer to the rhythm, the melody, indeed the style of those narratives. . . . [She also] has a flair for the English language which makes the question of strict accuracy definitely secondary. . . . Mrs. Lowe-Porter states that in effect a rigidly literal translation may debase the original "to a sort of bastard English."

Hatfield concludes, "A synthesis of these two translators would be splendid but hardly possible" (rev. of *Death in Venice*).

Despite the criticism of Lowe-Porter's translations, then, her contribution must be duly acknowledged. Indeed, Lowe-Porter, along with Alfred A. Knopf, Mann's American publisher, brought Mann to the English-speaking world, a literary event that is discussed in Jeffrey B. Berlin's "On the Making of *The Magic Mountain*." In this article, which provides and evaluates correspondence not previously known to exist, the relationship between Mann, Knopf, and Lowe-Porter is redefined. See also John C. Thirlwall's useful but incomplete and sometimes inaccurate *In Another Language*, along with Klaus Jonas's tribute to her ("In Memoriam"). In 1990 the University of California Press reprinted Lowe-Porter's translation of Mann's *Lotte in Weimar* as well as his late work *The Black Swan* in the translation of Willard R. Trask. Both contain brief new introductions. Other out-of-print Mann works are being issued by the University of California Press.

Several of Mann's more important essays are available in translation, but most of the essay volumes are out of print or the essays are contained in somewhat obscure magazines or journals. Exceptions are a few new translations, notably Walter D. Morris's *Reflections of a Nonpolitical Man* and Patrick Carnegy's *Thomas Mann: Pro and contra Wagner*. Both are available in paperback. For some general remarks about the *Reflections*, several instructors use as a guide Walter Laqueur's "Artist in Politics," a review of this translation (see also Michael's helpful review). Regarding *Thomas Mann: Pro and contra Wagner*, which is also often adopted for classes (see Cerf's essay in this volume, as well as Bridges's extensive review of the Carnegy work), Erich Heller writes in his introduction to it: "[T]his book, in bringing together most of what Thomas Mann said about Richard Wagner, is at the same time an essential fragment of the novelist's intellectual biography" (11). Another available translation is Clayton Koelb's *Thomas Mann's "Goethe and Tolstoy."* Koelb's illuminating introductory remarks and commentary trace, among other things, the genesis of what some consider Mann's greatest essay.

In addition to Mann's narrative works, essays, and speeches, a modest number of his letters and a selection from his diaries, both of which are discussed in more detail later, are available in translation. For example, a reprint of Richard Winston and Clara Winston's abridged edition of *Letters of Thomas Mann* appeared in 1990 in paperback, issued by the University of California Press. The publisher also has in preparation, scheduled for release in 1993–94, a translation of Hans Wysling's 1984 edition of the significant Heinrich Mann–Thomas Mann correspondence (see Reich-Ranicki's study on this subject). This translation, however, is not expected to include the numerous newly found Thomas–Heinrich letters that Wysling published in the first volume of the *Thomas Mann Jahrbuch* (1988). Finally, many instructors still use as reference volumes translations of the Mann-Hesse, Mann–Erich Kahler (*Exceptional Friendship*), Mann–Karl Kerényi (*Mythology and Humanism*), and Mann-Amann correspondences, all of which are notable but, unfortunately, out of print.

Reference Works

The most complete listing of Thomas Mann's own writings is in Hans Bürgin's bibliographical volume *Das Werk Thomas Manns*, which is continued by Erich Neumann for the years 1957 to 1965 along with an addendum ("Fortsetzung und Nachtrag zu Hans Bürgins Bibliographie"). Bürgin's work is currently being revised by Georg Potempa, with the assistance of Gert Heine, for publication in 1992 by the Cicero Press in Germany. While Bürgin listed approximately 1,550 titles in his bibliography, Potempa and Heine have almost doubled that number in their work. Non-German-reading instructors especially, and students also, should know that Bürgin's work provides bibliographical references to Mann's speeches and essays that have appeared in English. Potempa and Heine, however, will not include translations in their first volume; their second part is in preparation, but it is not expected to appear in the immediate future. For only first editions, see Berlin's "Thomas Mann" bibliography in the revised edition of Wilpert and Gühring's *Erstausgaben deutscher Dichtung.*

For further information about letters, Georg Wenzel's bibliographical volume *Thomas Manns Briefwerk* is available. The work is no longer current, but instructors agree that it contains a wealth of information, particularly in the form of introductory materials and notes. The forthcoming Potempa-Heine bibliography of primary materials will include a section of published letters. Even more significant for letters, however, is Hans Bürgin and Hans-Otto Mayer's indispensable five-volume *Die Briefe Thomas Manns: Regesten und Register*, which supplements Wenzel's bibliographical volume. Unfortunately its cost makes the work unavailable at many libraries. The value of the *Regesten und Register*, of which volumes 4 and 5 were completed and edited by Yvonne Schmidlin and Gert Heine, rests, among other things, on its concise summaries of all Mann's extant letters (about 14,000), as well as the publication information and archival location of the various documents (for further details, see K. W. Jonas's review). The methodology of Bürgin and Mayer's work has given rise to much scholarly debate, evidenced, for example, by Hartmut Steinecke's "Brief-Regesten: Theorie und Praxis einer neuen Editionsform." Similar discussion proves to be enlightening in the classroom too, as is consideration of the methodology for editing letters proper. For the latter, instructors find the cogent argument in Jürgen Grerolin's "Briefe als Texte" a good basis for the introduction of this topic in class.

Other useful bibliographical volumes are Ernst Loewy's *Thomas Mann: Ton- und Filmaufnahmen*, Georg Potempa's *Thomas Mann: Beteiligung an politischen Aufrufen und anderen kollektiven Publikationen*, and Günter Gattermann's nine-volume *Katalog der Thomas-Mann-Sammlung der Universitätsbibliothek Düsseldorf*. Like the *Regesten und Register* volumes, the Gattermann edition, published in 1991, is expensive; still, it consists of more than 3,500 pages of valuable information.

The secondary literature about Mann is of course extensive, but because of the precise work of dedicated Thomas Mann scholars, private collectors, and archivists, it is remarkably orderly. Klaus Jonas's two-volume *Die Thomas-Mann-Literatur*, prepared in cooperation with the Thomas-Mann-Archiv in Zurich, takes into account secondary literature until 1975. A third volume of Jonas's work, for the period 1976 to 1989, is expected to be published by Erich Schmidt Verlag in 1992–93. Equally important is Harry Matter's two-volume *Die Literatur über Thomas Mann*, which appeared almost simultaneously with the publication of volume 1 of Jonas's work. While Jonas's and Matter's bibliographies focus on the same Western materials, their approaches are different, with Jonas's being more selective. And unlike Jonas, Matter concentrates on East European publications. Their books largely complement each other, and for completeness the teacher or scholar should consult both—although Jonas's work is the first choice of instructors polled. (With regard to such reference works, students find that Jonas's "Making of a Thomas-Mann-Bibliography" adds "a very human element" to the realm of bibliography;

"his commentary brings another exciting element to the class." In another sense, Jonas's "Auf den Spuren Thomas Manns" is equally intriguing.)

While reviewers (and several are cited in the Hans-Albrecht Koch and Uta Koch "Thomas Mann" bibliographies) note some addenda to both the Jonas and Matter bibliographies, other bibliographers—discussed below— have brought the Jonas and Matter works forward chronologically. But the forthcoming third volume of Jonas's work will ultimately supersede most of these continuations. (See also Jonas's supportive review of Matter's bibliography, as well as Vaget's positive comments about Jonas's volumes.)

In addition to the annual MLA bibliographies and the quarterly listings in *Germanistik*, at present the following bibliographies function well as more comprehensive supplements to the Jonas and Matter volumes: Antal Mádl and Judit Györi's "Bibliographie" in their *Thomas Mann und Ungarn*, Hans-Albrecht Koch and Uta Koch's "Thomas Mann," and three significant works by Hermann Kurzke: "Auswahlbibliographie zu Thomas Mann," "Auswahlbibliographie 1976–1983," and *Thomas-Mann-Forschung 1969–1976*. The latter work, which is divided into several well-organized chapters that consider various aspects of Mann and his work, contains what one respondent called "accurate and concise discussions" of more than three hundred Mann studies. Finally, Kurzke's *Thomas Mann: Epoche, Werk, Wirkung*, reissued in a revised second edition in 1991, also provides bibliographical references along with selective and, as another respondent said, "indispensable, succinct discussions" of Mann's life and work (for a fuller but brief perspective, see Hasselbach's review). Not to be overlooked are the selective bibliographical references in Hans R. Vaget's *Thomas Mann: Kommentar zu sämtlichen Erzählungen* and Volkmar Hansen's *Thomas Mann*, both of which also contain significant commentary, although some criticism has been leveled at parts of Hansen's work (see Kristiansen's review). Along with Kurzke, both Vaget and Hansen, however, were recommended by nearly all the respondents of our survey. Additionally, key bibliographical references, slanted more toward studies in German, are appended to the forty-four state-of-the-art essays by mostly different international scholars in Helmut Koopmann's 997-page *Thomas-Mann-Handbuch*, an "indispensable" volume for study about Mann.

Related to these bibliographies are a number of studies that discuss the state of Mann scholarship. Although Götz Beck's perceptive and valuable "Fiktives und Nicht-Fiktives" disputes a few points in Herbert Lehnert's *Thomas-Mann-Forschung*, Lehnert's elaborate and painstaking volume remains, more than twenty years after its publication, not only as a work that still merits consideration but also as a model of its kind, an outstanding resource about trends in Mann scholarship. Lehnert's exceptional understanding of Mann also is displayed in his review articles "Hundert Jahre Thomas Mann: 1" and "Hundert Jahre Thomas Mann: 2," both of which briefly expand his earlier *Forschungsbericht*. Noteworthy too is Lehnert's review article "Neue Quellen für die Thomas Mann Forschung," which sketches a readable and vivid picture about some newly published Mann materials (diaries, letters, phonograph records, etc.). Also valuable is Klaus Schröter's review article "Literatur zu Thomas Mann um 1975."

In addition, Kurzke's *Thomas-Mann-Forschung 1969–1976*, already noted, along with his "Tendenzen der Forschung seit 1976" and Koopmann's "Zur Thomas Mann Forschung 1961–1979," indicates many of the perspectives and trends taken in Mann studies. At the same time, Hans Wysling's "Fünfundzwanzig Jahre Arbeit im Thomas-Mann-Archiv" is typically illuminating, presenting a brief, crisp evaluation of the state of Mann scholarship. Moreover, Koopmann's "Forschungsgeschichte" accesses Mann scholarship by dividing it into four periods: 1903–33, 1933–45, 1945–75, and 1975–90. Like Wysling, Koopmann is a Mann specialist, and in thirty-six pages he ably guides the reader along the best and most traveled road of Mann studies. Another perspective is available in Erik Lunding's review article "Thomas Mann und Hispano-Amerika." And Inta Ezergailis's "Introduction" (*Critical Essays*), which is partly based on a significant review article by Hans Vaget ("Thomas Mann und kein Ende"), while not purporting to be comprehensive, remains a useful, brief summary for the non-German-reading instructor.

Background Materials

Explanation of the historical events Mann experienced—including two world wars—in addition to his own rich and varied personal life continues to challenge instructors. There remains, as one instructor expressed it, "a vast amount of material to cover and a responsibility to at least partially inform students about the major events of the period as well as Mann's colorful and exciting life."

Ten often cited works that provide background materials for instructors teaching in English are Russell A. Berman's *Rise of the Modern German Novel* ("adroit and penetrating"), Malcolm Bradbury and James McFarlane's *Modernism 1890–1930* ("wide-ranging essays"), Peter Gay's *Weimar Culture* ("still an excellent starting point"), Ronald Gray's *German Tradition in Literature 1871–1945* ("insightful and powerful"), Golo Mann's *History of Germany since 1789* ("sensitive and comprehensive"), Roy Pascal's *From Naturalism to Expressionism* ("a masterly analysis," "of exceptional value"), Kurt Reinhardt's *Germany: Two Thousand Years*, Bärbel Schrader and Jürgen Schebera's *"Golden" Twenties* ("a wealth of material"), Fritz Stern's *Politics of Cultural Despair*, and Stefan Zweig's *World of Yesterday* ("poignant, wonderfully evocative portrait of an era"). An additional thirteen works identified by respondents as valuable for background materials are

Alan F. Bance's *Weimar Germany*, Dagmar Barnouw's *Weimar Intellectu-als and the Threat of Modernity*, Gottfried Bermann-Fischer's *Bedroht—Bewahrt*, Ernst Bramsted's *Aristocracy and the Middle Class in Germany*, Gordon A. Craig's *Germans*, Ralf Dahrendorf's *Society and Democracy in Germany*, Jost Hermand and Frank Trommler's *Die Kultur der Weimarer Republik*, Anton Kaes's *Weimarer Republik* ("over seven hundred pages of materials"), Walter Laqueur's *Weimar: A Cultural History*, Gustav Lindtke's *Die Stadt der* Buddenbrooks, Peter de Mendelssohn's *S. Fischer und sein Verlag* ("indispensable," "majestic"), William Simpson's *Hitler and Germany* ("helpful selection of source material in English translation along with useful classroom-oriented questions and discussion"), and Hans-Ulrich Wehler's *Das deutsche Kaiserreich*. For instructors not familiar with the canon of German literature and related topics, J. G. Robertson and Edna Purdie's *History of German Literature* and Mary Garland's *Oxford Companion to German Literature* are recognized as excellent guides.

To highlight Mann's life and works, some instructors assign as required reading for students his short autobiographical volume from 1930, *A Sketch of My Life*; the concise 1940 Princeton University lectures, "On Myself" (still untranslated); the 1950 University of Chicago lecture, "The Years of My Life"; and selected family memoirs. For some instructors, one approach to the (auto)biographical material is to ask students to present brief reports about the perspective taken by Mann and his family, almost all of the latter having written about their lives. Here a number of articles and book-length memoirs are also available in translation, including Erika Mann's *Last Year of Thomas Mann* and "Letter to My Father"; Erika Mann and Klaus Mann's "Portrait of Our Father" and *Escape to Life* (recommended as an introduction to Klaus Mann is Ilsedore Jonas's important biographical note in the *Dictionary of Literary Biography*); Golo Mann's *Reminiscences and Reflections*, as well as his earlier, still noteworthy article "Memories of My Father"; Heinrich Mann's "My Brother" (for Heinrich Mann the beginning instructor should consult Rolf Linn's and Jürgen Haupt's volumes); Katia Mann's *Unwritten Memories*; Klaus Mann's *Turning Point*; and Monika Mann's *Past and Present*. "The story of the Mann children," writes Peter Demetz, for example, in his pertinent and compelling introduction to Krishna Winston's translation of Golo Mann's *Reminiscences*, "amply reflects the balance, or rather imbalance, inherent in many of Thomas Mann's narratives and characters, if not in his own personality, between vulnerable intellectuality and bourgeois steadfastness" (x). As one instructor comments, "approaching Mann via the family memoirs always places before us, like newly found, mostly rare paintings, vast, often delicate landscapes that we should view and review with students." But instructors also point out the largest drawback: most of these memoirs, with the exception of Golo Mann's *Reminiscences*, are out of print, which necessitates putting them on library reserve. (Several other short family and collegial reminiscences in translation are collected—among other things—in Charles Neider's still important *Stature of Thomas Mann*.)

In addition, the German student has several other memoirs available, some more detailed and more reliable than others. Included here are Heinrich Mann's *Ein Zeitalter wird besichtigt*, Julia Mann's *Aus Dodos Kindheit*, and Michael Mann's *Fragmente eines Lebens*, as well as Viktor Mann's less reliable but still significant and often read *Wir waren fünf*. Thomas Mann himself has commented on the accuracy of Viktor Mann's book (see his letter of 12 November 1951 to the editor of the *Deutsche Woche* ["Richtigstellung"]).

Related to these materials are many monographs about the Manns. In English, instructors recommend Marcel Reich-Ranicki's "classic" *Thomas Mann and His Family* and Nigel Hamilton's *Brothers Mann*, as well as two shorter studies: Stanley Corngold's "Mann Family" ("crisp and succinct") and Richard Winston's "Being Brothers" ("unique and reliable"). (Incidentally, several instructors use George Steiner's and, to some extent, Peter Gay's reviews of *The Brothers Mann* as orientation pieces. Lehnert's review should be added to those works, however, because he terms Hamilton's biography "the work of a dilettante," noting that "not even the facts are always reliable" [249–50].) Otherwise, the full-length German volumes by Walter Berendsohn, *Thomas Mann und die Seinen: Porträt einer literarischen Familie*, and Marianne Krüll, *Im Netz der Zauberer*, are available to students. Some instructors venture further, considering such other reminiscences as Gottfried Bermann-Fischer's "Bewegte Zeiten mit Thomas Mann" lecture, delivered at the University of Bern on the occasion of Mann's hundredth birthday in 1975, or Brigitte B[ermann] Fischer's *My European Heritage*, the latter appearing in Harry Zohn's "distinct" 1986 translation. Similarly, Georges Motschan's *Thomas Mann—von nahem erlebt* describes the writer's experiences when he functioned as Mann's chauffeur in 1949, the first year of Mann's return to Germany after exile. Even Hilde Kahn-Reach, Mann's secretary in Pacific Palisades, has written about her experiences with Mann ("Thomas Mann: Mein 'Boss'"). For further information about Erika and Klaus Mann, see also Eberhard Spangenberg's *Karriere* and Helga Keiser-Hayne's "Beteiligt euch," along with Peter Hoffer's *Klaus Mann*.

Accounts of Mann's life are numerous in German but fewer in English. Although books like Esther H. Lesér's especially perceptive and revealing *Thomas Mann's Short Fiction* and Hamilton's volume, noted above, provide much information, they are limited in scope. Michael Mann's article "Truth and Poetry in Thomas Mann's Work," however, offers a "highly concentrated image" unlike many others. In one instance he writes:

> The tendency toward autobiographical identification with his subject, so characteristic of Mann's literary and cultural criticism, presumes a

peculiar mix to exist between "self" and "world"—a problem which
never ceased to preoccupy the author, solved in different ways at different times.   (85)

Many instructors currently refer to Richard Winston's *Thomas Mann*, but
this work examines only the years 1875 to 1911 (see Gay's general review).
Winston's projected volume for the remaining years stands unwritten because of his untimely death. (Instructors who want to add a personal note
about Winston should see Schiffer's "In Memoriam.") However, two comprehensive Mann biographies in English, both expected to appear in the
early 1990s, are in progress: Anthony Heilbut's for Knopf and Donald A.
Prater's for Oxford University Press (Prater's work will also be published in
German by Hanser Verlag). Until these appear, Hans Bürgin and Hans-
Otto Mayer's *Thomas Mann: A Chronicle of His Life*—in need of adjust-
ments in the light of the availability of new information but nevertheless a
remarkable piece of scholarship—also continues to serve instructors well.
Unlike the still useful chronological list of important events in Mann's life,
which Hans Wysling appends to Mann's *Dichter über ihre Dichtungen*,
Hans Vaget includes in his *Kommentar*, and Hermann Kurzke provides in
his *Thomas Mann: Epoche*, Bürgin and Mayer's *Chronicle* includes quotations from Mann's writings, thus providing "a kind of concise 'autobiography' of the man, illuminating his life and works in a way that will have
some appeal not only for his already established reading public and scholars but also for those who know relatively little about him" (ix).
    A few instructors still refer to the somewhat deficient German biography
by Roman Karst, but many more cite Eberhard Hilscher's and Hermann
Stresau's more perceptive biographical works on Mann. An even greater
number of respondents use Klaus Schröter's popular *Thomas Mann in
Selbstzeugnissen und Bilddokumenten* as well as Peter de Mendelssohn's
1975 magnum opus *Der Zauberer*, the latter covering only the years 1875
to 1918 because of the biographer's sudden death. To be sure, *Der Zauberer*, consisting of 1,185 pages, has—since its publication—given rise to
much criticism, not the least of which stems from its lack of notes. But
despite its drawbacks, Mendelssohn's biography has come to be regarded
as the standard work. Moreover, some of its faults were abated when, in
1992, Fischer Verlag published the remaining extant chapters of Mendelssohn's *Der Zauberer*, edited by Albert von Schirnding. This long-
awaited second volume not only makes available those remaining chapters
that Mendelssohn had written but was unable to see into print himself,
such as his posthumously published "Das Jahr Dreiunddreissig," but also
provides some of the needed critical apparatus. Mendelssohn's illuminating
"Ein Schriftsteller in München" should not be overlooked. (Interesting,
too, are remarks about Mendelssohn himself; see Freund.) André Banuls's
seventeen-page sketch, "Thomas Mann: Leben und Persönlichkeit"—

included in Koopmann's *Thomas-Mann-Handbuch*—is a good orientation for teachers and scholars (see also Franke, *Unbekannte*). Finally, Wysling's monumental *Narzissmus und illusionäre Existenzform*, while focusing on an elucidation of *Felix Krull*, offers a wide-ranging discussion of the figure of Mann too. As Steven Cerf comments in a review of the work, Wysling's "present book spans about half a century in Mann's creative life: it is an examination of the disparate philosophical and aesthetic attitudes exhibited by the novelist during the three different periods in which he worked on *Felix Krull*" (326).

Discussion of Mann's life and work brings up the "lively" and "popular" classroom topic of writing biographies. Here instructors take several perspectives, valuing guides like Mendelsohn's "Bekenntnis und Autobiographie" and "Lebensbeschreibung des Schriftstellers," as well as Koopmann's "Thomas Manns Autobiographien," Herbert Lehnert's "Fictional Orientations in Thomas Mann's Biography," and Rolf Renner's "Literarästhetische, kulturkritische und autobiographische Essayistik." While it is beyond our scope to evaluate general works here, their importance for teaching this phase of Mann warrants mention of at least Mendelsohn's important "Grenzlinien mit Wegweisern: Biographie und Autobiographie," Leon Edel's classic *Writing Lives*, Leroy Shaw's "Biographie als Literaturwissenschaft," and René Wellek and Austin Warren's comments in their *Theory of Literature*.

Letters represent an important source of information, and, as we know, Mann was a remarkable and prolific letter writer. Most of the editions of Mann's letters include illuminating but often specialized introductions, focusing primarily on the correspondence presented. The six key critical essays that discuss him as a letter writer are Bernhard Blume's "Der Briefschreiber Thomas Mann," Jacques Mercanton's "Thomas Mann in seinen Briefen," Georg Wenzel's "Thomas Manns Briefe" (in *Thomas Manns Briefwerk*), Jürgen Eder's "Thomas Mann: Briefwechsel mit Schriftstellern," T. J. Reed's "Einfache Verulkung, Manier, Stil," and Hans Wysling's concise and discerning "Zu Thomas Manns Briefwerk." Wysling observes, for example:

> Letter writing is in the first place an act of politeness for Thomas Mann. That he gave an answer to everyone has to do with his civic sense for law and order. He thought it proper. But he also needed reactions, a contact with his readers. . . . That his correspondence took on an inflationary character in his later years and could only be accomplished with the help of secretaries is due to these two things, a feeling of what is proper and a hunger for an echo. . . . But a sense of duty and obligation alone cannot be the driving force. Thomas Mann loved to write letters. . . . He loved informal talks, the uniting and genial conversation. (85)

Erika Mann's three-volume edition of her father's letters to a variety of individuals (*Briefe*, published during the 1960s) still remains a primary source for documentation. However, Fischer Verlag is currently reviewing a concept for a new edition of selected letters that would replace Erika Mann's work. Just how such a new edition could be prepared initiates lively class discussion. But many other collections of Mann's individual letters and correspondences are extant and published, such as Wysling's edition of Mann's correspondence ("Briefwechsel") with Kurt Martens—to whom *Tonio Kröger* is dedicated—or Wysling's "remarkable" *Thomas Mann: Briefwechsel mit Autoren*, which contains Mann's short correspondences with twenty-four authors, including Freud, Hofmannsthal, Brecht, and Broch. As Wysling points out in his introduction to the latter edition, Mann never entered into an "intensive" correspondence with the great figures of the period, but the letters nevertheless represent important cultural documents and remain significant for further studies. As in all his editions, Wysling provides exact, extensive, and invaluable notes. (While the *Thomas Mann: Briefwechsel mit Autoren* volume includes a listing of the major editions of published letters, for additional letter materials, the bibliographies cited earlier should be consulted.) Also informative is Hans Wysling and Cornelia Bernini's *Jahre des Unmuts: Thomas Manns Briefwechsel mit René Schickele 1930–40*. Additionally, Vaget's edition of the Mann–Agnes E. Meyer letters, especially revealing for Mann's relations with America, is scheduled to be published in 1992 by Fischer Verlag.

Finally, we should mention that some of the letter editions are available in paperback and hence are even more feasible for adoption in class; examples are Erika Mann's three-volume edition of letters, noted above, and the instructive correspondence between Mann and his publisher Gottfried Bermann-Fischer that spans the period from 1932 to 1955.

Additional extant documents include the two-volume edition of Erika Mann's own letters (*Briefe und Antworten*) and one-volume editions of Klaus Mann's *Briefe und Antworten*, Gottfried Bermann-Fischer and Brigitte Bermann-Fischer's *Briefwechsel mit Autoren*, and Samuel Fischer and Hedwig Fischer's *Briefwechsel mit Autoren*. All these volumes contain some letters to and from Thomas Mann, but they are, as instructors confirm, also profitably used to elucidate the figures and events of the period. In a similar sense, Julia Mann's *"Ich spreche so gern mit meinen Kindern"* contains the first publication of her fascinating correspondence with Heinrich Mann.

Though not as valuable as his letters, Mann's diaries should not be overlooked. Aside from Mann's own notations, the thorough and precise editors of these volumes provide extensive annotations. Eight diary volumes (*Tagebücher*) have been published, covering the years 1918 to 1921 and 1933 to 1950. Editions for the years 1951 to 1955 are expected to appear by 1994. The critical essays by Inge Jens ("Es kenne mich die Welt"), Inge Jens and

Walter Jens ("Die Tagebücher"), and Hans Wysling ("Thomas Mann als Tagebuchschreiber") are especially informative on the value and role of the diaries; see also the rich essays about Mann's diaries in Eckhard Heftrich's *Vom Verfall zur Apokalypse*, Hans Mayer's *Thomas Mann*, and Rolf Renner's *Lebens-Werk*. Ronald Speirs also perceptively discusses the diaries in "Aus dem Leben eines Taugenichts." Additionally, Ernst Pawel's review of the American edition of Mann's diaries, which is aptly entitled "Including Laundry Lists," remains especially useful to beginning instructors. (Incidentally, appended to several of the diary volumes are a number of Mann's difficult-to-locate or previously unpublished essays, speeches, drafts, and revisions.) Finally, instructors are encouraged to examine Klaus Mann's diaries covering the years 1931 to 1949. While not focusing principally on his father, Klaus Mann's notations provide a different perspective on the period and the family. (See also Fredric Kroll and Klaus Täubert's *Sammlung der Kräfte*, the first volume of their Klaus Mann biography.)

For another source of primary materials, one can now consult the first volume of Mann's *Notizbücher*, which comprises more than three hundred pages in an edition prepared by Hans Wysling and Yvonne Schmidlin. From 1893 to 1937, with an addendum for the year 1947, Mann kept fourteen such notebooks. Because Mann burned all his diaries before 1933 (except those for 1918 to 1921), these notebooks, for which the editors also provide elaborate notes, are especially valuable. A useful introductory guide is Hans Wysling's "Thomas Manns unveröffentlichte Notizbücher." The second and final volume, *Notizbücher 7–14*, is scheduled to appear in 1992.

Several instructors rightly point out that students should be aware of Volkmar Hansen and Gert Heine's 440-page *Frage und Antwort: Interviews mit Thomas Mann 1909–1955* (see also Rieckmann's review). At the same time, Wysling's 439-page *Bild und Text bei Thomas Mann* (prepared with the assistance of Yvonne Schmidlin and long out of print, but reprinted in 1989) reproduces pictures and artwork along with the corresponding text of Mann's interpretation or use in his works. This layout allows instructors to show students some of the visual sources Mann used and how he transformed certain scenes and works of art into his fiction. (It is also an interesting volume to use in writing classes.) While Wysling includes in *Bild und Text* a remarkably informative introduction, the comments are expanded in his essay "Thomas Manns Deskriptionstechnik." And instructors should keep in mind Wysling's invaluable, but also long out-of-print, three-volume edition of Mann's self-commentary taken from published *and* still unpublished letters as well as other sources (*Dichter über ihre Dichtungen*). This publication is especially significant because it contains almost everything Mann said about his own works. Sections of it are being reprinted in inexpensive paperbacks by Fischer Verlag, making it feasible for classroom use.

General Introductions and Critical Studies

There are studies about virtually every phase of Thomas Mann's life and times. Even Mann's reception in different countries—France, Hungary, Japan, the former Soviet Union, Sweden, and Turkey, for example—provides much interesting scholarly and class discussion (see, respectively, the essays by Leibrich, Mádl and Györi, Murata, Gulia, Bergsten, and Aytac). For other perspectives, see Peter Pütz ("Thomas Manns Wirkung") and Hans Schulte ("Ist Thomas Mann noch lebendig?"). Günther Debon's "Thomas Mann und China" and Steven Cerf's "Thomas Mann und die englische Literatur" add still another dimension.

For introductory (and very advanced) purposes, instructors agree that T. J. Reed's *Thomas Mann: The Uses of Tradition* is a classic work (with all quotations accompanied by translations). Respondents also recognize as a first source Lesér's *Thomas Mann's Short Fiction*, noted earlier (also with the quotations in English). Her book provides basic and highly readable discussions, although Lesér's approach does not allow all perspectives about the stories to be taken into account. Nevertheless, according to Lesér, her volume "has two intended roles: as a reference work in which each story may be read individually with its comprehensive study materials, and as an organic study of Thomas Mann's intellectual development" (9). Even though her bibliographical apparatus lacks some significant items, her commentary is built on more than fifty years of studying Mann. Along with copious notes, her volume includes a glossary of terms that beginning instructors and students welcome.

Otherwise, along with Richard Winston's introductory essay (in the 1971 edition of Mann's letters translated by Richard Winston and Clara Winston), survey respondents indicate that, in English, André von Gronicka's "completely reliable and discerning" *Thomas Mann: Profile and Perspectives* should be among the first works consulted. At the same time, the three Henry Hatfield books about Mann (*Thomas Mann, From* The Magic Mountain [see also Vaget's review], and a collection of scholarly essays) and Erich Heller's *Ironic German* remain more or less standard reading for instructors. R. J. Hollingdale's critical study and Martin Swales's shorter but also insightful *Thomas Mann* could be profitably used.

Further helpful essays in translation on a wide variety of topics are included in the collections edited by Harold Bloom (*Thomas Mann*) and Inta Ezergailis (*Critical Essays*). Ezergailis's volume includes T. J. Reed's important "Thomas Mann and Tradition." While Reed's position is argued more fully in his indispensable Mann volume, noted above, instructors with limited time find that this essay summarizes and highlights some key issues.

Also appropriate for orientation is Thomas Willey's discerning "Thomas Mann's Munich" as well as, for art and the artist figure, the following:

Burton Pike's "Thomas Mann and the Problematic Self," Horst Daemm-rich's "Mann's Portrait of the Artist," Peter Heller's "Thomas Mann's Conception of the Creative Writer," T. J. Reed's *Thomas Mann: The Uses of Tradition*, William H. Rey's "Tragic Aspects of the Artist in Thomas Mann's Work," and Peter Pütz's *Kunst und Künstlerexistenz bei Nietzsche und Thomas Mann* (see Kurzke's *Thomas Mann: Epoche*, esp. 82–110); see also Maurice Beebe's *Ivory Towers and Sacred Founts* ("especially good on the artist figure"). Another useful work is Christa Kamenetsky's "Thomas Mann's Concept of the 'Bürger' " (see again Kurzke, *Epoche*, esp. 44–53).

Several instructors continue to enjoy the insight and brevity afforded in some older but nevertheless reliable works by Lydia Baer ("still a remarkable work"), Walter Berendsohn (*Artist and Partisan* is "often too brief, but contains some good thought"), Joseph Brennan ("compact"), Ignace Feuerlicht ("often summary-like, but good; adheres to guidelines of the Twayne series"), Ronald Gray ("perceptive observations"), Frank Hirsch-bach ("enlightening about Mann's polarities"), Fritz Kaufmann ("not always correct; several aspects remarkable"), R. Hinton Thomas (*Mediation* is "still very useful"), and Andrew White ("helpful, very brief overall presentation"). As instructors emphasized, however, these works should be read in conjunction with current studies, which consider the present state of Mann scholarship. In fact, survey respondents were very firm here, because, as they pointed out, many libraries are likely to own these older volumes. At the same time, respondents stressed that, if these works are used properly, they can provide "much good thought."

Among the other recent and more important books in English that instructors noted were Harvey Goldman's *Max Weber and Thomas Mann* ("instructive," "adroit discussions of *Tonio Kröger* and *Death in Venice*") and Ilsedore Jonas's *Thomas Mann and Italy* ("commanding and elucidating"). Also cited, though less frequently, were Judith Marcus's *Georg Lukács and Thomas Mann* ("distinguished") and Inta Ezergailis's *Male and Female*.

Because many instructors refer in some way to *Doctor Faustus*, *The Magic Mountain*, and *The Buddenbrooks*, special note should be made of the following important book-length studies, several of which have received outstanding positive acclaim: Gunilla Bergsten's *Thomas Mann's Doctor Faustus: The Sources and Structure of the Novel* (respondents and Kirchberger, in her review, called this work "distinguished"); Patrick Carnegy's *Faust as Musician: A Study of Thomas Mann's Novel* Doctor Faustus (respondents agree with Hans R. Vaget who, in his review, finds the book a "useful, intelligent, and—at times—brilliant discussion" [524]); John Fetzer's *Music, Love, Death, and Mann's* Doctor Faustus (in his review, Cerf maintains that Fetzer "addresses the basic aesthetic and emotional issues of Mann's most difficult creation . . . with sophistication and erudition" [160]; similarly, Siefken's review notes that the book "presents its case with great elegance, skill, and erudition" [1052]); Herbert Lehnert and

Peter C. Pfeiffer's Doctor Faustus: A Novel at the Margin of Modernism; Hermann J. Weigand's A Study of Thomas Mann's Novel Der Zauberberg (originally published in 1933, it remains a standard reference); Harold Bloom's collection of essays, Thomas Mann's The Magic Mountain, a part of the Modern Critical Interpretations series; Hugh Ridley's Thomas Mann: Buddenbrooks; and Martin Swales's Buddenbrooks: Family Life as the Mirror of Social Change, which is in Twayne's Masterwork series. The Bloom, Ridley, and Swales volumes, while significant, are not by any means as acclaimed as the Bergsten, Carnegy, Fetzer, Lehnert and Pfeiffer, or Weigand works. Each of these eight texts includes all quotations in English.

For introductory studies in German, instructors agree that Kurzke's Thomas Mann: Epoche, the essays in Koopmann's Thomas-Mann-Handbuch, and Vaget's Thomas Mann Kommentar are, like Hansen's Thomas Mann, works that "warrant immediate consideration." For introducing The Buddenbrooks, Ken Moulden and Gero von Wilpert's Buddenbrooks-Handbuch is equally indispensable. Additionally, Wysling's "Schwierigkeiten mit Thomas Mann" is considered illuminating.

The other "most significant" German works that respondents cited are, first of all, Inge Diersen's Thomas Mann: Episches Werk, Weltanschauung, Leben ("balanced and very readable"), Helmut Jendreiek's Thomas Mann: Der demokratische Roman ("brilliant analyses of Mann and his works," "detailed, thorough, and dependable"), and Helmut Koopmann's Die Entwicklung des "intellektualen Romans" ("classic"). Also mentioned were Koopmann's Thomas Mann: Konstanten seines literarischen Werks and Der schwierige Deutsche (both "penetrating and insightful"), Lehnert's Thomas Mann: Fiktion, Mythos, Religion ("scholarly discussions"), and Rolf Renner's Lebens-Werk ("thorough and instructive," "a most serious critical examination deserving of high praise"). Following these, Hans Mayer's Thomas Mann ("sweeping") is highly regarded.

Das erzählerische Werk Thomas Manns, edited by Klaus Hermsdorf and others, brings together in a single volume all the concise afterwords of the Aufbau Verlag edition of narrative works that was completed in 1975. Instructors and students will benefit from these commentaries, which discuss a work's genesis, sources, effect, and other topics. Several instructors keep the above books, as well as Peter de Mendelssohn's Nachbemerkungen zu Thomas Mann, which contains his illuminating commentaries, originally in the 1980 edition of the complete works, on library reserve. Also frequently placed on library reserve is Eva Schiffer's Zwischen den Zeilen, which offers "a unique perspective" that "generally interests both beginning and more advanced students." Here, too, Klaus Schröter's Thomas Mann im Urteil seiner Zeit, long recognized as a major contribution, continues to be consulted. Finally, as to German volumes with essays on various topics, instructors acknowledge, above all else, Beatrix Bludau, Eckhard Heftrich, and Helmut Koopmann's edition Thomas Mann 1875–1975, which presents the distinguished papers delivered at the international symposia held in Munich, Zurich, and Lübeck in 1975 on the occasion of the hundredth anniversary of Mann's birth.

Mann often made clear that Nietzsche, Schopenhauer, and Wagner were the three major figures who influenced him. In introducing and teaching the ideas of these world figures and their effect on Mann, instructors benefit from many works. Survey respondents point to Stanley Corngold's "Mann as a Reader of Nietzsche" and "Thomas Mann and the German Philosophical Tradition" as well as Adrian Del Caro's studies (one with Renate Bialy), cited in his essay and the works-cited list in this volume. Keith May's *Nietzsche and Modern Literature* is also mentioned, along with Roger Nicholls's somewhat one-sided *Nietzsche in the Early Works of Thomas Mann*. Additionally, instructors single out Børge Kristiansen's "Thomas Mann und die Philosophie," Peter Pütz's "Thomas Mann und Nietzsche" (see Reed's review of Pütz's *Thomas Mann und die Tradition*), Wysling's "Schopenhauer-Leser Thomas Mann," Vaget's "Thomas Mann und Wagner," and Peter Wapnewski's "Der Magier und der Zauberer: Thomas Mann und Richard Wagner." Also recommended are William Blissett's "Thomas Mann: The Last Wagnerite" and André Banuls's "Schopenhauer und Nietzsche." Finally, instructors rightfully acknowledge that students should know of Goethe's major influence on Mann; the first reference sources respondents suggest are Hinrich Siefken's *Thomas Mann: Goethe— "Ideal der Deutschheit,"* H. Stefan Schultz's still useful "Thomas Mann und Goethe," the essays in Vaget and Barnouw's *Thomas Mann*, and Wysling's "Thomas Manns Goethe-Nachfolge." (For Mann's attitude toward Schiller, respondents recommend as an introduction the "fundamental" studies by Lehnert ["Thomas Mann und Schiller"] and Sandberg.)

Lecturing about Mann's exile years and political activities also challenges the instructor, first because of the many important perspectives and second because of the great amount of documentary and critical materials available. Instructors observe that, if only a few of Mann's shorter works are assigned, frequently time does not permit extensive attention to be focused on the period of exile. In fact, some instructors and students welcome brief commentaries. With this in view, ten basic studies of article length or shorter in English, confronting a variety of related issues, are Henry Hatfield's "Thomas Mann and America," Koopmann's "German Culture Is Where I Am," Victor Lange's "Thomas Mann: Politics and Art" and "Thomas Mann in Exile," Lehnert's "Thomas Mann in Exile 1933–1938" and "Thomas Mann in Princeton," Michael Mann's "Thomas Mann and the United States of America," Hinrich Siefken's "Thomas Mann's Essay 'Bruder Hitler,' " and Theodore Ziolkowski's "Thomas Mann as a Critic of Germany" and "Thomas Mann and the Emigré Intellectuals."

Five fundamental commentaries that help a number of instructors place this subject into sharper focus are Hans Eichner's "Thomas Mann and

Politics," Hans Mayer's "On the Political Development of an Unpolitical Man," and three essays by T. J. Reed: "Unpolitics: War Thoughts 1914–1918," "Republic: Politics 1919–1933" (both chapters in his *Thomas Mann: The Uses of Tradition*), and "Thomas Mann: The Writer as Historian of His Time." Also very helpful are Martin Swales's "In Defence of Weimar" and Keith Bullivant's "Thomas Mann and Politics in the Weimar Republic." At the same time, Berlin's "In Exile" compares Mann's exile years with those of Heinrich Eduard Jacob, thereby underscoring the difficulties less famous emigré writers encountered in America.

The available sources in German about Mann's political activities are extensive. Erich Frey's sketch provides a helpful orientation. Otherwise, in addition to some of the books already cited, like Hermann Kurzke's *Thomas Mann: Epoche*, instructors single out Kurzke's *Auf der Suche nach der verlorenen Irrationalität* and "Die politische Essayistik," Hans Wisskirchen's *Zeitgeschichte im Roman*, Theo Stammen's "Thomas Mann und die politische Welt," Kurt Sontheimer's "Thomas Mann als politischer Schriftsteller," Peter de Mendelssohn's "Der Schriftsteller als politischer Bürger," Paul Egon Hübinger's *Thomas Mann, die Universität Bonn und die Zeitgeschichte*, Hans Wysling's "Thomas Mann—Der Unpolitische in der Politik," Ernst Keller's *Der unpolitische Deutsche*, and Matthias Wegner's *Exil und Literatur*. Useful too is Herbert Wiesner's cross-chronology of important historical happenings compared with Mannian events.

Valuable primary and secondary sources are also available in several archive and Mann society publications with which German literature majors, especially, should be familiar: *Blätter der Thomas Mann Gesellschaft* (1958–), *Hefte der Deutschen Thomas-Mann-Gesellschaft* (1981–1987), *Thomas Mann Jahrbuch* (1988–), and the *Thomas-Mann-Studien* volumes published by Francke Verlag; to date, ten *Thomas-Mann-Studien* volumes are available.

As expected, respondents mentioned numerous studies that specifically elucidate *Tonio Kröger*, *Tristan*, and *Death in Venice*. Their responses bear out once again the celebrated dictum that Hans Wysling, director of the Mann archives in Zurich from 1961 to 1993 and high priest of Thomas Mann scholarship, first exclaimed in a 1975 lecture at the University of Basel: "Die gesamte Thomas-Mann-Literatur vermag heute niemand mehr zu überblicken" 'Today it is no longer possible to be acquainted with all that has been written on Thomas Mann' (*Thomas Mann heute* 7). While we cannot list all the respondents' recommendations here, instructors should alert students to important critical materials; indeed, the review of such analyses often facilitates successful teaching. To this end, secondary literature about *Tonio Kröger*, *Tristan*, and *Death in Venice* is cited here—German sources follow later—only if a particular study met three criteria: (1) several instructors recommended it, (2) the text was in English, and (3) the study was article-length.

Tonio Kröger: H. A. Basilius, "Thomas Mann's Use of Musical Structure and Techniques in *Tonio Kröger*"; Lilian R. Furst, "Thomas Mann's *Tonio Kröger*"; Lida Kirchberger, "Popularity as a Technique"; K. W. Maurer, "Tonio Kröger and Hamlet"; James R. McWilliams, "Conflict and Compromise"; Patrick O'Neill, "Dance and Counterdance"; T. J. Reed, "Text and History"; Winthrop H. Root, "*Grillparzer's Sappho* and Thomas Mann's *Tonio Kröger*"; Martin Swales, "Punctuation and the Narrative Mode"; Mark G. Ward, "More Than 'Stammesverwandtschaft'?"; Elizabeth M. Wilkinson, "*Tonio Kröger*"; Kenneth Wilson, "The Dance as Symbol and Leitmotiv in Thomas Mann's *Tonio Kröger*"; and Anthony Woodward, "The Figure of the Artist in Thomas Mann's *Tonio Kröger* and *Death in Venice.*"

Tristan: Stevie Anne Bolduc, "A Study of Intertextuality: Thomas Mann's *Tristan* and Richard Wagner's *Tristan und Isolde*"; Peter J. Burgard, "From *Enttäuschung* to *Tristan*"; Inta Ezergailis, "Spinell's Letter"; Henry Hatfield, "Thomas Mann's *Tristan*"; Lida Kirchberger, "Thomas Mann's *Tristan*"; Marcia Morris, "Sensuality and Art: Tolstoyan Echoes in *Tristan*"; James Northcote-Bade, "Thomas Mann's Use of Wagner's 'Sehnsuchtsmotiv' in *Tristan*"; Sophia Schnitman, "Musical Motives in Thomas Mann's *Tristan*"; Richard Sheppard, "*Tonio Kröger* and *Der Tod in Venedig*: From Bourgeois Realism to Visionary Modernism"; and Albert Sonnenfeld, "*Tristan* for Pianoforte: Thomas Mann and Marcel Proust."

Death in Venice: Alan F. Bance, "*Der Tod in Venedig* and the Triadic Structure"; Frank Baron, "Sensuality and Morality in Thomas Mann's *Tod in Venedig*"; Albert Braverman and Larry Nachman, "The Dialectic of Decadence: An Analysis of Thomas Mann's *Death in Venice*"; D. Bronsen, "The Artist against Himself: Henrik Ibsen's *Masterbuilder* and Thomas Mann's *Death in Venice*"; Margaret Church, "*Death in Venice*: A Study of Creativity"; David James Farelly, "Apollo and Dionysus Interpreted in Thomas Mann's *Der Tod in Venedig*"; Kurt Fickert, "Truth and Fiction in *Der Tod in Venedig*"; Graham Good, "The Death of Language in *Death in Venice*"; André von Gronicka, "Myth plus Psychology"; Hunter G. Hannum, "Archetypal Echoes in Mann's *Death in Venice*"; Geoffrey Harpham, "Metaphor, Marginality, and Parody in *Death in Venice*"; Tom Hayes and Lee Quinby, "The Aporia of Bourgeois Art"; Dominick La Capra, "Mann's *Death in Venice*"; Wolfgang Leppmann, "Time and Place in *Der Tod in Venedig*"; William H. McClain, "Wagnerian Overtones in *Der Tod in Venedig*"; Eugene McNamara, "*Death in Venice*: The Disguised Self"; J. R. McWilliams, "The Failure of a Repression"; Heidi Rockwood and Robert Rockwood, "The Psychological Reality of Myth in *Der Tod in Venedig*"; Macha L. Rosenthal, "The Corruption of Aschenbach"; Walter Stewart, "*Der Tod in Venedig*: The Path to Insight"; R. Hinton Thomas, "*Die Wahlverwandtschaften* and Mann's *Der Tod in Venedig*"; Isadore Traschen, "The Uses of Myth in *Death in Venice*"; Constance Urdang, "Faust in

Venice"; Marc Weiner, "Silence, Sound, and Song in *Der Tod in Venedig*."
Many studies written in German about *Tonio Kröger*, *Tristan*, and *Death in Venice* are, of course, also available. First sources that instructors noted are Hans Vaget's essay "Die Erzählungen," as well as his famous *Mann Kommentar*. Ehrhard Bahr's *Thomas Mann: Der Tod in Venedig*, Werner Bellmann's *Thomas Mann: Tonio Kröger*, and Ulrich Dittmann's *Thomas Mann: Tristan*, all of which are in the Reclam *Erläuterungen und Dokumente* series, provide a wealth of commentary and reference studies. At the other extreme, several instructors cited Heribert Gorzawski's *Stundenblätter* Tonio Kröger and Martin Thunich's *Thomas Mann: Tonio Kröger*, although there were mixed views about each: some respondents consider these works much too basic, while others recommend Gorzawski and Thunich because of their simplicity and specific pedagogical orientation.

Instructors also pointed out several interpretative articles and books in German that they consider timeless: the important studies by Manfred Dierks ("Der Wahn"), Helmut Koopmann ("Hanno"), Fritz Martini, Franz Mautner, Wolfgang Michael ("Stoff und Idee"), Hellmuth Petriconi, Peter Pütz ("Der Ausbruch"), Wolfdietrich Rasch ("Jugendstil" and "Erzählung"), Ernst Schmidt ("Künstler und Knabenliebe" and "Platonismus"), Oskar Seidlin, Hans R. Vaget ("Thomas Mann und die Neuklassik"), Werner Vordtriede, Walter Weiss, Benno von Wiese, Hans Wysling ("Dokumente," "Aschenbachs Werke," "Mythus," and "Geist und Kunst"), and Viktor Žmegač. Also singled out as highly useful were the studies, in German, by Reinhard Baumgart, Tamara Evans, John Frey, Hans Jürgen Geerdts, Heinz Gockel, Hellmut Haug, Yaak Karsunke, Hertha Krotkoff, Karl Laage, Herbert Lehnert ("*Tristan, Tonio Kröger* und *Der Tod in Venedig*"), Hans-Bernhard Moeller, Rolf Günter Renner (*Das Ich als ästhetische Konstruktion*), Jens Rieckmann ("Brüderliche"), Bruno Rossbach ("Der Anfang" and *Spiegelungen*), Hans-Joachim Sandberg ("Der fremde Gott"), Franz Sonner, and Hans Wanner. Of course, some of these older studies, while still extremely valuable, need to be approached in the light of new interpretations and research findings.

Furthermore, a few specialized or unusual topics in *Tonio Kröger*, *Tristan*, or *Death in Venice* are treated in English by the following critics: Russell A. Berman ("Montage"), George Bridges ("Problem of Pederastic Love"), John Conley, Catherine Cox, David Eggenschwiler, Peter Egri, R. F. Fleissner, Bernhard Frank, Margaret Gullette, Lorraine Gustafson, James Hepworth, Christopher Hoile, Lida Kirchberger ("*Death in Venice* and the Eighteenth Century"), Herbert Lehnert ("Another Note," "Notes," "Thomas Mann's Early Interest," and "Tonio Kröger and Georg Bendemann"), Kathy Phillipps, Heidi M. Rockwood, Charlotte Rotkin ("Form and Function" and "Oceanic Animals"), Lee Stavenhagen, Rainulf Stelzmann, Cedric Watts, Paul Weigand, Heinz Wetzel ("Erkenntnisekel" and "Seer"), Michael Winkler, Richard Winston (*Thomas Mann*), Brucia Witthoft, and Kathleen Woodward. Unusual topics in German are discussed by Frank Baron ("Das Sokrates-Bild"), Bernhard Boschert and Ulf Schramm, Bernd Effe, Peter R. Franke, Fritz Gesing, Roland Harweg, Eberhard Hermes, Volker Knüfermann, Dieter P. Lotze, Frederick Lubich, John Margetts, Hubert Ohl, Henry Olsen, Walter Schmitz, Marianne Thalmann, Karsten Witte, and Frederick Wyatt. See also Jochen Reichel's reader, *Der Tod in Venedig: Ein Lesebuch*, which offers a unique literary history of Venice. Because these works were recognized as useful, instructors with additional time may benefit from them.

On the theme of homosexuality, respondents suggest, as introductory works, the studies by Karl Werner Böhm, Frank Busch (see Siefken's review), Mechthild Curtius, Ignace Feuerlicht ("Thomas Mann and Homoeroticism"), Gerhard Härle (*Gestalt* and *Männerweiblichkeit* [see J. W. Jones's review]), Claus Sommerhage, and Hans Wanner.

Finally, three festschriften should interest instructors of Mann: *Wegbereiter der Moderne* (edited by Helmut Koopmann and Clark Muenzer), *Thomas Mann und seine Quellen* (edited by Eckhard Heftrich and Helmut Koopmann), and *Horizonte* (edited by William Lillyman, Hannelore Mundt, and Egon Schwarz). These volumes, honoring, respectively, Klaus W. Jonas, Hans Wysling, and Herbert Lehnert, contain complete bibliographies of the honorees' publications to date. Since nearly all the survey respondents recognize Jonas's, Wysling's, and Lehnert's pioneering and creative scholarly work as both highly informative and exemplary, it is useful to have such a complete listing. Moreover, students learn much from studying the methodology of Jonas's many editions of Mann's letters (along with his bibliographies and editions of other authors' letters) as well as from examining the approach and development of Lehnert's critical essays. Like the work of Jonas and Lehnert, Wysling's "brilliant studies and editions" are "models of their kind." Students greatly benefit by studying the approaches and thought of these three scholars. All three volumes also contain significant contributions about Mann.

Audiovisual Aids

The most frequently used aid to teaching Mann is Luchino Visconti's film adaptation of *Death in Venice*. Visconti's work created a heightened interest in Mann. Fischer Verlag reports that from 1960 to 1970, the average number of copies of *Death in Venice* sold each year was 24,000. After Visconti's film version appeared, in March 1971, Fischer sold 77,800 copies in that year (Mertz 31). However, the survey revealed mixed opinions about the value of Visconti's version. A considerable number of perceptive article-length studies with varying appraisals have been written about the film, the most important of them by Jean Améry, Thomas Bleicher, Kurt von Fischer, Angus Fletcher, Carolyn Galerstein, David Glassco, David Grossvogel, Joachim Günther, Alexander Hutchison, B. M. Kane, Hans Mayer ("*Der Tod in Venedig*"), Anthony Mazzella, Robert Plank, Andrew Porter, Douglas Radcliff-Umstead, Philip Reed, Rolf Renner ("Verfilmungen der Werke von Thomas Mann"), Irving Singer, Hans R. Vaget ("Film and Literature"), Roger Wiehe, and Ernest Wolf. See also John F. Fetzer's essay in this volume. For a listing of newspaper reviews as well as further commentary about Visconti's work, see Gabriele Seitz's *Film als Rezeptionsform von Literatur*. Also recommended is Werner Faulstich and Ingeborg Faulstich's *Modelle der Filmanalyse*.

For discussion about Benjamin Britten and Myfanwy Piper's operatic rendering of *Death in Venice*, which was first performed on 16 June 1973, see the articles by Patrick Carnegy, Steven Cerf, Donald Mitchell, and Christopher Palmer. The opera may be used in a variety of ways in the classroom.

Few instructors seemed aware of the Inter Nationes film *Thomas Mann and the Germans*, written by Peter de Mendelssohn. It is readily available in English and most interesting. Together with a succinct sketch of Mann's life, the film provides vivid, exciting scenes of Mann delivering speeches, as well as an engaging interview with Katia Mann. Similarly, few instructors knew of the Inter Nationes film *Dichtung und Wahrheit: Thomas Mann*—Tod in Venedig, which includes, in English, an interview with Wladyslaw Moes, the son of Baroness Moes from Warsaw, who was the real-life prototype for Tadzio. It also features an interview with Janek Fudakowski, who was the model for Jaschu. Instructors who use the film report much success and student appeal.

Teachers also benefit from recordings of Mann's works, which are readily available for *Der Tod in Venedig*, *Herr und Hund*, and selections from *Buddenbrooks*, *Der Zauberberg*, *Der Erwählte*, *Tonio Kröger*, *Felix Krull*, and the essay "Lob der Vergänglichkeit." The last four items are especially attractive, for Mann himself is the reader. Similarly, Mann's *Deutsche Hörer: Radiosendungen aus dem Exil 1940–45* and *Versuch über Schiller*, both with Mann as the speaker, are recommended.

Video Yesteryear offers a video in German with English subtitles for *Tonio Kröger*, but most instructors agree that it is poorly done. The video of *Unordnung und frühes Leid* (*Disorder and Early Sorrow*), however, is recommended. For commentary, see the works by Seitz and by Renner listed earlier in this section. To augment their class discussions, many teachers wisely use photographs of Mann and the times as well as facsimiles of his manuscripts. The most popular work for this purpose is Jürgen Kolbe's *Heller Zauber: Thomas Mann in München 1894–1933*, which, aside from excellent photographs, contains extensive valuable commentary, including, as a brief introduction, the distinguished lecture Hans Mayer originally presented at the Villa Stuck in Munich, on 20 October 1987, on the occasion of the exhibit's opening.

A variety of other volumes also contain significant photographs and commentary. In a certain sense, each volume's set of pictures permits the instructor to approach Mann from a different perspective. Several survey respondents recommend the following: Sigrid Anger's *Heinrich Mann*, Richard Carstensen's *Thomas Mann sehr menschlich*, Eva Chrambach and Ursula Hummel's *Klaus und Erika Mann: Bilder und Dokumente*, Marianne Krüll's *Im Netz der Zauberer*, Antal Mádl and Judit Györi's *Thomas Mann und Ungarn*, Thomas Mann's *Diaries* (American edition) and *Letters* (1971 American edition, translated by Richard Winston and Clara Winston), Wilfried F. Schoeller's *Heinrich Mann: Bilder und Dokumente*, Bärbel Schrader and Jürgen Schebera's *"Golden" Twenties: Art and Literature in the Weimar Republic*, Klaus Schröter's *Thomas Mann in Selbstzeugnissen und Bilddokumenten*, and Wolfgang Tschechne's *Thomas Manns Lübeck*. Much discussion can be motivated by consideration of Ilsedore B. Jonas's stimulating "'Ich sah ein kleines Wunder . . . .': Porträts von Thomas Manns Lebensgefährtin." Still another perspective is available from Ulrich Hohoff and Gerhard Stumpf's *Thomas Mann im amerikanischen Exil: 1938—1952*, which is based on the November 1991 exhibit, at the University of Augsburg, of Klaus W. Jonas and Ilsedore B. Jonas's Thomas Mann collection of more than eleven hundred volumes and three thousand documents.

Since the issuance of Mann's earliest works, Fischer has remained his German publisher. In this regard, volumes recommended for photographs are J. Hellmut Freund et al., *Almanach 83: Bilder aus dem S. Fischer Verlag 1886–1914*, and Bernhard Zeller, *S. Fischer, Verlag*, the latter covering the founding of the firm through its return from exile. Friedrich Pfäfflin's *Hundert Jahre S. Fischer Verlag 1886–1986* contains photographs of book covers, usually quite interesting for instructors and students alike.

Finally, while the 1953 privately printed and limited facsimile edition of Mann's *Die Betrogene* is a rare volume and not available to all instructors, Zeller's facsimile edition of *Schwere Stunde* is more accessible and proves well suited to student viewing regardless of which Mann works are

Part Two

APPROACHES

GENERAL ISSUES

Teaching Mann's Short Fiction: A Historian's Perspective

Roderick Stackelberg

Historians frequently assign literary works in their courses as an effective means to introduce students to the dominant attitudes, social practices, and value systems of the past. Literary works written in the period under study may give students a more direct appreciation of how life in the past was different from (or similar to) the present than works of historical exposition written by a later generation. This may paradoxically be true even of works, such as Thomas Mann's prewar short fiction, that seem to be concerned only with the interior life, not with external conditions.

Literature provides insight into society in at least three distinct, though related and overlapping, ways: first, through its mimetic description of social reality (for instance, students may learn something of Hanseatic patrician culture from reading *The Buddenbrooks*); second, through its explicit or allegorical critique of social or political institutions, ideologies, practices, and conventions (Mann's developing social consciousness after World War I is exemplified in the social criticism offered by specific characters, such as Settembrini in *The Magic Mountain*, or in his allegorical critique of fascism in *Mario and the Magician*); and third, through the author's values and attitudes, either openly expressed or reflected, often unconsciously, in style, method, and choice of subject matter (they may yield insights into the social context in which a given work was written). Analyzed, from this last perspective, for its ideological presuppositions, Thomas Mann's prewar short fiction, despite its apparent indifference to contemporary issues, can give students insight into the social and political culture of imperial Germany.

I raise the following kinds of questions with my students: What is the relation between culture and politics? What are the social and political assumptions implicit in the works of literature they read? What kind of political culture or ideology do these works imply or reflect? The predominant message of Mann's prewar short fiction seems to be that the sociopolitical realm of practical affairs is corrupting. Involvement in public affairs, in business or politics, cannot bring fulfillment except to baser types. Sociopolitical questions and problems are not an appropriate subject matter for art. The consequence of such attitudes is the silent acceptance of prevailing ideology and the sociopolitical status quo.

This quietist ethos was later elaborated in Mann's wartime *Reflections of a Nonpolitical Man*, a celebration of *machtgeschützte Innerlichkeit*, inwardness protected by power. His juxtaposition of German culture and Anglo-French civilization perpetuated a theme that can be traced back to at least the early nineteenth century. Culture and civilization are at odds—culture represents a higher, more creative activity than civilization does. Civilization and politics may improve the comforts and amenities of living; culture and metaphysics give life its meaning and purpose. Civilization is the product of rational, secular self-interest; culture is produced by self-overcoming, transcendent idealists. Germany embodied the values of culture; the West, those of civilization. Germans embraced idealism, the quest for moral perfection, as a superior alternative to Western utilitarianism and liberalism, both of which stood condemned as egoistic, success-oriented doctrines. If the democratic tradition of the West exalted the individual's merely external political rights, authentic German culture embraced the inner freedom that liberated the individual from selfishness and material temptation. The French Revolution sought to liberate humanity only from its external chains; the German idea of freedom was to liberate humans from the interior chains of sensuality and weakness of will. Moral regeneration, not political reform, was the goal of idealists from Friedrich Schiller and Johann Gottlieb Fichte to Wagner and Nietzsche. Indifference to politics was a virtue in the German tradition, in which freedom stood not for the right to gratify one's inclinations but rather for the absence of desire to do so. The voluntary fulfillment of duty, not the assertion of individual rights, was the hallmark of the German conception of freedom (Bruford 236). "I have absolutely no interest in political freedom," Thomas Mann had written to his brother on 27 February 1904 (Hamilton 87); political oppression, he suggested, was conducive to great art. The artist, aristocrat, and heroic idealist personified the German tradition, as the journalist, business executive, and politicized intellectual personified the West.

With my students I inquire into the sociopolitical sources of such apolitical or antipolitical attitudes. These attitudes may be interpreted as reflecting the static and hierarchical structure of Wilhelmian society and the undemocratic nature of Wilhelmian politics. But they also form part of a much older conservative tradition of disdain for the "materialistic," "egotistical," and "acquisitive" values of the Enlightenment and the French Revolution. The apolitical, contemplative ethos that developed both in reaction to and as a result of absolutism and particularism can be traced back to the eighteenth century and earlier. Even classicism, with its emphasis on achieving peace of mind through harmony, balance, and withdrawal into art, represented a gesture of resignation in the face of ossified social and political conditions. Romanticism represented more desperate attempts to rebel against or escape from a refractory reality that precluded true community. Nineteenth-century German literature mirrored a repressive political tradition in which most Germans had little opportunity to participate in the political process or initiate reforms.

Contempt for political action grew out of the impossibility of achieving democratic reform through the political process. The characteristic German literary themes of inwardness, alienation, rejection, self-cultivation, and heroic renunciation reflected a generalized disillusionment with existing conditions. At its most extreme, this culture of rejection was expressed in a morbid fascination with death as the only way to achieve the unity and fulfillment that life in the world as it is could not provide. Such an attitude may be interpreted as both reaction against and result of the rigidity of social and political institutions. It is impossible here to separate cause from effect, for Germany's authoritarian institutions and undemocratic ideology sustained, abetted, and conditioned each other in dialectical fashion. The separation of culture and politics into mutually exclusive spheres and the juxtaposition of an uplifting ideal and spiritual realm to the degrading material realm of public affairs in turn reinforced the very conditions such a contrast reflected. Modernization, that combination of industrialization, liberalization, rationalization, secularization, and democratization, was widely equated with the triumph of materialism and the loss of authentic culture and soul.

To what degree do Mann's aestheticism and neo-Romanticism reflect European cultural trends in general rather than specifically German conditions? The fin de siècle culture of decadence and the growing assault on Enlightenment rationalism form part of a general crisis of liberalism at the turn of the century. This "revolt against positivism," as H. Stuart Hughes has called it (33), may be interpreted as a loss of bourgeois confidence, a reaction to the growing gap between the liberal ideal of the autonomous individual free to pursue *Bildung* and self-development, on the one hand, and the social reality of urban poverty, mass politics, recurring economic crisis, and class conflict, on the other. Mann's prewar stories, which have aptly been called "the consummation of German bourgeois Romanticism"

(Lichtheim 90), illustrate aspects of this malaise and form part of the general reorientation of European thought toward various types of irrationalism and anti-intellectualism before the First World War. The psychological dislocations occasioned by the growth of industrial society may not have been qualitatively different in Germany than in other European countries, but Germany provided more extreme examples of Europe-wide trends. The country's static, illiberal political institutions, coupled with the rapid pace of industrialization and the consequent growth of working- and middle-class pressures for democratic change, meant that in Germany the social question appeared particularly intractable and that the "cultural despair" (Stern) of the educated and propertied classes would be correspondingly greater than in Western Europe. The popularity of *The Buddenbrooks* may be attributed at least in part to its success in capturing this mood of dissolution, degeneration, and decline. Oswald Spengler's *Decline of the West*, conceived before the war but not published until 1918, provides perhaps the most comprehensive statement of conservative misgivings about democracy and modernizing trends.

What insights does Mann's short fiction provide when viewed in the light of this "culture of political despair" (Anchor 77–96) and the culture-civilization dichotomy? The central theme of his early works is the search to achieve through withdrawal into art the personal fulfillment that participation in inhospitable social reality cannot provide. The unspoken question Mann seems to pose is how the human personality can find its unique development in a fundamentally inimical social environment. Mann's response apparently revives the typically German alternatives of artistic self-cultivation and isolation from society at large. His lack of critical social consciousness recalls the Romantic alienation, Schopenhauerian pessimism, and Wagnerian morbidity characteristic of the German literary tradition. Yet the short novels *Tristan* (1903), *Tonio Kröger* (1903), *Death in Venice* (1912), and *Mario and the Magician* (1930) may in fact mirror Mann's progression from "aesthetic isolationism" and subjectivism in the era before World War I to his "militant humanism" and increasing integration of social concerns into art in the postwar period (Berman, *Rise* 271, 278). The works may be read as documents of the shift from Wilhelmian monarchism to Weimar democracy, a shift that many of Germany's elites refused to make or accept. Although Mann's conversion to liberal democracy has been described as "a painfully slow affair" (Lichtheim 150), he eventually came to reject the excessive subjectivity—the "cult of the private sphere that necessarily denigrated political interests" (Berman, *Rise* 270)—of prewar German literary culture.

Mann's readiness to accept the republic and to embrace Western values may have been presaged by precisely the ambivalence and irony that raise his prewar fiction to the level of great art. It is the ambivalence and irony that provide an implicitly critical edge even to the prewar works in which the irreconcilability of culture and politics, art and life, the ideal realm and the world of affairs, is assumed. As Mann suggests in *Tristan* and *Tonio Kröger*, life is associated with ugliness, and activity is equated with sin (125, 161). This irreconcilability of ideal and reality, of thought and action, is most starkly apparent in the contrasting figures of Spinell and Klöterjahn, in *Tristan*. Spinell, the idealist who abhors the "crude appetite for reality" (105), exemplifies the escapist alternatives of aestheticism and self-cultivation, while Klöterjahn's feet are firmly planted in the real world of commercial rationality and practical affairs. With whom does Mann side? Not with the philistine Klöterjahn, to be sure, but his portrait of Spinell can hardly be said to serve as a model for emulation, either. It is a portrait that frequently borders on caricature. While art may provide a refuge from life, a haven of private fulfillment, it is Klöterjahn, through his infant son, who literally has the last laugh, and Spinell's aestheticism is revealed as one-sided self-absorption and escapism. Mann lovingly describes the seductive appeal of Wagnerian aestheticism (as also in *The Blood of the Walsungs*, 1921) but leaves no doubt that surrender to its appeal is tantamount not to redemption but to sickness and death. Ultimately, *Tristan* may serve as the record of a "sick" society in which its most conscientious members cannot reconcile social or political involvement with their artistic or human integrity.

Ambivalence is at the very center of *Tonio Kröger*, in which the private sphere of artistic creation and the public sphere of social activity remain unreconciled. But Kröger, unlike Spinell, registers despair at his inability to join the realm of practical affairs. Spinell hates the "unconscious types" (124), while Kröger longs for the "fair-haired and the blue-eyed, the bright children of life, the happy, the charming and the ordinary" (192). Of course, both stories, and *Death in Venice* as well, attest to the strained relations between intellectuals and society in imperial Germany. *Tonio Kröger*, too, conveys that bad conscience about the pursuit of happiness that is typical of the German literary and intellectual tradition. Kröger embodies the recurring cultural imperative not to give in to worldly or even human desires and longings. "Living and working are incompatible," Kröger believes, and the artist must have died "to be wholly a creator" (152). But in *Tonio Kröger* the tension between the two realms seems more susceptible to mediation than in *Tristan*. There is at least a hint here that the artist can be true to his calling without totally disengaging from social reality.

In the last episode Tonio Kröger heads for the soulful, puritanical, disciplined north, eschewing the sensual, passionate, instinctual charm of the south. In *Death in Venice* this north-south dichotomy reemerges in full force. Gustav Aschenbach succumbs to the lure of the south. Here nature and reality are again depicted as a danger to the artist. But Mann's ambivalence is expressed in his exploration of a rigid, repressed personality that struggles unsuccessfully against the instinctual forces within; in this work the authoritarian personality, if not authoritarian society, is dissected and critiqued. Although puritanical Prussianism still wins out, Mann reveals the self-destructiveness inherent in Aschenbach's ethos of self-denial and in his pathological obsession with order. Aschenbach's death is more a caricature than an apotheosis of *Liebestod*. In *Death in Venice* Mann seems to be trying to break the Wagnerian spell and reconcile the hostile opposition between art and life. His irony allows a reading of *Death in Venice* as an effort to achieve a sensibility in which nature and reality can be affirmed, not repressed or denied. Aschenbach's fate is clearly a warning of where the repression of nature and feeling can lead. Transposed into the realm of politics and society, Aschenbach's end anticipates the self-destructiveness of the Germanic ethos of duty, denial, and discipline. The element of self-criticism in *Death in Venice* marks another, though still very ambiguous, step toward the reintegration of culture and politics, the individual and society, art and life, effected by Mann after the First World War.

The contrast between Mann's prewar and postwar outlook is most striking in his adaptation to the changed political circumstances after the war. His acceptance of the republic in the 1920s is proclaimed in essays that reject Romantic isolation and call for participation in democratic society. Estrangement from the world of affairs gives way to greater commitment and engagement. Culture and politics are no longer treated as mutually exclusive spheres. The implicit critique of fascism in *Mario and the Magician*, in which Mussolini's charismatic dictatorship is allegorically derided as a form of hypnotic domination, may serve as an example of his postwar integration—subtle and complex, to be sure—of social and political concerns into art. Mann's conversion to liberal democracy meant that he no longer simply conceded the political sphere to the state. The politicization of culture serves as a belated antidote to Romantic isolation. Mann's later social involvement throws the aesthetic subjectivity of his earlier works into relief. Despite their timeless themes, his prewar works of fiction appear as time-bound documents of social loneliness in a fractured polity. Through their depiction of alienation, however, students may gain valuable insight into German history and society.

As a teacher of history, I am less concerned with Mann's personal odyssey than with the social and political context in which that exemplary intellectual voyage took place. *Tristan*, *Tonio Kröger*, and *Death in Venice* provide splendid literary illustrations of themes that I stress in my course on German history through literature from 1770 to 1918. Each of these stories depicts aspects of Germany's antipolitical idealist tradition, with its moral imperative of regenerating humankind through art and transforming reality by infusing existence with timeless moral and spiritual ideals. The leading protagonists are idealist types, though it is both a function of Mann's artistry and a sign of the crisis of the idealist tradition that they should appear not as paragons but as partially deformed and fallible individuals. Spinell, sensitive, refined, conscientious, wholly dedicated to the cultivation of art and beauty, is ultimately a caricature of the inwardness that Mann celebrates in his *Reflections of a Nonpolitical Man*. Tonio Kröger's schizoid temperament reproduces the dualisms of a nation unable to reconcile the conflicting claims of tradition and modernity, morality and power politics, spirit and nature, thought and action, community and society, aristocracy and democracy, ideal and reality. Gustav Aschenbach's exaltation of morality and "dignity" over knowledge, rationality, and skepticism may represent the triumph of will over intellect, but his repressive ethos of "*durchhalten!*" (201) eventually helps to do him in.

Students readily take to the challenge to read these stories for signifiers of antidemocratic attitudes and the restrictiveness of the political sphere. There is a danger of overinterpretation, of course, but I have found these stories, in many ways foreign to the experiences of American students in the late twentieth century, an excellent medium for introducing what may simplistically be called "the German ideology." Students quickly pick up on the recurring dualisms in the German tradition and participate in extrapolating values from the culture-civilization dichotomy. Perhaps because they read Mann's stories at the end of the course, they have no difficulty recognizing themes that have already become familiar to them: the search for a spiritual path out of everyday tensions; the craving for the authentic life that social reality does not provide; the denigration of the active life, and the flirtation with death as the only way to achieve complete fulfillment; the need for the individual to carve out a sphere for himself or herself apart from society; the dangers to the (aristocratic) personality from the (democratic) masses; the importance of discipline as the way to build moral character and achieve true freedom. The preoccupation of these stories with the inner life throws into relief the impotence and indifference of the individual within the public sphere. In this way, stories that dramatize personal psychological neuroses may also be read as documents of social pathology.

The ambivalence and complexity of Mann's stories and their leading characters have the advantage of permitting students to appreciate both the creative and the destructive potential of the German tradition of idealizing art and authoritarian politics. A useful class exercise is to contrast the values that Mann treats in so ironical and ambiguous a fashion with the values common to the American tradition as experienced by contemporary students. It sometimes comes as a shock to students to discover that the characters the young Thomas Mann created and at least partially identified with subscribed to assumptions that today appear suspect and discredited. The biological determinism and ethnic stereotyping implicit in Tonio Kröger's rejection of the idea of another visit to Italy is a case in point: "And I can't stand all that dreadful southern vivacity, all those people with their black animal eyes. They've no conscience in their eyes, those Latin races . . ." (164). Passages such as this offer a vehicle for relating the pervasive racialism and anti-Semitism of the Wilhelmian era to idealist patterns of thought. Even Mann shared the characteristic idealist disdain for empirical reality in favor of essential ideas and ideal types. Thus he not only attributed fixed mental and psychological traits to different nationalities but assumed that these traits were reflected in physical features and transmitted through bloodlines. For Tonio Kröger, the blond and blue-eyed Ingeborg Holm stood for the normality, purity, and ideal of wholeness that he found so attractive yet so difficult to attain.

A study of Mann's recurring north-south characterizations in his short fiction enables students to gain an appreciation both of Germany's unique self-understanding and of the potentially invidious consequences of the "Nordic myth." The north is typically endowed with a higher, deeper spirituality, a discipline and a conscience lacking in the animalistic, hedonistic, impulsive south—or in the rational, self-interested West. "Conscience, dear lady—conscience is a terrible thing!" says Spinell in explaining to Frau Klöterjahn why he rises so early, but of course he doesn't mean it (103). Tonio Kröger celebrates his father's northern temperament: "contemplative, thorough, puritanically correct, and inclined to melancholy" (191). If the south epitomizes vitality and the West embodies intellectual skepticism, the Germans personify morality. Just how problematic, however, even the "superior" traits of the German national character are to Mann may best be gleaned from a careful reading of *Death in Venice*.

In Mann's description of Gustav Aschenbach, students readily discern what are still sometimes considered to be the typically German character traits of self-discipline, self-sacrifice, and the subordination of self to a normative authority. At the same time, Aschenbach's story may be read as a warning against both the self-aggrandizing and self-destructive tendencies inherent in these very same "admirable" traits. Aschenbach personifies the conscientious—or compulsive—perfectionism for which Germany was renowned, the rigorous, disciplined, incorruptible adherence to high standards of workmanship that for years rendered the label "Made in Germany" the guarantee of highest quality all over the world. Yet such perfectionism can only be achieved against the grain, by overcoming one's natural inclination to surrender to the enjoyment of life: "Aschenbach did not enjoy enjoying himself" (231). How different Aschenbach's reasons for traveling abroad are (before his fateful last journey to Venice) from those of the average American: "His attitude to foreign travel . . . had always been that it was nothing more than a necessary health precaution, to be taken from time to time however disinclined to it one might be" (198). His conscience would not have permitted him to travel solely for pleasure. Vacations are for the serious business of recuperation, not for fun. This iron resolve to pursue an ideal of perfection against his natural inclinations—a state of mind expressed by Mann through the metaphor of the clenched fist (201)—constituted the essence of his art and, by extension, of the Germanic ethos as well. All great works "owe their existence to a defiant despite"; this was "the formula of his life and his fame" (202).

Aschenbach's works reflect the ascetic ethos of heroism, self-denial, and self-overcoming that looms large in the Prussian-Germanic tradition and that contrasts sharply with contemporary American values. What would Aschenbach—indeed, what would Mann—have thought of the American pursuit of personal happiness and profit? It would have seemed shallow, egoistic, and immoral. A failure of the sense of duty, of the Kantian moral imperative. A triumph of reason and the senses instead of the will. From Aschenbach's attitudes it is easy to see how a democratic culture of collective individualism could come to be viewed as self-indulgent, uncreative, chaotic, and un-German. Nor is it difficult to show—though Mann does not make this connection explicit—how anti-Semitic attitudes could be derived from the identification of Jews, the quintessential outsiders, with the materialism, commercialism, sensualism, intellectual skepticism, and left-wing (i.e., egalitarian and libertarian) politics that good Germans (and good Christians) renounced, even if their natural inclinations should tempt them toward the gratification of their worldly and bodily desires.

Tadzio, the object of Aschenbach's obsession, represents an entirely different way of life: natural, relaxed, unapologetically self-indulgent, but without a trace of servility. Aschenbach's fatal attraction may be read as a form of self-criticism, a realization that his life up to now had been arid, inauthentic, and vain. He now renounces his earlier slavish addiction to duty, convention, and the achievement of "dignity." He recognizes that the fame he has strenuously sought and attained has come at the cost of personal autonomy. Toward the end his repudiation of his past and its previously unacknowledged hypocrisy even entails dismissal of the basic idealist faith in the edifying and regenerative function of art: "the use of art to educate the nation and its youth is a reprehensible undertaking which should be forbidden by law" (261). Yet by inserting this passage into Aschenbach's dreamlike recollection of a Platonic dialogue, Mann typically creates the ironic distance that makes students wonder whether he really means it. And isn't Aschenbach's renunciation of past ideals merely a function of lust? "What could art and virtue mean to him now, when he might reap the advantages of chaos?" (255). In this way Mann's irony and ambivalence make room for discussion and debate. What was to blame for Aschenbach's demise? Was it his need for total control, the psychic toll taken by the "constant harnessing of his energies" (201), that brought him to this fateful pass, or was it his failure of self-restraint, his surrender to impulse and emotion? Is repression or gratification to blame? In Freudian language, was he the victim of his hypertrophied superego or of his uncontrollable id? Is Mann's story a defense of or an attack on the Prussian-Germanic ethos of self-discipline and self-denial? Is it a critique of or a plea for emotional permissiveness and, by extension, freedom and democracy?

Does Aschenbach's self-caused death in Venice redeem the value of knowledge and skeptical rationalism, which he was proud of having overcome in his works, or does it show the nihilistic depths to which these corrosive "Western" (and "Jewish") values can lead when no longer held in check by "moral courage"? Was Aschenbach too disloyal to his ideals or too out of touch with material reality? Did Mann conceive of this morality tale as a Nietzschean denunciation of the destructive consequences of asceticism or as a warning of what can happen if one follows the Nietzschean precept to "live dangerously"? Though students may not agree on the answers, their understanding of the problematic of freedom and authority—so crucial to the German historical experience—is enhanced. Most important, perhaps, they come to see how the German social, cultural, and political tradition could give rise dialectically to both high creativity and great (self-)destructiveness.

Why would a historian choose Thomas Mann's short fiction rather than a social novel or, conversely, other, more obvious examples of literary escapism to introduce students to Wilhelmian culture and politics? Certainly *The Buddenbrooks* lends itself to the analysis I have suggested, but its length may prohibit its use in a history class. Mann's short fiction has the advantage of brevity. As outstanding examples of the culture of inwardness, these short works epitomize the bourgeois Romanticism of the German literary tradition in the nineteenth and early twentieth centuries. Despite the timelessness and universality of their themes, they may be used in class to illustrate specific features of imperial German politics and society. Precisely because of their high literary quality—the product of the creative artist's unique combination of talent, sensibility, imagination, and integrity—they lend themselves better to this purpose than the more ephemeral and less ambitious literary output of the time does. The acuity and scrupulosity of Mann's examination of German bourgeois consciousness at the turn of the century capture the complexity and ambiguity of social reality in a way that lesser works can't match. His stories provide both examples and incipient critiques of the culture of apolitical inwardness and ascetic idealism that Mann himself defended until the end of the First World War. Of course, some students will choose to read Mann's works as descriptions of the human condition rather than of a particular social constellation; the confrontation between such alternative readings always leads to lively discussion and enhanced insight. If students relate the problematic of thwarted personality addressed in Mann's short fiction to their experiences in contemporary America, so much the better.

Assigning Mann's short novels in history class thus serves two valuable educational functions at once: it gives students unique insight into the culture of German imperial society at the turn of the century even as it exposes them to the mastery and creativity of great literary works of the past.

Philosophizing and Poetic License in Mann's Early Fiction

Adrian Del Caro

Schopenhauer and Nietzsche were major philosophical influences on Thomas Mann, and it is important to determine how Mann used his sources in the early fiction. In "Thomas Mann and Tradition" T. J. Reed warns against an "iceberg assumption" whereby "any detectable literary allusion implies the hidden presence and functional relevance of the larger whole" (222). I make no such assumption but emphasize instead that teachers of Mann are dealing with literature in the German tradition. Reed explains that Mann "is not out to understand exhaustively, but to make piecemeal use of what attracts him" (224). What attracted Mann and many others of his generation was the rich philosophical legacy of the nineteenth century.

Since undergraduates cannot be expected to assimilate philosophical texts on their own, brief but salient excerpts from Schopenhauer's *World as Will and Representation* (notably, selected paragraphs from the third and fourth books) should suffice as handout material supplemented with lecture. Since Nietzsche's major ideas are scattered throughout the works, I find excerpts from *The Birth of Tragedy* useful, especially insofar as the Apollonian-Dionysian polarity is brought out; here the students should at least grasp the Apollonian as Schopenhauer's principle of individuation and the Dionysian impulse as the disrupter of all form.

Additional secondary readings for the reserve list that I have used with success are the works of Erich Heller (*Ironic German*), R. J. Hollingdale, and Roger Nicholls. These highly readable texts are available in English, and they represent a thorough understanding of Schopenhauer and Nietzsche in the works of Mann. To offset the preponderance of philosophical interpretation provided by these sources, I also recommend Reed's "Thomas Mann and Tradition," especially for tempering the Schopenhauer slant presented by Heller in particular (222–23). Another valuable approach for helping students sift through the facts of reception in order to appreciate Mann's fictional intent is offered by Stanley Corngold in *The Fate of the Self*. Finally, the writings of Georg Lukács on both Mann and Nietzsche are useful for demonstrating not only how Mann used his sources but also how he later disavowed his main influence, Nietzsche (see "Search"; *Destruction* 309–99). Although I place these sources on reserve, I distribute handouts before class that contain particularly striking theses or observations concerning material under discussion, to provide focus to the students' preparation and guidelines for critical reading.

One additional "secondary" source I place on reserve is Mann's *Reflections of a Nonpolitical Man*. Though it is asking too much to have undergraduates or graduates read this work, teachers who avoid this text are doing their students a disservice. In *Reflections* Mann passionately reveals his character and shows himself without the benefit of the aesthetic flora that conceals him in most of the fiction. Here, too, he explains why Schopenhauer, Wagner, and Nietzsche are his three major influences and why he, writing during World War I in defense of Germany's "nonpolitical" character, considered himself to be a man of the nineteenth century. To ignore *Reflections* is to ignore that German artists, writers, and intellectuals also experienced the First World War, and without some lecture devoted to this work, students could easily come to believe that Mann's practice of literary aestheticism from roughly 1900 and into the war was without emotional and professional consequences for him. Nothing is further from the truth.

Whether or not he erred in doing so, Mann himself forced the analogy between his "burgherly" status as a writer and what it meant in his day to be a German. Both Reed ("Thomas Mann and Tradition" 229) and Corngold ("Mann as a Reader of Nietzsche" 146, 159) point out how strongly Mann relied on Nietzsche for his fundamental ideas and how Mann's later disavowal of this influence was a political act. The political apprenticeship of Mann shows the extent of the change the devoutly aesthetic, self-contained writer of the early fiction undergoes. Specifically, it reveals the way in which the favorite theme of decline, appropriated from Nietzsche, evolves from the relatively innocuous treatment reflected in *Tristan* and *Death in Venice* to the full-blown condemnation of Germany, personified by the syphilitic Nietzscheanized composer Leverkühn in *Doctor Faustus*.

Mann's affinity with Nietzsche rested on a similar style and not merely on borrowed ideas. In his essay "Bilse und ich" Mann responded to criticisms concerning his lack of creative invention by insisting that the genuine writers of the past used materials already given and that they based themselves on reality. The talent of invention, however, cannot "qualify as the criterion of the writer's profession" and is merely secondary (13–14; my translation). As Corngold formulates it, in "Thomas Mann and the German Philosophical Tradition," Mann "saw his entire *oeuvre* as a reinterpretation of the cultural past" (9). Now consider Nietzsche's remarks in praise of Goethe, another favorite of Mann as well. In *Human, All Too Human* Goethe is described in contradistinction to those who allowed "revolution" to enter the world of letters: "no novel material or characters, but the ancient and long-familiar continually reanimated and transformed: this is art as Goethe later *understood* it, as the Greeks and, yes, the French *practised* it" (104). Mann espoused a classical position vis-à-vis art, based not only on his perception of Goethe but almost certainly on what he had learned from Nietzsche with respect to Goethe and art.

Mann's assessment of Nietzsche, when he elevated him to the role of advocate for the German ethos, was fundamentally flawed, more a matter of desire than fact. The *Reflections* are also "meditations" reminiscent of Nietzsche's own *Untimely Meditations*; Mann attributed to Nietzsche the defense of German ideals that he, Mann, desperately needed, or, as Reed has written, "this is debased Nietzsche, paralleling the contradiction which runs through all his thought, and Mann realized it" ("Tradition" 229). Corngold has also observed that during World War I, "what Mann assimilates of Nietzsche . . . is mainly a style and not a lucid criticism of culture" ("Thomas Mann" 13). I have discussed this aspect of Mann's relation to Nietzsche in the context of what I call his political apprenticeship ("Apprentice" 25–27). Mann was capable of "tinkering" with his philosophical sources, and it would be unfair to judge him as an expert.

With respect to the characters in *Tristan*, who undergo constant reformulation in the later fiction, I find this statement by Reed to be helpful: "Nietzsche was virtually the only begetter of Mann's fundamental ideas— on art, disease, genius, vitality, human typology; and of his basic attitudes—critical, analytical, ironical, self-querying" ("Tradition" 228). Mann's poetic license presents us with literary products depicting human typology focused particularly on art versus vitality, on the Spinell-Gabriele nexus set against Herr Klöterjahn and his robust child. He created types out of Nietzschean material and placed them into a laboratory environment where they are allowed to play out their destinies under ironic scrutiny. Once the basic polarities of this story are set forth, classroom discussion could be devoted to the absence of any "moral" to the story. It does not escape students' attention that Mann condemns and ironizes on both sides—that is, he makes Spinell look effete and ridiculous, but he makes Klöterjahn appear brutal and insensitive. Beyond art being paired with decline, and vitality with appetite, what are readers supposed to make of this strange encounter in a sanatorium? Is Mann or any other writer required to go on record with a socially redeeming message?

Roger Nicholls addresses the Schopenhauer-Nietzsche-Wagner connection. Mann had claimed that Wagner's *Tristan and Isolde* had its origins in Wagner's reading of Schopenhauer, so that the opera expresses "Schopenhauer's metaphysical escape from the wheel of Ixion, the domination of the will" (Nicholls 43). Indeed, all three intellectual mentors are compressed into the thematics of the story *Tristan*. The three great teachers are discovered, in relatively small quantities, in the tissue of Mann's characters, and they react in ways that intrigue the reader.

But here a sample of Schopenhauer's thought will shed light on the fate of the sanatorium dwellers. The type of knowledge brought about by tragic experience pierces phenomena, and the veil of Maya no longer deceives. This knowledge sees through the *principium individuationis*, the ego, resulting in "the complete knowledge of the real nature of the world, acting as a *quieter* of the will, [and producing] resignation, the giving up not merely of life, but of the whole will-to-live itself" (1: 253). In *Tristan* music is the catalyst of this Schopenhauerian surrender because, according to the philosopher, music is as *immediate* an objectification and copy of the whole *will* as the world itself . . . for this reason the effect of music is so very much more powerful and penetrating than is that of the other arts, for these others speak only of the shadow, but music of the essence.   (1: 257)

A rationale for Frau Klöterjahn's musicality, and her decline, is thus partially given. But Mann orchestrates a polarity between declining life and ascending vitality.

Schopenhauer claimed that knowledge based on art exists "outside and independently of all relations, but [that it] alone is really essential to the world, the true content of its phenomena, that which is subject to no change" (1: 184). In so claiming, he elevated artists to humanity's elect. But Nietzsche rejected Schopenhauer because art is prescribed *against life*, against experience in this world, as an ultra-Platonism. Schopenhauer uses art to combat the will, and the effective struggle to subdue will results in withdrawal from life. By the time of *Human, All Too Human*, Nietzsche had formulated biting criticisms of the artist-escapist, and his actual disavowal of Wagner and Romanticism corresponded with his rejection of metaphysical aesthetics. The artist, wrote Nietzsche, "possesses a weaker morality than the thinker. . . . He appears to be fighting on behalf of the greater dignity and significance of man; in reality . . . he considers the perpetuation of his mode of creation more important than scientific devotion to the truth in any form, however plainly this may appear" (80). Now consider Spinell's extreme aestheticism and his machinations designed to win Frau Klöterjahn for music at all costs. He goes into raptures at the glimpse of beauty (99) and stays in the sanatorium not for his health but for the "style" of the place (102). He is coy, preferring only to "glimpse" (105), and though he possesses knowledge of music, he must confess, painfully, that knowledge and artistic skill, such as Frau Klöterjahn's, "seldom go together" (118). Frau Klöterjahn, aesthetically inoculated by Spinell, begins to suspect that his influence is affecting her health (110). But Spinell is ruthless, devoted only to his artist's ideals, just as Nietzsche described them.

Under the title "Ennoblement through Degeneration" in *Human*, Nietzsche provided Mann with a wealth of material in only three pages. According to Nietzsche, strong communities composed of homogeneous individuals are exposed to the danger of growing stupidity, which "haunts all stability like its shadow." Morally weaker individuals ensure spiritual progress by inoculating the stable community: "Degenerates are of the highest importance wherever progress is to be effected." But Nietzsche also cautioned that the community must be strong enough to accept the inoculation without succumbing to it (clearly Frau Klöterjahn is not strong). He continued by moving from the community to the individual:

"rarely is degeneration, a mutilation, even a vice and physical or moral damage in general without an advantage in some other direction" (107). Frau Klöterjahn's father is an artist, and Spinell has a Nietzschean explanation for the family's decline (108). His pathological greed for aesthetic intoxication is instrumental in his seducing Frau Klöterjahn to death; he is bent on "redeeming" her from the slavery of life, of the will.

Spinell uses Nietzschean language in his letter to Klöterjahn: "You are the stronger man. In our struggle I have only one thing to turn against you, the sublime avenging weapon of the weak: intellect and the power of words" (125–26). Herr Klöterjahn is the exaggerated opposite of Spinell, the "stupid," strong type, described as robust, hearty, hungry, fleshy, and unconscious. Herr Klöterjahn and his infant son, who has "won and held his place in life with colossal energy and ruthlessness" (97–98), represent that unconscious vitality that flourishes at the expense of the weaker— namely, the declining mother. Gabriele is delicate, ethereal, and artistically gifted, but, at the same time, her beauty is the refined mark of death close at hand (114–15, 118–19). Mann is not concerned with demonstrating philosophical ideas in their validity but primarily with examining the effects he is able to coax from the material. The requisite mixtures and composites are allowed to enact the plot, resulting in a grotesque *Liebestod* (love death or love-inspired death), after which Spinell is compelled to flee from the jubilantly vital (but predictably stupid) baby. Weighing Schopenhauer against Nietzsche provided a wealth of polarities that Mann fictionalized to suit his own needs. For example, denial of life versus affirmation of life is a consistent pattern in many stories, but aesthetic refinement versus robust lack of consciousness as seen in *Tristan* is Mann's own creation— Nietzsche did not provide him with theoretical models of either type.

Tonio Kröger represents an internalized treatment of the artist's vocation and art in relation to life. Nicholls calls Tonio's longing for life "the resolving theme" of his experiences (36). Bearing in mind that Mann's conception of the artist draws on both Schopenhauer and Nietzsche and that Nietzsche opted forcefully in favor of life, I cannot accept David Luke's observation that Nietzsche "had been the supreme protester . . . against life," though I grant him the rest (x). Mann's poetic license in *Tonio* is on a more serious plane than the tragicomical, ludicrous, and grotesque applications of *Tristan*, since *Tonio* is an autobiographical work. Tonio, like Hamlet, is a character who suffers deeply, and the suffering stems from knowledge. According to Schopenhauer, suffering occurs when the will is hindered: "Therefore, in proportion as knowledge attains to distinctness, consciousness is enhanced, pain also increases, and consequently reaches its highest degree in man." Genius, of course, suffers most (1: 310).

Nietzsche also held that suffering is a mark of higher consciousness, the grist not only of art but of life itself. This idea he tirelessly elaborated in *The Birth of Tragedy* and continued to espouse throughout his career;

insofar as suffering results from obstacles, and one becomes stronger, more vital only by overcoming obstacles, suffering must be.

When students are exposed to talk of "suffering," they have a right to know that within the German Romantic tradition, stretching from Wilhelm Heinrich Wackenroder (1773–98) to Schopenhauer, Wagner, and Nietzsche, suffering is frequently the fate of the alienated artist or genius, who feels uncomfortable in the bourgeois (German: *bürgerlich*) world but out of touch with life when immersed only in art. I find it helpful to spend time on the illumination of the term *bürgerlich*, since students do not readily appreciate why *Bürger* and *Künstler* constitute a dichotomy. Mann himself comes to our aid with his discussion of *bürgerlich* in *Reflections* (71–105).

Tonio vacillates between denial and affirmation of life. He suffers as a child because his idolized friend does not love him (137), he suffers under the realization that his best artistic efforts would not impress Inge Holm and what she represents (148), and he suffers finally from the "carnal adventures" in which he engages when his heart feels dead and without love (151–52). At the same time, however, he is fulfilling the Nietzschean challenge of creativity by turning his suffering into gold (152). Tonio is not the kind of man who can live "happily, charmingly, and artistically, little suspecting that good work is brought forth only under the pressure of a bad life, that living and working are incompatible and that one must have died if one is to be wholly a creator" (152). In Zarathustra's speech "On the Way of the Creator" (part 1) we find the source of this idea: "Go into your loneliness with your love and with your creation, my brother; and only much later will justice limp after you. With my tears go into your loneliness, my brother. I love him who wants to create over and beyond himself and thus perishes" (177).

Tonio's vitality is his deepest instinct. He abandons himself to adoration of Inge Holm because "it would enrich him and make him more fully alive" (144). But his is a highly reflective experience of life, the artist's, "enthroned above mere inarticulate, unconscious life" (151). And of course, in his best moments Tonio senses that his "heart" is alive (178, 189). While the vitalism is suggestive of Nietzsche's influence, Mann successfully blends Schopenhauer and Nietzsche with respect to both suffering and tragic insight. The latter occurs, for Schopenhauer, with the destruction of the *principium individuationis* and the lifting of the veil of Maya, and in similar fashion for Nietzsche, who adopted Schopenhauer's terms. Even as a boy Tonio has penetrating insight, unlike the elegant Herr Knaak (146), and the polarity of insight versus gracefulness animates his polarized soul. Tonio's inner monologue is a characteristic fusion of Schopenhauerian insight and Nietzschean criticism directed at the superficial life. Reflecting on Herr Knaak's "imperturbable" gaze, one is reminded of Nietzsche's characterization of humans as herd animals, imperturbable because they merely graze. Herr Knaak's eyes did not look deeply into things, they did not penetrate to the point at which life becomes complex and sad; all they knew was that they were beautiful brown eyes. But that was why he had such a proud bearing! Yes, it was necessary to be stupid in order to be able to walk like that; and then one was loved, for then people found one charming. (146)

Mann allows for a Nietzschean explanation of Tonio's heightened insight and his lack of gracefulness: "The old Kröger family had gradually fallen into a state of decay and disintegration, and Tonio Kröger's own existence and nature were with good reason generally regarded as symptomatic of this decline" (150). Tonio's state of decline resembles Gabriele's in *Tristan*, since her musical talent supposedly derives from the ascendance of art at the expense of life, except that now Mann is writing about himself, the artist whose creative talent and insight causes his alienation.

In his talk with Lisaweta, Tonio alludes to Hamlet in describing "a state of mind in which a man has no sooner seen through a thing than so far from feeling reconciled to it he is immediately sickened to death by it" (160). And when he experiences his revisitation of youth in the presence of Inge and Hans, he curses his insight for the last time (186). Nietzsche's warning is that too much knowledge—or, rather, knowledge not directly in the service of life—is nihilistic, without value. Tonio navigates between icy intellectuality, aloofness, indifference (152, 156, 160), and his true understanding that he is not a nihilist, that he "affirm[s] the value of living emotion" in spite of literature's dismissive articulation (160–61).

Nietzsche was his century's strongest critic of *l'art pour l'art*, the notion that art is basically without purpose and should not be harnessed to any cause. He explained in *Twilight of the Idols* that *l'art pour l'art* justifiably describes the need to keep morality out of art, but he vehemently denied that art serves no purpose; all art, he insisted, strengthens or weakens certain valuations, affirming valuations when life is affirmed and denying valuations when life is denied. The artist's basic instinct, therefore, aims at life, not art, so that art is the great stimulus to life and undeserving of the term *l'art pour l'art* (529). Tonio demonstrates, as Mann's alter ego, that he embraces this philosophy and dislikes the condition of his art and the art of his day:

> I tell you I am often sick to death of being a portrayer of humanity and having no share in human experience. . . . Can one even say that an artist *is* a man? Let Woman answer that! I think we artists are all in rather the same situation as those artificial papal sopranos. . . . Our voices are quite touchingly beautiful. But— (156)

In this disavowal of *l'art pour l'art*, students should recognize Mann's place within the culture of the fin de siècle; here, too, students have an opportunity to glimpse the irony and complexity of his nature. His own writings were predominantly aesthetic, and he allowed his alter ego Tonio to admit this when Tonio referred to his past as a writer as "all these long, dead years" (183). But Mann, who was always popular with his readers, found a large audience for his basically aesthetic fiction. He knew, as the artist endowed with insight knows, that he practiced neutrality in art to the point of feeling neutered, as Tonio's words imply, and this question of neutrality versus life affirmation motivated Nietzsche's critique of the modern person. In *Twilight* he condemned morality as antinature, explaining that the church, which uses castration as a cure against passion, is therefore basically hostile to life. For the fin de siècle, religion was not viable, and the value vacuum dramatized by Nietzsche's claim that God is dead was effectively filled with devotion channeled into art for art's sake. The hollowness and insidious decadence associated with the cult of beauty received tragic treatment in *Death in Venice*.

For *Death in Venice*, which is structured like tragedy, the most useful source is *The Birth of Tragedy*. Here Nietzsche treated the main elements of Aschenbach's greatness and decline; Schopenhauer's views are present in the hero's disciplined "taming" of the will, his Apollonian composure and embodiment of the *principium individuationis*. The Wagnerian dimension is suggested by the power of music, its fascinating lure as the catalyst of Aschenbach's *Liebestod*. Throughout his Venice sojourn Aschenbach is depicted as struggling between knowledge, the Socratic impulse criticized by Nietzsche, and tragedy, which is signaled by his surrender to Dionysus. He does not allow knowledge to paralyze him (204).

Mann's description of Aschenbach in chapter 2 is a masterpiece of fiction from philosophy, applying his conception of Schopenhauer's principle of individuation and Nietzsche's Apollonian to the hero. But since Aschenbach lives one-sidedly, Mann punctuates the short novel with hints about how Aschenbach begins to deny the will (198). Once his resolve starts to falter, so that he is removed from his place and work, others are successful at imposing their will on him (213, 222, 229, 256). Aschenbach, like other Mann heroes, is not on his own turf, and new obstacles help him consummate his tragic fate.

Like Venice itself, Aschenbach is the artist in whom decadence is concealed. After penning his exquisite prose under the inspiration of Tadzio-Eros, Aschenbach feels like a worn-out debaucher (236). Students tend to view Aschenbach as a weakling and a failure unless they recognize that, in theoretical terms, both Apollo and Dionysus must be present as fundamental life principles. To stimulate interest in, and some degree of sympathy for, Aschenbach's tragic fate, we might consider the "page and a half of exquisite prose" (236) written in defiance of his normal style, his epic and pedagogical dimension (the exemplary Apollonian versus the disruptive, unstructured Dionysian). We never learn the content of this writing, but we do know it was Aschenbach's last (see Berlin's essay in this volume). The precise circumstances of this curious production, which deserve careful scrutiny, can be discussed in connection with Zarathustra's message that "one must die at the right time" (183). I also encourage discussion on the nature of tragedy itself and on Schopenhauer's and Nietzsche's reasons for elevating it; this strategy allows the short novel's dimensions to emerge for themselves and avoids the problem of ascribing to the work a contrived "socially redeeming" message. Students can be informed about Nietzsche's critique of the innovations of Euripides in *Tragedy*, especially as they pertain to the original transcendental nature of tragedy's effect and Nietzsche's rejection of poetic justice.

In his conversation with Lisaweta, Tonio remarks how people generally consider the artist to be a special, exalted type, while "it never enters their heads that the origins of this so-called 'gift' may well be extremely dubious and extremely disreputable" (158). Nietzsche was bent on defrocking the artist, the poet especially. Zarathustra calls the poets liars whose best reflection rests on lust and boredom (240). In *Tragedy*, while Nietzsche was still an ardent admirer of Wagner, the greatest artist of his time, the two artistic impulses were the Apollonian and the Dionysian. The Apollonian represents restraint, poise, and duration as seen in the plastic arts, while the Dionysian represents precisely the *disruption* of the principle of individuation, since its artistic counterpart is unrestrained, bodiless, intoxicating—that is, music. Aschenbach the Apollonian artist must succumb to the primeval sway of the Dionysian, just as Socrates, before his death, finally acknowledged the importance of the irrational, the purely lyrical, by playing the flute.

Mann uses music to suggest that Aschenbach is drifting further from his Apollonian inner stronghold. Tadzio's speech is like music (233), the "aging lover" Aschenbach "no longer wished to be disenchanted" (237). Venice is the city "where composers have been inspired to lulling tones of somniferous eroticism" (245), and the great Dionysian dream is "permeated and dominated by a terrible sweet sound of flute music" (258). During the intoxication of the Dionysian festivals, Nietzsche claimed, the revelers were incited by flute music, wine, and orgiastic behavior into a condition of complete oneness with the Primal Unity, and individuation was temporarily dissolved. True art lay beyond individuation and consciousness, and true artists were those who served as their own work of art, as mediums and speakers for the Primal Unity.

This view allowed Nietzsche to state that "it is only as an *aesthetic phenomenon* that existence and the world are eternally justified" (*Tragedy* 52). The weight that young, Romantic Nietzsche attached to art in *Tragedy* should help to place Aschenbach's decline and surrender into perspective; his "defeat" occurs at the expense of Apollo, but his "triumph" occurs under the auspices of Dionysus. Aschenbach's flaw, if we must search for one, lies in his having structured and sustained a will held under rigid control and in having learned to impose this will in order to live sovereignly. But harking back once again to *Tonio Kröger*, we see that the appearance of beauty commonly associated with the Apollonian artistic impulse was suspect in Tonio's eyes; the result was observance of, but not participation in, life. This decadence finally succumbs to beauty as though to a drug, so that the illicit gondolier who cannot collect his fee tells Aschenbach: "You will pay, signore" (214). When it comes time to pay, Aschenbach is too weak, too bankrupt to pay with any currency but life itself.

A final word of caution: Mann's characters are composites of Schopenhauerian and Nietzschean material, so that their actions cannot always be predicted according to either impulse. But that is precisely the genius of Mann's working with sources, the elusive x of his artistry. Nietzsche avoided ideals, and part of Mann's success lies in his having avoided ideal characters. If undergraduates can be directed to some of the major philosophical sources of Mann's fiction, all of which exist in translation, and if they are given enough information in handouts and lectures to provide a modest basis for illuminating major themes, the result should be heightened readability and an enriched understanding of Mann's craft. To a small extent, encouraging students to consider even short excerpts of Schopenhauer and Nietzsche will require them to temporarily abandon the familiar medium of literature for the less accommodating terrain of philosophical discourse, but teachers should not approach Mann's sources as though they themselves were the subject under scrutiny. By the same token, Mann infused his fiction with the ideas of his spiritual mentors, and some understanding of where the philosophizing ends and the fictionalizing begins is basic to the experience of his craft.

Mann and Wagner

Steven R. Cerf

The publication of *Thomas Mann: Pro and contra Wagner*—a collection of forty-six Mann essays and letters in English translation based on the anthology *Thomas Mann: Wagner und unsere Zeit*—enhances our understanding of the novelist's lifelong preoccupation with Wagner. As Mann repeatedly emphasized, Wagner, along with Goethe and Nietzsche, served as a constant source of artistic inspiration. If Goethe provided a literary model of self-confession and longevity and Nietzsche represented the ironist and critic, unaligned and uncommitted, then it was Wagner, through his extended music dramas, who personified epic narrative. Mann perceived the failure of the nineteenth-century German novel to attain the lofty position enjoyed by that art form in England, France, and Russia as a potential hiatus in his own culture. He believed this hiatus to be filled by the richly interwoven complexities of Wagner's operas.

By mirroring Wagner's leitmotific structures in the strategic word repetition in his first novel, *The Buddenbrooks* (1901), Mann was indirectly announcing his indebtedness to the composer as the founder of the *Gesamtkunstwerk*, or "total work of art." Wagner had viewed his music dramas, which lasted three and a half to five hours, as "total"; by placing equal weight on the text and the score, he could create integrated stage works that would be more than vehicles for beautiful song. One of the ways that the composer, who set his own texts to music—with his own stage directions and scenic designs in mind— could provide unity was by the repetition and continuous musical development of leitmotifs. And it was this narrative technique that attracted Mann the "naturalistic" novelist.

These repetitions not only created an aura of mesmeric unity but also suggested the complex blend of memory and experience that is the hallmark of psychological art. With their powerful evocations of primitive emotions and frank eroticism, Wagner's works captivated most of the modernist artists of the nineteenth century, from Baudelaire to Shaw. We shall see that *Tristan and Isolde*, in particular, had an irresistible fascination for Mann, and he was scarcely alone in his obsession with this opera: Wagnerism, a passion to the composer's supporters, was considered a veritable disease by his detractors. Although Wagner's operas, with their by and large medieval and mythic settings, did not have the contemporary sociopolitical dimensions of novels by the likes of Dickens, Thackeray, Dostoevsky, Tolstoy, Balzac, and Zola, they were imbued, in Mann's view, with the same monumental greatness of spirit—and it is this epic breadth that inspired the novelist throughout his career.

Although Mann's longest work, *Joseph and His Brothers*, is not particularly conducive to undergraduate-classroom study, it provides a telling link between Mann and Wagner. The congruences between the novelist's biblical

tetralogy and Wagner's *Ring of the Nibelungen* cycle are salient and may
be touched on for the students' information. Both artists worked intermit-
tently. Mann began his novel cycle in December 1926 and did not complete it until January 1942; Wagner's *Ring* occupied him between 1848 and
1874. Mann drew on Jewish sources as Wagner had drawn on Teutonic
myth. Mann's project, like Wagner's, began as a relatively small undertaking, assuming gargantuan proportions only gradually; both tetralogies were
composed mostly in exile. I have dealt with the thematic, structural, and
stylistic similarities between the two cycles in "Mann and Myth: The Author's Response to the *Ring*," an article in *Opera News*.

A helpful introduction to Mann's fascination with Wagner is his 1933
essay "The Sorrows and Grandeur of Richard Wagner," which is the longest single essay he devoted to his musical prototype. When the novelist
delivered his talk in Munich in February of that year, just two weeks after
Hitler's assumption of power, Mann had no idea that this speech—an icon-
oclastic yet ultimately enthusiastic assessment of Wagner's works—would
lead to his exile from Germany. Commissioned by Munich's Goethe Society
to mark the fiftieth anniversary of the composer's death, the essay unflinch-
ingly assessed Wagner's achievement in using both his strengths and weaknesses to forge some of the most titanic works of the nineteenth century.

In a class discussion of this text, or excerpts from it, one might ask how
the Mannian appraisal of Wagner served as an attack on the official, un-
critical Nazi attitude toward chauvinistic ideas in Wagner's prose writings.
Other questions central to the essay might be asked: Why is Mann eager to
point out how Wagner's craft taps not only the German spirit but a collective human consciousness? Why does Mann emphasize the ahistorical and
timeless qualities of Wagner's oeuvre? Why does he emphasize the composer's cosmopolitan character traits—aspects that the National Socialists
found repulsive?

An account of the Nazi reaction to Mann's Wagner address might be of
interest to the students. In what may have been an organized Nazi campaign to discredit Mann's essay, forty-five Bavarian cultural leaders signed
a letter that appeared in a Munich newspaper in the middle of April ac-
cusing the novelist of "defamation." The signatories protested the novelist's
treatment of Wagner's human frailties and his Freudian approach to the
composer's operas. The penultimate paragraph of the page-long text
strongly objected to Mann's thesis that the music drama was created for a
larger world, representing a blend of the German with the modern. Two
days later, a Berlin newspaper published Mann's resolute reply from Swit-
zerland, in which he defended his analytical approach as not being in the
slightest way deprecatory or at odds with a genuine reverence for Wagner's
work. In October, Mann made his home in Zurich, his flight paralleling
Wagner's escape from Germany to the same city after the revolutionary
uprisings of 1848–49. (The essay and the letters referred to here may

be readily found in the anthologies mentioned in the opening sentence of this article.)

Two synthetic discussions of Mann and Wagner are included in Helmut Koopmann's *Thomas-Mann-Handbuch*; taken together, they provide a helpful overview of Mann as lifelong Wagnerite. In his "Der Fall Wagner" ("In the Case of Wagner"), a section in his treatment of Mann and the literary tradition, T. J. Reed draws the important distinction between the novelist's reverential attitude toward Wagnerian opera and his Nietzschean skepticism toward Wagner the phenomenon. On the one hand, Mann was enthralled by the works themselves, a seminal childhood experience at a performance of *Lohengrin* having converted him instantly to Wagnerism and the fantasy of its transcendental world (10: 841). On the other hand, as Mann grew older, he questioned both the seductive effects of the Wagnerian music drama and Wagner's own lack of self-criticism (Reed, "Der Fall Wagner").

Walter Windisch-Laube's more detailed "Wagner-Bilder" ("Wagner-Pictures"), included in a comprehensive discussion of Mann and music in the *Handbuch*, gives a helpful catalog of direct references to Wagnerian works in Mann's fictional output. What becomes immediately evident from this essay is how Mann's intimate familiarity with the entire Wagnerian canon allowed him to incorporate, with ease, a spate of allusions to Wagnerian opera in any number of his imaginative works. Windisch-Laube also refers to several secondary works dealing with the Mann-Wagner interrelationship (327–32).

Ironically, it is in two shorter works that Mann sought to evoke specific Wagnerian operas: *Tristan* (1903) and *The Blood of the Walsungs* (1921) are parodic treatments of *Tristan and Isolde* and *Die Walküre*. In *Tristan*, Mann evokes Wagner's mature Romantic opera in three discrete ways: through actual verbal renderings of the three most significant moments in the score, through leitmotific devices associated with different characters and events, and through a parodic treatment of the opera's plot.

In studying the short novel, whether in general-access courses in translation or in seminars for German majors, it is beneficial to begin by dealing with such themes as dilettantism, the relation between mortal sickness and art, fin de siècle malaise, and the specific application of these to the text. At later stages in class discussion, however, the curiosity of the reader-student requires a closer understanding of Wagner, in general, and of *Tristan and Isolde*, in particular.

For a discussion of the eighth and most important section of the short novel, it is valuable to single out the three portions of the score that Gabriele plays on the piano—the prelude (116–17), the Love Duet, or "Liebesnacht" (117–19), and the Love Death, or "Liebestod" (119)—and to play some recorded selections of them in class while showing how they are evoked verbally.

A mood evocative of the opening of the second act of *Tristan and Isolde* has been created at the outset of the eighth chapter before Gabriele plays highlights from Wagner's opera. The majority of patients and staff at Einfried—the sanatorium's name being a satiric rendering of Wagner's home in Bayreuth, Wahnfried—have departed on a sleigh ride. Just as the horns of King Mark's hunting party are heard at the beginning of act 2 (Wagner 56–57), reference is made to the bells accompanying the departure of the sleighing party (112). Rätin Spatz temporarily serves as chaperone—a Brangäne-like figure watching over the "illicit lovers." And before Gabriele plays the piano, Spinell invokes the darkness (113–14) in much the same way that Isolde welcomes the onset of night (Wagner 64–65).

By devoting just under ten minutes to listening to the opera's prelude in class, instructors can point out the difference in Mann's two-paragraph-long description of this passage. In the first paragraph, emphasis is placed on the actual orchestral opening of the opera. Considered a ne plus ultra of erotic portraiture by late-nineteenth-century intellectuals, this highly chromatic prelude evokes the interior mood of the all-encompassing Romantic passion that consumes the mythic lovers. It is indeed this emotion that is at the center of Mann's telescopic description; his succinctness, his attention to both the emotional tension of the prelude and its structure will come out in class discussion. The second paragraph chiefly describes Gabriele's Romantically expressive pianistic execution—her vitality pours out of her life and into her art. Ernest Newman's musical discussion of this selection (207–14) is particularly helpful in showing the fidelity of Mann's verbal rendering.

The second selection that Gabriele plays is the "Liebesnacht"—to be found, both literally and figuratively, at the center of the opera (Wagner 66–93). The instructor might prepare and distribute a librettistic handout based on the second scene of the second act, with underlinings of those passages from the text that Mann chose to excerpt for his own one-page-long rendition. This teaching aid illustrates the telescopic nature of Mann's evocation of the longest love duet in the operatic canon, with its themes of all-consuming love and death. The words and lines culled, in what Steven Scher calls Mann's "paraphrasing technique" (*Verbal Music* 112), will reveal not only Wagner's ideas on transcendental love but his indebtedness to Novalis's (Friedrich von Hardenberg's) *Hymns to the Night* and Schopenhauer's *World as Will and Representation*.

Gabriele concludes with the final piece from the opera, Isolde's "Liebestod," covered in a single-paragraph description of both the music being played and Gabriele's performance. Listening to this six-minute selection in class while following its evocation in the short novel will demonstrate the aptness of Mann's emphasis on the erotically charged crescendoing of Isolde's solo as she is, at last, reunited with her lover in transfigured death.

A next step might be to ask in what ways the seriousness of each description is undercut by the humorous intrusion of reality that occurs either during or after each work is performed. After the prelude, Rätin Spatz immediately leaves the room because of a flare-up of her stomach ailment (117). In the midst of the love duet, Gabriele briefly interrupts herself to ask what the duet is all about (118); and afterward, the Pastor's wife, Frau Höhlenrauch, the mother of nineteen, enters and exits the room in a zombie-like stupor (119). With the completion of the "Liebestod"—the actual final portion of the opera—the sleighing party returns to the same bell sounds that had heralded its departure. The ironic humor created by the insistent undercutting of serious musical evocations creates a situation in which Wagner's opera is viewed simultaneously in a serious and a comedic vein.

The class might then consider a discussion of how themes and style are linked in Mann's use of the Wagnerian leitmotif. In contrast to the verbal music that appears only in the eighth chapter, the leitmotific structure is all-pervasive within the short novel. In fact, in the first and third descriptions discussed above, the words *Sehnsuchtsmotiv* ("yearning motif") and *Liebesmotiv* ("love motif") are employed to refer to those clusters of notes that Wagner used as building blocks for his mammoth drama. The following questions might be considered: How does Mann employ leitmotifs, or repetitive verbal patterns, throughout the work? Which ones are most memorable and why? Wherein does their aesthetic attraction lie—for both the author and the reader? How do they define individual characters or actual events? How does Mann both develop leitmotifs and link them?

The little pale blue vein on Gabriele's forehead, for example, is a motif that Mann repeats and builds on. Not surprisingly, attention is paid to this symbol of Gabriele's artistic sensibility and mortality, the vein becoming ever more prominent as she plays through the "Liebestod." Additional examples of leitmotific clusters include Spinell's physical appearance (his carious teeth, for instance), Klöterjahn's euphemistic turns of phrase, and the various habits, appearances, and backgrounds of the patients at Einfried. Clearly, differences exist between Mann's specific, naturalistic use of leitmotifs and Wagner's more suggestive and evocative ones. Nonetheless, the aesthetic delight in recognizing repeated patterns of words or notes as a set of structural principles stems from the reader's or listener's role as initiate.

A conclusion of the discussion might focus on the sharp contrast between the short novel's thematic concerns and those of the mammoth Wagnerian counterpart. In Wagner, the Romantic myth, no matter how elaborate, complex, and musically forward-looking, is all of a piece. After all, as already mentioned, Wagner was the proponent of the *Gesamtkunstwerk*. A good example of the artistic integration in *Tristan and Isolde* is the structural balance of the libretto: if the first act belongs to Isolde—who recites her narrative and curse and provides the potion—then the last act is Tristan's, with his yearning for a final, transcendent reunion with his beloved in death. The centrally positioned act 2, which belongs to both lovers, is the one extended archetypal moment in which they exchange vows of love on earth.

In *Tristan*, the robust Wagnerian protagonists are replaced by slender, tubercular characters removed from the heightened amorous passions holding sway over their operatic counterparts. Furthermore, the parity and surefootedness of the eponymous characters, crucial features in the Wagnerian opera, are intentionally replaced by imbalance. Violating the symmetry of Wagner's opera, in which Tristan and Isolde are accorded equal status, the single-word title of the short novel at once signals Mann's indebtedness to Wagner while pointing to the humor inherent in his ironic approach—it immediately privileges Spinell and his obsessive devotion to the score. It also carries reverberations of a form of self-absorption and self-love that make a human love object expendable or even obsolete. (In fact, the opening of the short novel separates another pair of mythical lovers, giving us a Leander without a Hero.)

Spinell, repeatedly referred to as the "putrefied infant" by the other patients at Einfried, and Gabriele, his gravely ill "accompanist"—with emphasis on her subsidiary role—are the stark antitheses of their "heroic" Wagnerian counterparts. Whereas Tristan seeks death at the end of each of the opera's acts (by taking a potion that he believes to be lethal, by not defending himself against Melot, and by ripping off his own bandages when Isolde approaches), Spinell in the final paragraph looks absurdly helpless as he flees the "jubilant shrieks" of the offensively healthy Klöterjahn child (132).

The following questions might be considered to juxtapose Mann's thematic concerns with those of Wagner: In what ways is Mann's tale a human diminishing of nineteenth-century grandeur and myth? What realistic dimensions does the specificity of Mann's tubercular sanatorium impose on Wagner's otherworldly and rarefied setting? In what ways are the sickly Spinell and the frail Gabriele "reduced" portraits of Wagner's immortal lovers? Answers and attendant discussions may vary.

For instance, that Gabriele plays a piano reduction of highlights only is emblematic of Mann's "modified" narrative—with more "modest" protagonists. Moreover, an effective way of contrasting the self-assurance of the operatic lovers with the more conflicted behavior of Mann's protagonists would be to juxtapose the romantically exuberant stage directions found throughout the "Liebesnacht" with the posture of Spinell and Gabriele at the conclusion of the eighth section. In contrast to Wagner's passionately embracing lovers (80–93), Spinell sinks down on both knees in a semihistrionic swoon, while Gabriele remains awkward and confused as she stares at her admirer (120). (This is Wagner with the flesh left out.)

Mention might also be made of the themes that Mann shares with other turn-of-the-century artists in response to Wagner. Four book-length studies that provide an intellectual and historical context for Mann's own impressionistic reception are Erwin Koppen, *Dekadenter Wagnerismus*; Elliott Zuckerman, *The First Hundred Years of Wagner's* Tristan; Raymond Furness, *Wagner and Literature*; and David Large and William Weber, *Wagnerism in European Culture and Politics*.

Exposure to the Wagnerian score is necessary for a deeper appreciation of the text, as is some discussion of Mann's enthrallment with this opera in the years before he wrote the short novel and of his need to free himself from a slavish devotion to it. In his brief 1911 article "Coming to Terms with Richard Wagner," Mann revealed that he indeed had not missed a single performance of *Tristan and Isolde* in Munich for many a year during the last decade of the nineteenth century (10: 840).

Elliott Zuckerman distinguishes between two basic strands in Wagner reception: "Wagnerism" and "Tristanism." Wagnerism, essentially public in nature, supports any variety of Wagner's theories with little concern for the composer's music. Tristanism, private in nature, depends on a "succumbing" to the works themselves and particularly their music. Moved by "personal infatuation" rather than by "ideological commitment, . . . the Tristanite has only to be overwhelmed" (30). Mann could thus view his ironic short novel, in part, as an artistic leave-taking from his own "Tristanism" or intoxication. A telling fact is that at no point in the work is Wagner or the actual title of the opera referred to by name.

Two monographs are of particular help in preparing to teach *Tristan*. Ulrich Dittmann's guide, *Thomas Mann:* Tristan, includes those excerpts from the second act of the libretto that Mann paraphrased for the eighth chapter (Dittmann 59–62). Frank W. Young's study *Montage and Motif in Thomas Mann's* Tristan pinpoints Mann's strategies for interweaving both Wagner's libretto and the score into his short novel. Young's chapter titles speak for themselves: "Paraphrase-Parody of Wagner's *Tristan and Isolde*," "Other Parodistic Allusions," "The Musical Quality in Mann's Prose," and "'Tristan' as a 'Musical Score.'"

In addition, teachers might encourage students to read *The Blood of the Walsungs*. Though this short novel is in many ways slighter than *Tristan*, it, too, has an erotic Wagnerian opera as its source. A student excited by *Tristan* might decide to write a paper on *The Blood of the Walsungs*. Although, on the surface, differences between these two short works abound (*The Blood of the Walsungs* takes place in an urban environment and actually, in part, in an opera house during a performance of *Die Walküre*), the student will be struck by Mann's need, once again, to liberate himself from Wagnerian intoxication through parody.

A coda for class discussion could be provided by the following passage from Mann's 1933 essay "The Sorrows and Grandeur of Richard Wagner," a passage Mann saw fit to repeat in his only other full-length essay on Wagner, "Richard Wagner and *Der Ring des Nibelungen*" (502):

> A passion for Wagner's enchanted oeuvre has been a part of my life ever since I first became aware of it and set out to make it my own, to invest it with understanding. What it has given me in terms of enjoyment and instruction I can never forget, nor the hours of deep and solitary happiness amidst the theatre throng, hours filled with frissons and delights for the nerves and the intellect alike, with sudden glimpses into things of profound and moving significance, such as only this art can afford.   ("Sorrows" 100)

Students will recognize that Mann succumbs to Wagner as a "Tristanite"; as an artist, he transforms his rapture into narrative.

Gender, Sexuality, and Identity
in Mann's Short Fiction

Robert K. Martin

Teaching Mann's short fiction offers instructors the opportunity to describe a number of concepts of sexuality that developed in the late nineteenth and early twentieth centuries, particularly in Germany. *Tonio Kröger* invites discussion of the ways in which adolescence may precipitate a crisis in gender identity, one that may have considerable social consequences. Looking at the relations between nationality, sexuality, and aesthetics in this story, as in the later *Death in Venice*, should suggest that sexual orientation is a fundamental representation of experience in the modern world. At the same time, a fully historicized discussion of the stories brings out the contingency of sexual identities—that is, enables students to see that concepts of masculinity and femininity, heterosexuality and homosexuality, are social constructions dependent on differences in context.

In its very title, *Tonio Kröger* (first published in 1903) announces its concern with inner divisions, which it locates in oppositions both of nationality and culture and of gender. The eponymous hero is cast as a person of two identities and, hence—in a rigidly dualistic world—of no identity. This conceptualization of the character owes something to Mann's own biography but also to the cultural currents of his time. That such a story had deep personal significance is evident from Mann's frequent return to the pattern, in a figure such as Johnny Bishop in the story of the striking title *The Fight between Jappe and Do Escobar* (1911); in Aschenbach's mixed heritage and his "exotic racial characteristics" (200) inherited from his Bohemian mother, as well as in the larger north-south, heterosexual-homosexual distinctions of *Death in Venice* (1912); and, most strikingly, in Hans Castorp's love for the Slavic schoolboy Pribislav Hippe, in *The Magic Mountain* (1924).

In a letter of 19 March 1955 to an old friend, Hermann Lange, Thomas Mann recalled the circumstances that had given rise to *Tonio Kröger*— above all, his love for his schoolmate Armin Martens, the first love of his life and the tenderest, most blissful-painful. Although Martens did not know what to make of Mann's enthusiasm, *Tonio Kröger* is a monument to that love (*Briefe* 3: 387). The story was first conceived during, or in connection with, a trip to Lübeck and Denmark in 1899, which undoubtedly awoke memories of Martens and of Mann's relation to his father (of whom he speaks in the same letter). Mann returned to the story the following year, just after he fell in love with the painter Paul Ehrenberg. These youthful loves, and the conflicts they produced, are visible in the divisions of *Tonio Kröger*. However troubling and moving these personal experiences, they did not take place outside a social context. Lübeck remained for Mann what he termed it in *Tonio Kröger*, a "Vaterstadt," or father-city.[1]

The assignment of gender to nations was largely of Nietzschean origin, but it had come to have wide significance in political thought of the late nineteenth century. Mann's quarrel with his brother Heinrich, although partly political, was, until the 1920s, largely based on a distinction between *Kultur* and *Zivilisation*, or between a masculine Germany and a feminine or effeminate France. Tonio is described as both "the son of Consul Kröger" and the son of a "dark, fiery mother" from "somewhere right at the bottom of the map." Although he owes his artistic expression to his maternal, or feminine, side, he has also internalized the opinions of patriarchal culture so that he "found his mother's blithe unconcern slightly disreputable" (136, 138). It is precisely this willingness to condemn a part of himself, a part that he sees as lacking in self-control and correctness, that will make Tonio into a "verirrter Bürger" 'bourgeois manqué' (164). Caught between Denmark and Italy, between father and mother, between masculine and feminine, between bourgeois and artist, Tonio cannot be at peace, even though it is his androgynous nature that will enable him to be an artist, enough *of* the world to have a subject and enough out of the world to record it.

Students might be asked to look at the debate over sexuality in turn-of-the-century Germany and its consequences for Mann's depiction of his autobiographical hero. As James D. Steakley has shown, homosexuality, which had until then been seen as one of a number of transgressive sexual *acts*, was conceptualized as an identity and given physical and cultural characteristics. Karl Heinrich Ulrichs, the best known of the early theorists of homosexuality, writing in the 1860s, believed that male homosexuals were in effect spiritual androgynes—that is, that they had "a female soul confined in a male body" (Steakley 16).[2] The rather crude biologistic formula has evolved in Mann into a subtle analysis of divided identity and social marginality. By the 1890s the personal accounts of Ulrichs and others had become the basis for a widespread political movement (the first in world history) for homosexual rights and parallel establishment of a society for the scientific study of homosexuality. It is useful to recall some dates that coincide with Mann's early manhood: the publication of the first homosexual journal, *Der Eigene*, in Berlin, 1896; the founding of the first homosexual rights organization, by Magnus Hirschfeld and others, in Berlin, 1897 (the same year that saw publication of Havelock Ellis and John Addington Symonds's study *Sexual Inversion*); the first publication, in 1889, of a yearbook on homosexuality, the *Jahrbuch für sexuelle Zwischenstufen*, providing an opportunity for the dissemination of a broad range of scholarly material; the publication of a widely distributed brochure on the "third sex," in 1901; and the mass circulation, in Berlin, of a questionnaire on homosexuality, in 1903. Alongside these acts of self-definition and political self-awareness one must place the suicide in 1902 of the steel magnate Friedrich Alfred Krupp, a close friend of the kaiser's, after his expulsion from Capri for homosexual activity. In the midst of these developments, *Tonio Kröger* does not come as a simple reflection on aesthetics.

If the new discourse on homosexuality (the word itself was first used in the 1860s) created a new sense of identity, it also associated that identity with abnormality and encouraged a medicalization of sexuality. There were two alternative sources of understanding male friendship: one Greek and transmitted through the Renaissance and neoclassicism, the other German and Romantic. Both are present in Mann's work of this period. The model of Plato's *Symposium*, crucial to the English Romantics as well—Shelley wrote the first English translation—would serve Mann as the basis for the sexual aesthetics of *Death in Venice*, with its sense of a conflict between love and life and its yearning toward a life inspired by love.

In *Tonio Kröger* the Greek theme, perhaps because it is fundamentally pederastic, is only discreetly present, in the allusion to Bertel Thorwald-sen's "noble and charming sculptures" (178), copies of classical originals, and, even more faintly, in the allusion to Storm's poem "Hyazinthen" ("Hya-cinths"), with its evocation of the beautiful young man killed by the jealous Apollo (147). But it is responsible, above all, for the place given Lisaweta, Mann's version of Diotima, the "wise woman" in the *Symposium*, who of-fers her philosophy of transcendent love through art: "the purifying, sanc-tifying effect of literature . . . the way our passions dissolve when they are grasped by insight and expressed in words" (159).[3] Students might be asked to explore the relation of Mann's text to such models as Plato and Plutarch.

If the Greek tradition plays a relatively small part for Tonio, the German tradition of male friendship is crucial. Like the Greek tradition, it is en-coded in the text largely by allusion, above all to Schiller's *Don Carlos* (1787). Students can usefully draw on their other reading to describe such patterns of reference. Tonio's attempt to induce interest in the drama on the part of his friend Hans—like his later citations of *Hamlet* (159–60), with its evocation of Hamlet's association with Horatio—inscribes the two boys' relationship in the tradition of ideal, or Romantic, friendship. Hans's inability to respond to the play, and his willingness to shun Tonio for a more "ordinary" friend, Erwin Jimmerthal, may indicate the irrelevance of this tradition for the twentieth century. For Tonio what is most moving about the play is the friendship between the two boys and its eventual betrayal by the marquis (140–41). He identifies with Don Carlos's famous speech of longing and despair, "I have no one—no one / on this great wide earth, no one" (1.183–84), and thus anticipates his own rejection by Hans—even if the situation is very different from that in the play. German literature of the late eighteenth century, marked by an intensity of emo-tion located particularly in scenes of friendship and love, offered a poten-tial model for the development of a friendship ideal in the early twentieth century. That the play might have implications of love rather than simple friendship was clear to its earliest critics, and Schiller incorporated a long commentary on the question in his "Third Letter on *Don Carlos.*" Although Schiller denies that the play establishes that "passionate friendship could be as moving an occasion for tragedy as passionate love" ("Dritter Brief" 230), he remarks that he has put that subject aside for a future work and devotes himself simply to showing that the friendship in the play cannot be passionate, since it is not based on equality (at least after the boys' childhood). Don Carlos indeed offers "a thousand tendernesses and true brotherly love," but the young marquis returns them coldly (1.215–16). If Schiller argues against a reading of *Don Carlos* as a play of passionate male friendship, it is precisely because he believes too deeply in such a concept to see it in this conflict.

In addition to these literary and aesthetic models, another way of understanding homosexuality was to view it as effeminacy, or the failure to conform to increasingly rigid gender boundaries. Students should be encouraged to consult studies of Greek sexuality, such as K. J. Dover's, so that they may consider the absence of the concept of the "homosexual" and explore the anxieties that accompanied the emerging model for homosexuality and the corresponding construction of a strictly delimited and enforced heterosexuality. The recollection of Tonio's childhood moves from boyhood infatuation with the idealized and unattainable Hans to the dancing class, symbolic site for the inculcation of gender identity. The class is presided over by a dark double of Tonio's, François Knaak, whose name, like Tonio's, speaks of his divided origins and marginal status. But by becoming the foppish dancing instructor, Knaak turns his status as outsider to his advantage and provides an example of the way society uses such marginal figures as part of a structure of social control. (The narrator in *The Fight between Jappe and Do Escobar*, in which Herr Knaak is presented at greater length, remarks that "although [Knaak] did not belong to society, he was paid by society as the guardian and instructor of its ideal of deportment" [8: 435].) Knaak is a parody, or negative image, of both the artist and the homosexual: his art is reduced to blind repetition of learned patterns in the pay of the bourgeoisie, while his sexuality is simultaneously concealed and proclaimed.

Knaak is a figure of the third sex, as illustrated by Hirschfeld in his studies of the bodily characteristics of "intermediate types" (see Steakley), with "plump . . . hips swaying to and fro" revealing what might be thought of as his feminine nature (145). His appearance here, like that of the old man with the "scarlet necktie and a rakishly tilted Panama hat" on Aschenbach's boat to Venice, serves as a warning to Tonio of what he risks becoming if he does not adhere to the rules of the fathers (208). At the same time, as the outrageously effeminate male, Knaak enforces the rules of gender, which are here inscribed in the parts assigned in the dance. When Tonio dances the *moulinet des dames* and betrays his own gender uncertainty, he is met with the derisive response "Miss Kröger," along with a mixture of French and German, indicating his distance from both sexes, as they were socially constituted (147). Knaak, with his assumption of the role of what Michel Foucault calls "surveillance," illustrates the fragility of gender definition as well as the phenomenon of the "house-nigger," in which society can claim tolerance by allowing isolated figures the appearance of freedom, provided of course that they serve only to perpetuate the system of exclusion from which they are temporarily exempt (*Surveiller*).

Tonio's dilemma is not that he is a woman but that he locates himself in the territory between the genders. Faced with the humiliation that awaits anyone daring to violate the boundaries of gender in 1903, Tonio compensates for his own anxieties by an exaggerated regard for the ordinarily masculine and feminine, in the figures of Hans and Ingeborg. His love for them is an expression of his rejection of himself and his internalization once more of patriarchal values. Since he can see himself only as a foreigner, someone located outside the boundary of normality, he must constantly reassert his own sense of belonging. The Polish-Slavic figures of *Death in Venice* similarly pose a personal and national threat, one that recurs in the Kirghiz eyes of *The Magic Mountain*. One of the many leitmotifs of *Tonio Kröger* is the phrase "he was no gypsy in a green caravan" (142; see also 138, 152), in which the gypsy serves as a figure of the homeless and countryless and that represents for Tonio a talisman against his own sense of not belonging. Tonio's paternal, Germanic heritage renders him incapable of enjoying the pleasures of the senses, leaves him seized by "revulsion [and] hatred," seeking a "purity" (151) that is free of the body and that he thinks he can find in the blankness of Hans and Inge, much as Aschenbach identifies with Saint Sebastian, in the pursuit of "elegant self-control" (203) and the stifling of desire. In Tonio, students can explore the pattern of self-hatred that can lead the homosexual to idealize figures of "normal" sexuality and the person of mixed race to idealize the racially pure. Here Mann is brilliantly insightful, providing a startling view of the psychological forces that would be manipulated by fascism a generation or more later.

For Tonio the figure of the father is always present, even in his dreams, reminding him of his "degenerate way of life"—using that crucial term *entartet* later exploited by the Nazis. Tonio is unable to resist the judgment, since he has incorporated the paternal and conventional within himself, and repeatedly thinks that his father's criticism is "as it should be" (166). At the same time, the authority of the father has failed: the paternal home is now a *public* library, and in the paternal city he is without papers, subject to interrogation. Tonio's role as artist is one with his role as homosexual; in both he is imagined as marginal, an observer of life rather than a participant in it.

The "dance" of heterosexual reproductive life is not one in which he will participate, although it may furnish the materials for his art. But the decision to affirm his identity as artist and homosexual is a difficult one in a conventional society in which such a choice can only confirm his position as outsider and stranger. He sees the artist as a castrato ("those artificial papal sopranos" [156]) whose beauty can be obtained only by the loss of his masculinity. This sense of the painful inscription of loss on the body of the homosexual is one of the stereotypes of modern male homosexuality, that of the aesthete who dies to life. Another, more social image sees the homosexual as a victim of an intolerant community. The story alludes to such a figure in Tonio's references to himself, incorporating an Old Testament sense of transgression, as "a marked man" with "a sign on [his] brow," the object of a "curse" (157). Through such language we can see the enormous shift that is being worked out in Mann's story: the appearance, as Foucault put it, of the homosexual as "une espèce" and not merely a participant in certain acts (*La volonté* 59). Tonio has the signs, and the social fate, of the modern homosexual.

Like many of the early accounts of sexuality, particularly those initiated by Richard von Krafft-Ebing and perfected by Freud that students can be encouraged to explore, *Tonio Kröger* is in effect a case study, the detailed analysis of the making of an individual psychology as revealed in long confessional conversation, in this instance with Tonio's artist-friend Lisaweta. Unlike many of the contemporary accounts, Tonio's story is not medicalized. Tonio is not sick; he is unhappy. And his unhappiness is depicted by Mann as the result of a division within himself. But the conclusion is not tragic, unlike Willa Cather's "Paul's Case," of a similar date. Tonio recognizes that mixed in with his love of the ordinary is contempt for it and an inchoate recognition of the tyranny of the conventional. Tonio's repeated denial that he is a "gypsy in a green caravan" foreshadows in an eerie way the fate of all that is strange in Nazi Germany: gypsies, Jews, political opponents, and homosexuals met similar fates in the death camps. That these groups could be identified as "entartet" and marked for extermination was the result of a national movement that identified the superiority of the (Aryan) male body with the concept of the normal (see Mosse). Mann's own resistance to such tendencies was confirmed, after a period of hesitation, at the time of the First World War, largely through the example of the American poet Walt Whitman, whose work offered a model of homosexual self-affirmation without associations of elitism or a cult of the body. Mann's first work reflecting this shift, and the new celebration of a nonfetishized body, is *The Magic Mountain*, in which the Tonio-Hans love is reworked, and partially inverted, as Hans Castorp's love for the Slavic Pribislav Hippe. Significantly, Whitman is a major presence in this novel and its hope for a new future after the destructive war (cf. Martin). In Mann's earlier years, before the recovery of a democratic model for the understanding of male love, he identified schoolboy love as both the site of first desire and a source of permanent alienation. One of the things that is most remarkable about *Tonio Kröger* is the force of its defense of that love, whatever its price. Without naming names, Mann created a work occupying a special place in the history of homosexual self-conceptualization.

Death in Venice, published nine years later, is not concerned primarily with gender, partly because of its focus on an aging hero and partly because of its origins in Greek thought, to which the concept of gender is largely foreign. What *Death in Venice* dramatizes, however, is a personal and social response to Greek love, what Mann would have known as *Knabenliebe*.

The sexual geography of *Death in Venice* will be familiar to readers of *Tonio Kröger*: the journey south and, implicitly, east, is a journey to the feminine and the repressed. Although Aschenbach is the descendant of "military officers, judges, government administrators," his mother was "the daughter of a director of music from Bohemia" (200), at once artistic and foreign. Unlike Tonio, who as a young man is immersed in the maternal world of feeling, Aschenbach has constructed his life out of resistance to this darker self. Students might be encouraged to read Nietzsche's *Birth of Tragedy* in order to gain some greater understanding of the sources of this dualism in Mann's thinking. Relatively advanced students could trace the concept of the "feminine" through nineteenth-century works by Nietzsche and Schopenhauer, both crucial to Mann, to more recent texts by Derrida.

Although German Romantic literature is filled with a longing for the south, epitomized in Goethe's "Kennst Du das Land, wo die Zitronen blühn?" (1784), such feelings took on particular meanings in the emerging homosexual tradition. It is against this background, and especially the model of August von Platen, that *Death in Venice* is constructed. Platen, whom Mann evokes in *Death in Venice* as "that poet of plangent inspiration" (210), is remembered for his cycle of sonnets on Venice, deeply moving evocations of Platen's search for an ideal love in verses of extraordinary purity and power, as well as for his poem "Tristan," which promises death to anyone who has seen Beauty. Mann devoted an important essay to Platen in 1930, quoting "Tristan" but also calling attention to Platen's search for a place in a homosexual tradition; Mann's essay is a remarkable indication of the significance of his own formal choices and their origins (cf. Seyppel; Williams). Platen is evoked here as a figure of the German gay reception of Italy. Travel can mean for the homosexual both escape from the bounds of conventional life and the possibility for erotic encounters, especially in a society perceived as less repressed. It would be useful to ask students to pursue this theme in a number of writers, including perhaps André Gide, D. H. Lawrence, Herman Melville, and James Baldwin.

The friendship tradition evoked in *Tonio Kröger* is enlarged in *Death in Venice* to focus on the Greek tradition, seen as the basis of intellectual growth, of erotic love between an older man and a youth. The story presents the two conflicting views of homosexuality that have dominated in

Western culture: on the one hand, an ideal sexuality that is at the basis of all Western thought, that has given rise to the masterpieces of classical philosophy; and, on the other hand, a sexuality that is regularly condemned, in a model that from culture to culture shifts from the theological to the medical. The dilemma that *Death in Venice* poses is the difficult negotiation between these apparently contradictory images. At the end of a highly classicized age, the early twentieth century was faced with the paradox of a culture built almost entirely on the very sexuality that was being increasingly contested. Students could usefully think about the significance of the Olympics, for instance, by looking at Pindar and other poets in celebration of Greek athletes, down to A. E. Housman's consciously classical "To an Athlete Dying Young" and Patricia Nell Warren's popular novel *The Front Runner.* Some students might think about the ways in which sports are constructed as heterosexual in our culture, while others might look at concepts of "Platonic love" in, say, Shakespeare and E. M. Forster's *Maurice* or "The Classical Annex."

To historicize attitudes toward the male body as an arbiter of beauty, students could study works in the classical section of a local museum, perhaps alongside "physique" photography, and also explore the role of Johann Winckelmann in the creation of a taste for the Greek that combined beauty with love. Students able to read German might look at Christoph Geiser's *Das geheime Fieber* and then combine explorations of Caravaggio's paintings with Derek Jarman's film. Mann illustrates the persistence not only of the concept of ideal male beauty in Western philosophy but also of images of that beauty in Western art (a parallelism between philosophy and art and the body and soul of Mann's story). Although Aschenbach has resisted the claims of the body, they have never been totally repressed but merely sublimated. They return, for instance, in his book on Frederick the Great, whose life provides an excellent opportunity for class discussion of paternal control of homosexuality and the ways in which gays can learn to be even more rigid and masculine than their heterosexual peers, who may have less to prove. (This could lead to some interesting projects on homosexuality and the military, starting perhaps with István Szabó's film *Colonel Redl.*) The two greatest subjects of homosexual art, Sebastian and Ganymede, are evoked (203, 236), indicating Aschenbach's (and Mann's) place in a tradition of the representation of the male body as object of desire. Some of the images in James Saslow's study will help establish the importance of Ganymede as a subject for Renaissance painting and could be looked at in conjunction with Goethe's monologue for Ganymede.

Readers should ask whether the virtual overburdening of the text with philosophical and art-historical allusions does not bespeak, on the one hand, a need to legitimize an otherwise forbidden topic by an appeal to the great homosexual tradition and, on the other hand, a displacement of desire for Tadzio onto acts of connoisseurship, as Reed has suggested (*Mann,*

Der Tod in Venedig: *Text* 135). The text evokes a "long-haired boy of about fourteen,"[4] with a face that "recalled Greek sculpture of the noblest period" (216). Soon thereafter he is seen to have "the head of Eros, with the creamy luster of Parian marble" (220). Do such comparisons act to ennoble or to evade? Aschenbach's desire for Tadzio is situated in a tradition of idealist philosophy, in which the individual incarnate beauty serves as a means toward a higher, more abstract Beauty. Mann allows the reader to wonder whether Aschenbach misinterprets when he sees the idea of Beauty in the body of Tadzio (Mann's German text plays on the ambiguity, through references to "das Schöne," or ideal Beauty, and "der Schöne," the beautiful man or boy, applied to Tadzio, while Venice, the corrupt and corrupting city, is "die Schöne," the beautiful woman)[5] and mistakes this representation of beauty for Beauty itself. The multiplied classical references, to Greek sculpture, to Hermes, to Eros, to Ganymede, provide a lineage that stands in sharp contrast to Aschenbach's internalized sense of social destruction and decay.

If one strand of Western thought sees homosexuality as the source of art and culture, another sees it as a pernicious disease threatening the body politic. For Mann, whose early views on homosexuality come out of a tradition that is more Spartan than Athenian, Aschenbach's tightly grasped fist (201) is also to be understood as the tightly closed sphincter, the self closed in and resistant to all that is foreign, but at the same time bearing the traces of the foreign within itself. The imagery of *Death in Venice* suggests a danger that comes simultaneously from within and from without. This apparently contradictory image repeats a larger social pattern in which homosexuality is both internal, the "fault" of some weakness of effeminacy, and external, the result of foreign influence or contamination. Modern conceptualizations of homosexuality thus often stress its "racial qualities," as in Richard Burton's famous "Sotadic zone," or the association of the homosexual with the Jew. Similarly, there is often a slippage from race to class, so that the bourgeoisie of the hotel is threatened not only by physical disease but by "a certain breakdown of moral standards, . . . an activation of the dark and antisocial forces" (254).

The contagious disease that threatens Venice thus stands for an alien culture, one that is at once Italian (the site of the story), Polish and Slavic (the nationality of Tadzio, and Germany's traditional enemy), and, finally, Indian, "originating in the sultry morasses of the Ganges delta" (252). Here again the ambiguity is evident: the cholera is both foreign and located at the very heart of Indo-European culture, as basic as Sanskrit. The story of the origins of the ambiguity is borrowed in part from Nietzsche's account, in *The Birth of Tragedy,* of the displacement of the ancient gods of Greece by a new Socratic culture. This transition is for Nietzsche the great displacement, the great moment in which a phallic culture gives way to one of cerebration. Aschenbach's dream of *"the stranger-god"* (or the foreign god) revives the Bacchic world and allows for the final defeat of "the composed and dignified intellect" (256–57). The phallic god will lead Aschenbach down dark alleys, not sparing his dignity but demonstrating the fleshly nature of all life. When discussing the illness in *Death in Venice*, students can be asked to look at contemporary accounts of AIDS. They need to understand that disease is finally a discursive field whose parameters are determined in large part by social needs. Students might be asked to think about the links between AIDS and Africa, or Haiti, and to consider such accounts in terms of a colonial history of the "dark continent" (they might read Gilman on this point). They can then be asked to extend their analysis to the politics of the body and to think about the anus as a forbidden and dangerous territory. How does *Death in Venice* possibly help us understand the control of disease as an element of social control? How does the fear of AIDS serve as a continuation of the fear of the apparently corrupt and corrupting body of the homosexual? How are such social views internalized (or introjected) by the gay subject, so that an Aschenbach can fear the very things he desires and see them as at once absolutely beautiful and grossly disgusting?

As one thinks about the text and its treatment of the other, one can move to address the issue of the absent female. How is the feminine constructed in *Death in Venice*? The feminine is the body of disease itself; Aschenbach's life is constructed around the strict maintenance of masculinity and a deep fear of any intrusions of femininity. Aschenbach's fear of effeminacy is expressed through the comic figure of the older man who attempts to retain youthful beauty and in his own sense that he himself is effeminized by giving in to beauty, by being "driven by a mad compulsion" (242). Aschenbach has created a new hero type: a youth with "an intellectual and boyish manly virtue" (more accurately, an intellectual and youthful manliness)—words that were in fact used to describe Mann's early work (202). Such manliness is at the heart of Aschenbach's self-conception. As he increasingly gives in to his passion, he reflects on his ancestors and their "decent manliness": "What would they say?" (245). Would they not accuse him of degeneracy (*Entartung*)? Can his asceticism not be his form of "manliness"? As he reflects on this, he turns to the story's most explicit identification of homosexuality, as "the kind of love that had taken possession of him," that had been "highly honored by the most valiant of peoples" (246). It is of course precisely this view of homosexuality, as an ultimate masculinity, that is challenged by Tadzio and Aschenbach's infatuation with him.

If Tonio Kröger is Thomas Mann as an adolescent, filled with Romantic love for Hans and a sense of exclusion from ordinary life, Aschenbach is the kind of man Thomas Mann had run the risk of becoming, through the continued repression of his sexual identity. Mann's stories have considerable biographical resonance, but they speak clearly to us today because they are written at the time of, and play a major part in, crucial debates over the emergence of a modern homosexual identity. Students, who are frequently in the midst of negotiating their own paths through what may seem like a sexual wilderness, can benefit from understanding that many of their dilemmas have a history, that the modern gay identity many of us take for granted was the product only of many years of anguish, experimentation, and loneliness. It is also important to see that identity in the making, as a way of reminding ourselves of its cultural contingency, of recognizing that after one becomes aware of one's difference, after one dances the *wrong part*, there is still a life to be lived, one indeed that may offer a vision of Beauty itself in all its splendor.[6]

NOTES

[1]David Luke translates the term as "native city," a phrase of far better English that also unfortunately loses the sense of the relation between the city and the parent. For Mann, Lübeck was always the world of the father, of heterosexual order and bourgeois life, while the maternal city was located elsewhere, in Munich, in Zurich, even in Venice. Luke's translation also misattributes the narrowness to the streets of the city rather than to the city itself, making the description physical rather than metaphysical. In these points Luke repeats the errors of H. T. Lowe-Porter. (In German, Tonio departed "von der engen Vaterstadt," while in Luke's version, he "left his native city and its narrow streets" [150]. In later use the term "Vaterstadt" is translated as "the city of his fathers" [174].)

[2]The original phrase was in Latin: *anima muliebris in corpore virili inclusa*. For a discussion of Ulrichs and other early writers on the subject, including Hirschfeld, see Steakley.

[3]The English translation again obscures some of the details of the German text. In the last phrase, passions do not "dissolve" but are "destroyed," and it is "die Erkenntnis" as well as "das Wort" that accomplishes this destruction. The term *Erkenntnis* is picked up by Tonio a few minutes later when he refers to his "Erkenntnisekel," or "nausea of knowledge" (160).

[4]The German text throughout uses the term *der Knabe*, which can be considered the equivalent of the Greek *pais*. Calling him "the boy" may make him seem presexual, when in fact he is situated at the moment the Greeks considered ideal: just past puberty, but before the disfiguring appearance of facial hair.

[5]Luke's translation obscures this pun on several occasions.

[6]For further reading, see Feuerlicht, "Homoeroticism"; Härle, *Mannerweiblichkeit*; Mayer, *Outsiders*; Sommerhage; and Vaget, *Kommentar*.

Humor and Comedy in Mann's Short Fiction

Werner Hoffmeister

> The comical as a source of joy, the humorist as a true
> benefactor of mankind—the older I grow, the more
> deeply I feel it, and I felt it early on.
> —Thomas Mann, *Pariser Rechenschaft*

It goes almost without saying that the process of understanding and appreciating a complex work of fiction is heightened when the pleasure of the text is enriched by the author's sense of humor and comic imagination. A little laughter in the classroom, be it a hearty guffaw or a belly laugh, a chuckle or just a smile, often may be the most revealing and most valuable response to a fictional situation, character, or manner of expression. A discussion with our students about the reasons for our laughter (Why do we laugh here? What's funny? What does the narrator's humorous overtone or manner of expression convey to the reader?) may lead to substantive insights about a work's characters, narrative strategies, and thematic structure. Trying to understand why we laugh at Herr François Knaak's lesson in dancing and deportment and why Tonio calls him "a preposterous monkey" (146) will tell the class something about Mann's view of the way bourgeois society tends to domesticate and conventionalize the arts and artistic skills. Trying to understand why, in *Tristan*, Detlev Spinell can express his feelings about Herr Klöterjahn effectively only in writing, whereas the latter can verbalize his response equally effectively only in an oral confrontation, not only may lead the students to recognize the comical incongruity of these two characters but may also offer the instructor the opportunity to explicate the Schopenhauerian opposition of will and idea that makes up the philosophical framework of the story.

By and large, college students tend to read literary texts primarily in terms of plot, characters, structure, theme, and ideas, and most classroom discussions focus on these properties, which are well suited for interpretive analysis. For a full appreciation of the specifically literary and imaginative fabric of a work, however, the students' attention needs to be directed to details of tone and texture, of voice and style. It is in this realm of textural details that Thomas Mann's prose is extraordinarily rich, intricate, and supple. Mann's humor and comic sense as well as his irony are significant components of his prose, and they function as meaningful constituents within larger thematic contexts and structural entities. Reading Mann should be an enjoyable and entertaining experience for our students; at the same time, we should attempt to make them grasp the interpretability of textural particulars and the functionalism inherent in the fabric of Mann's prose. The best way to achieve this goal is to concentrate the attention of the students on a particular narrative or scenic segment of the story and make them *hear* the text. A lively, finely tuned, well-modulated reading, preferably by the instructor (especially if the German original is involved), will expose the students to the semantic vibrations and overtones of the text, including its humorous or comic elements, and will elicit gut responses that may form the basis for an interpretive class discussion.

Critics have paid much attention to Mann's ironic stance as an ever-present feature of his fiction. While the presence of irony in his writings is undeniable and while discussions of irony lend themselves splendidly to conceptual analyses of philosophical and psychological dualities in a given work and, moreover, of Mann's view of society and human affairs, it may be safe to say that the formula of *Thomas Mann: The Ironic German* (Heller) has been overworked at the expense of the author's humor and comic-histrionic genius. As Ronald Peacock has observed, "Mann can see the funny side of anything, without needing to be ironical" (178). On several occasions Mann himself weighed the relative merits of irony and humor; he made the strongest plea for the appreciation of humor in his works in a radio discussion in 1953:

> It seems to me that irony is that spirit of art which draws a smile from the reader or listener, an intellectual smile, I would call it; whereas humor produces the laughter that wells up from the heart, and this I personally rate higher as an artistic effect, and I welcome it with greater joy when it is the effect of my own creations than the Erasmian smile that is evoked by irony.   (11: 802)

He adds that in his public readings he always felt happiest when he heard a "hearty laugh" in his audience. Anyone who has listened to his recordings of, for example, *The Infant Prodigy* (*Das Wunderkind*), *Railway Accident* (*Das Eisenbahnunglück*), or *Felix Krull* can attest to the calculated histrionic effectiveness of his humorous or comic tone of voice.

Of course, irony and humor can mix, and, with varying degrees of emphasis on the two components, they often do in Mann's writings. Nevertheless, it is useful for our hermeneutic practice in the classroom to recognize a basic categorical difference between, on the one hand, the ironic stance, with its subversion of surface statements through dissimulation, concealment, and duplicity of meaning, and, on the other hand, the humorous disposition, with its conciliatory and good-natured outlook. Whereas irony tends to launch some kind of aggression, to be critical, derisive, or even destructive, humor usually expresses a sympathetic or at least tolerant acceptance of things as they are, including human frailties and follies, pain and suffering. We see an abundance of ludicrous, pathetic, and grotesque figures in Mann's fiction, and there is plenty of pain, disease, and mental anguish. Yet the reader, in some strange way, derives pleasure from the manner in which a highly imperfect world is presented. Mann's humor, as a mode of his poetic imagination, makes the inadequacies and absurdities of human existence not only acceptable but aesthetically enjoyable as well. In some respects this kind of humorous imagination is in accord with Sigmund Freud's view of humor as being "liberating," "elevating," and "consoling"; it not only demonstrates the "assertion of the ego's invulnerability" in the face of adversity, it also "victoriously maintains the pleasure principle" ("Humor" 162, 163, 166).

The general term *humor* may cover a great variety of literary features that are pleasurably amusing, hilarious, comical, funny, witty, ludicrous, bizarre, or farcical. When we take a close analytical look at the literary texture in Mann's stories, we find that his humorous imagination manifests itself in two basically different modes. First, at the stylistic level, there is what we may call *narrative humor,* as a property of a personal narrator's voice, tone, attitude, viewpoint, and reader relationship. An outstanding example of such narrative humor is the brilliant opening chapter of *Tristan,* in which the narrator employs a stylistic mixture of mimicry, jargon, gossip, emotive exclamation, sly comment, and intimate observation to introduce the reader to a world of disease and death. The principal vehicle of humor here is the narrator's role-playing, his mimicking the sentiments of unidentified Einfried inhabitants. An exclamation such as "Dear me, what a whirl of activity!" with reference to Fräulein von Osterloh's diligence, or a statement such as "Ah yes, this is a lively place. The establishment is flourishing" (93, 94) displays what Franz Stanzel calls "contaminations" of a narrator's language by the speech of fictional characters (192). A particularly noteworthy case of such contamination, or "submerged quotation" (192), occurs when the narrator somewhat underhandedly introduces Spinell by affecting an inmate's puzzled impression: "There is even a writer here, idling away his time" (94). The narrator's mimicry here derides not only the "idle" and "eccentric" aesthete but also the bourgeois mentality that pronounces judgment on him. Later in the story, we are amused by the leitmotific use of the contamination technique when we repeatedly hear about Gabriele's trachea: "the trachea, and not, thank God, the lungs!" (95). The narrator thus mimics Herr Klöterjahn's wishful thinking.

Everything we learn about Einfried and its population is mediated through the playfully adaptable, finely modulated, slightly malicious voice of an anonymous narrator, who is highly audible as an amused and detached teller of the tale. Significantly, the detachment breaks down only in chapter 8, when the narrator himself, along with Spinell and Gabriele, appears to be swept away by the power of music conjuring up a mystic union in an "everlasting night of love" (118). Is this effect, however, actually an extreme case of "contamination" caused by the emotional crescendo of the two characters and, hence, another example of the narrator's virtuoso adaptability? It may well be, especially if we perceive subtle humor in the music scene because of its parodistic reenactment of Wagner's Romantic love-and-death motif and its presentation as an aesthetic act of sublimation and substitution by which Detlev Spinell, the "Platonic adulterer" (W. Hughes 75), lures Gabriele to her death.

While Mann's narrative humor is a kind of verbal mime that is part of the narrator's voice, the second principal mode of his humor is a function of character, action, and dialogue, and it comes in the form of *comedy*— that is, as a scenic-dramatic episode usually involving at least one comic character and presenting us with an amusing incongruity or collision of opposites. In terms of the narratological distinction between "telling" and "showing," narrative humor is a manner of telling the tale, whereas comedy (German *Komik*, the comical, the comic scene or situation) is produced through showing—that is, by means of a more or less "theatrical" presentation. Mann's fiction abounds in memorable comic scenes. We need only think, for example, in *The Buddenbrooks* of little Christian's histrionics at the dinner table or Alois Permaneder's visit and conversation with the Frau Konsulin; in *Felix Krull*, of the young draft dodger's simulation of an epileptic fit in front of the medical officers or his eye-opening encounter with Professor Kuckuck in a railway dining car. In these and many other delightful comic scenes, Mann has created impressive variations of comic incongruity or dissonance.

Tristan is as close to being a stage comedy as any of Mann's stories. The largely scenic presentation, the hilarious dialogues, and the portrayal of all characters except Gabriele as comic figures suggest why Mann, in a letter to his brother Heinrich (13 Feb. 1901), referred to the story as a "burlesque" (*Briefe* 1: 26). To the extent that a burlesque may involve an "incongruous imitation . . . of a serious literary work" (Abrams 17), Mann's story is a parodistic reenactment of the principal motifs and the triangular character constellation in Wagner's *Tristan and Isolde*. The target of ridicule, however, is not Wagner's work, but rather the turn-of-the-century middle-class milieu with its polarized human types: on the one hand, the sterile, parasitic, and pretentious aesthete and, on the other, the robust, complacent, and slightly vulgar nouveau riche bourgeois. Unlike *The Buddenbrooks* or *Tonio Kröger, Tristan* neither presents us with any genuine "Bürger" nor shows us any authentic artist; Gabriele is no more than a dying remnant of the Bürger tradition. The absence of a traditional Bürger and of a genuine artist points to the source of comedy in *Tristan*: measured against Mann's prototypical standards of either middle-class health and respectability or artistic awareness and creativity, all characters in *Tristan* are deficient, one-sided, or physically or mentally deformed. Without becoming fiercely moralistic or aggressively satirical, Mann's unmasking scrutiny (*Entlarvungspsychologie* in the Nietzschean vein) exposes the funny side of his characters' foibles, ailments, and shortcomings. This is true not only for the two major antagonists of the story, whose character traits—mindless vitality and sterile intellectuality—are set up in complementary distribution, but also for minor figures such as Fräulein von Osterloh, with her unfulfilled erotic wishes, the syphilitic gentlemen with their "unruly dancing gait" (94), or Pastorin Höhlenrauch, whose vital energies are totally exhausted after she has had nineteen children. Even very minor figures amuse us with comic disparities. Examples are Dr. Müller, who is relegated to taking care of the harmless and the hopeless cases (94) and so will hardly encounter any professional challenges, or the family physician, Dr. Hinzpeter, who indulges in a little professional hypocrisy when, in a "remarkably soothing, reassuring" manner (98), he euphemistically speaks of Gabriele's "trachea."

Aestheticians and philosophers from Kant, Jean Paul, and Schopenhauer to Bergson and Freud have been in general agreement that the quintessence of comedy and the comical consists in some laughable contrast, incongruity, or disparity. *Tristan* offers superb examples of comic contrast in scenic and dialogue form. When Spinell transposes and sublimates Gabriele's account of the youthful garden scene into a pristine fairy-tale idyll, it is the incongruity between ordinary factuality ("we crocheted and gossiped") and Spinell's fantasizing ("What beauty! Ah, dear me, how beautiful that is!") (108) that produces the comic effect. In gourmet Klöterjahn's later version, the girls' discussion revolved around a recipe for potato pancakes (129); thus we receive the most down-to-earth view of their activities by the fountain.

The most hilarious and thematically significant scenic comedy is acted out in the final clash between the two antagonists in chapters 10 and 11. Although the two are "on stage" together only in chapter 11, Spinell's epistolary attack is the first half of a comic collision in which each figure employs the rhetorical weapon most appropriate for himself. Spinell's provocative letter, in which the motif of the garden scene reemerges as a rather literary argument, is an amusingly eloquent and incisive analysis of and attack on Klöterjahn, the "unconscious" type (124). The latter's equally amusing and no less eloquent oral counterattack is impressive because of its blunt spontaneity and uninhibited name-calling. On the surface, in terms of the sequence of events, Klöterjahn appears to be the "winner" of the battle. But at the level of deep structure, there can be no winner because each man's weapons are inadequate to defeat the other. Spinell's high-flying intellectual attack, propelled by what Nietzsche considered to be the resentment of the weak and sick against the strong and healthy, can have no real effect on Klöterjahn, who is constitutionally incapable of understanding Spinell's letter. By the same token, however, Klöterjahn's crude verbal violence cannot defeat or destroy Spinell's awareness and perception. In the final analysis, the comic confrontation takes place between two incongruously equipped opponents, and the ultimate effect on the reader is one of comic absurdity.

The basic distinction between narrative humor and comedy can also be applied to *Tonio Kröger*. But while in *Tristan* the humorous tone of the narrator and comic configurations are pervasive, the employment of humor and comedy in *Tonio Kröger* is more limited and functions differently. Since the problematic hero of the story evokes strong feelings of identification and sympathy on the part of the reader, especially the young reader, humor and comedy are much-needed devices to counteract, aesthetically, possible overdoses of emotion and sentiment. Mann himself must have been aware of this problem, because he repeatedly referred to *Tonio Kröger* as a "lyrical" story (*Dichter über ihre Dichtungen* 1: 159, 160, 169), and in a letter to Kurt Martens (28 Mar. 1906) he said that he had written into the story a confession of his "love of life with a conspicuousness and directness that touches on the inartistic" (*Briefe* 1: 61). Whenever critics have expressed reservations about this work, they invariably have misgivings about an excess of sentiment or of essayistic discourse. A recent such complaint comes from Marcel Reich-Ranicki, who calls *Tonio Kröger* "a flawed, imperfect literary product," primarily because of alleged emotionalism, sentimentality, and lack of artistic control and detachment (66). Oddly enough, Reich-Ranicki and most other critics have given little attention to the role of humor and comedy in this highly popular story. Mann the humorist quite deliberately employed certain narrative strategies that protected him against the pitfalls of a mere *Stimmungsnovelle* à la Theodor Storm and the dangers of fictionalized essayism.

Tonio Kröger contains three memorable comic scenes that show Tonio in encounters with minor comic figures. Each of these scenes functions as a kind of comic relief within a context that might otherwise have become too burdened with Tonio's emotion and introspection. The first such scene, occurring when Tonio is in love with Ingeborg, is the dancing lesson with Ballettmeister Knaak, a "preposterous monkey" who has adapted his artistic skills totally to the demands and social conventions of "the best families" (144). His studied, polished comportment and "impressively controlled physique" (146) are an incarnation of Henri Bergson's concept of the comic figure who performs a "social masquerade" and makes us laugh at "rigidity . . . clashing with the inner suppleness of life" (Bergson 89). The second clearly comical scene takes place at the end of Tonio's wistful visit to his hometown, when police officer Petersen suspects him of being "an individial [sic] . . . of unknown parentage and doubtful provenance" (173). The episode is playfully connected with the leitmotif of the "gypsy in a green caravan." Tonio's near-arrest by a representative of law and order, whose literacy is a bit questionable, adds a light and farcical touch to a chapter that is dominated by a mood of nostalgia and melancholy. The third comic interlude occurs on board the steamer that takes Tonio to Denmark; it involves his encounter with the young businessman from Hamburg who, after consuming "astonishing quantities of lobster omelet" (175), falls into raptures about the "sstars" and the infinity of the universe. Tonio senses in him the sentimental bourgeois, who writes "deeply felt, honest, businessman's poetry" (177), and the reader is reminded of the "deeply felt and totally inept" poetry (163) of a similarly dilettantish lieutenant whom Tonio had ridiculed in his conversation with Lisaweta. The businessman's metaphysical effusion ends abruptly, of course, when the "uproar of the elements" (177) affects his stomach—an exquisite example of comic incongruity where mind and matter are at odds with each other. This comic situation, too, is embedded in a serious, in fact "lyrical," context, showing us Tonio's exuberance at being reunited, as it were, with the Baltic Sea. Moreover, it is Tonio himself who is now on the verge of becoming a comical figure, very much like the lieutenant and the businessman, when he is carried away by his emotions to compose a poem: "Inwardly he began to sing a song of love, a paean of praise to the sea. Friend of my youth, ah wild sea weather, once more we meet, once more together . . . But there the poem ended" (178). Deeply felt and totally inept stuff, the narrator seems to intimate, because Tonio's "heart was alive" and he ignored everything he had told Lisaweta about "refrigerating" feelings and passions in poetry (160). For a brief moment Tonio appears to us just like any other bourgeois dilettante who wants to make poetry out of emotions.

While the comic episodes in *Tonio Kröger* revolve around or are triggered by minor figures, narrative humor, as a quality of tone and texture, can appear anywhere in the story. It is most effectively used, however, as a device to make the reader adopt, now and then, an amused, slightly detached, or even mildly critical attitude toward the central figure, Tonio. Since Tonio basically elicits considerable affection and sympathy from the reader, Mann employs narrative humor to prevent total identification, to keep Tonio at a minimal distance. Because of the strong bond of affection, the narrative humor in *Tonio Kröger* is much more subtle than that in *Tristan*, and the narrator is much less intrusive and audible. Two examples from very different contexts must suffice to show how narrative humor functions here.

At the end of chapter 1, Tonio's thoughts about Hans Hansen's promise to read *Don Carlos* "sometime soon" are exposed to us in a passage of "erlebte Rede" (free indirect speech) as follows:

> Hans was going to read *Don Carlos*, and then they would have something in common, something they could talk about, and neither Jimmerthal nor anyone else would be able to join in! How well they understood each other! Perhaps—who could say?—he would one day even be able to get him to write poetry, like Tonio himself . . . No, no, he didn't want that to happen. Hans must never become like Tonio, but stay as he was, with his strength and his sunlike happiness which made everyone love him, and Tonio most of all! But still, it would do him no harm to read *Don Carlos*.   (143)

The dialectic movement of Tonio's reflections has a tripartite structure. In the first three sentences, he rejoices in the hope (or, as the reader feels, the delusion) that Hans will become a more intimate friend by sharing Tonio's literary interests. But the next two sentences state the antithesis: Hans is lovable because of the way he actually is. It is the last sentence that makes an effort at synthesis and, thus, is the agent of humor: "But still, it would do him no harm to read *Don Carlos*." Succinctly stated, the fourteen-year-old Tonio would like to have it both ways, and that is what Tonio Kröger's story is all about.

Tonio wants both respect from artists like himself and a little love from ordinary, middle-class humanity—this is, of course, a significant theme in chapter 4, when he divulges his problems to Lisaweta. On occasion the episode has been regarded as being too essayistic or cerebral, and Reich-Ranicki terms it the "theoretical" chapter within a "programmatic" story (97). The imaginative reader or student, however, will interpret this section not as a programmatic essay but rather as part of the fiction about Tonio Kröger, who is shown here at a certain critical stage of his development (see the essay by Rodney Symington in this volume). Tonio is not the mouthpiece of the author. Even his most cerebral or profound pronouncements ought to be considered inseparable from the fictional character. Most important, the presence of a listener, a slightly amused, curious, and keenly observant recipient of Tonio's discourse, generates an aura of fine humor that pervades the whole scene. Although Lisaweta interacts with Tonio only a few times, she ought to be present in the reader's imagination as Tonio's humorous and mildly critical confidante, a good listener who makes him relax with tea and cigarettes, teases him a little about his middle-class manners and garments, and, at last, pronounces a "judgment" that mildly ridicules Tonio's background as well as his scrupulous self-analysis. But the reader should not too literally interpret Lisaweta's neat formula of Tonio the "bourgeois manqué"; her assessment is somewhat one-sided because it doesn't do justice to the artist in Tonio. By the same token, Tonio's final reply, "*Ich bin erledigt*" ("I am shattered" or "demolished" or "annihilated" may be more appropriate than David Luke's translation "*I have been eliminated*" [164]), is a humorous overstatement that does not necessarily imply a serious authorial comment; it should be considered part of the humorous and playful rhetoric that is characteristic of all the exchanges between Tonio and Lisaweta, including those in chapter 5. Tonio may feel or pretend to be "erledigt" for the moment, but that chapter shows him quite determined, despite slight feelings of embarrassment vis-à-vis Lisaweta, to revisit the very territory of his middle-class origins that Lisaweta had ridiculed.

On the whole, then, Lisaweta's presence in chapter 4 serves as a humorous and relaxed corrective voice counterbalancing Tonio's all too intense and rigorous self-examination. Through the figure of Lisaweta, Mann offers us some interpretive leeway: the reader does not have to accept Tonio's dramatized and polarized notions of art and life quite as seriously as Tonio himself feels compelled to do at this stage of his development.

Humor and comedy thus protect the text against an excess of sentiment, emotion, and introversion, providing the reader with a perspective that is not identical to Tonio's. It seems that the young author of *Tonio Kröger* was well aware that this story of the artist as a young man, a story of alienation and anguish, called for some cheerful and pleasurable counterbalance. Indeed, the young artist Tonio himself knows about the interdependence of "Komik und Elend" (8: 290), comedy and misery; his first publication is a "well-made piece of work, full of humor and the knowledge of suffering" (152).

Jugendstil in Mann's Early Short Fiction

Edith Potter

Jugendstil, called art nouveau in France and Spain and the arts and crafts movement in England and the United States, was one of a number of short-lived movements that occurred around 1900 and that are discussed in detail, for example, by Richard Hamann and Jost Hermand in their exhaustive study *Stilkunst um 1900*. Jugendstil's influence on Thomas Mann's early short fiction is well documented. Hans Vaget even talks of a specialized secondary literature existing on Mann and Jugendstil (*Kommentar* 89). Mann's early works, therefore, offer an excellent opportunity to introduce students, through the study of a literary text, to this important movement and to acquaint them with the interconnections and interdependence of the arts (Koopmann, "Gegen" 204).

Other reasons suggest Mann as the ideal representative for such a study. His entry into the world of literature coincides with the beginnings of Jugendstil, since his sketch *Vision* (8: 9–10) and the short novel *Gefallen* (8: 11–42) were written in 1893 and 1894, just as Julius Otto Bierbaum's *Moderner Musenalmanach*, published in 1893, achieved a breakthrough for the literary Jugendstil in Germany.

Not only the timing but also the setting is significant. Mann lived in Munich—which, along with Berlin, Darmstadt, and Vienna, was one of the centers of Jugendstil in the German-speaking countries. He was associated, first as a "lektor" (assistant editor), and then as a contributor, with *Simplicissimus*, which together with *Pan*, *Die Insel*, and *Ver Sacrum* was one of the important magazines for this movement. He knew its artists, among them Thomas Theodor Heine and Olaf Gulbransson, and had his books illustrated by them. Furthermore, the cover of the first two-volume edition of *The Buddenbrooks* was designed in pure Jugendstil by Otto Eckmann. The famous photo of the two Mann brothers Heinrich and Thomas was made in the Elvira Studio in Munich, designed by August Endell (Lehnert, *Vom Jugendstil* 469, 481); the studio's interior and exterior were among the most discussed manifestations of Jugendstil (Selz and Constantine 138–39). As early as 1899 Mann mentions the Vienna Jugendstil periodical *Ver Sacrum* in his letter of 7 June to Kurt Martens (*Briefe* 1: 10), expressing his admiration for Maeterlinck's "Tintagiles Tod" as well as for its illustrations.

As is well known, Jugendstil was a protest movement against the historicism practiced in the nineteenth century. It demanded art and literature that grew out of their own time. Adherents of Jugendstil reacted in a particularly hostile way to the crass naturalism of the 1880s and early 1890s, rejecting its ugliness and its emphasis on the underside of life. The protest was also directed at the ostentatious tastes and smug attitudes prevalent during the Wilhelmian age (J. M. Fischer, "Deutsche Literatur" 244–49).

Jugendstil was a highly decorative style, featuring floral motifs, asymmetric sweeping bold lines, arabesque designs, and a two-dimensionality, as well as the evocative line found in the Japanese color prints that exerted a great influence on art at that time (Selz 59; Ernst Michalski, qtd. in Hermand, *Jugendstil: Forschungsbericht* 11, 16–17). It emphasized youth, spring, and a celebration of life; creating the mood of a new beginning, the artists preferred the exquisite and the rare to the pedestrian. Water lilies, irises, orchids, reeds, nymphs, swans, and flamingos recur again and again, lending their exotic, ephemeral, and ornamental qualities to illustrations. Eckmann's well-known design "Five Swans" (Hiesinger 53) could serve as a characteristic example of Jugendstil; exuberant depictions of dancers and sun worshipers, such as those by Hodler and Fidus, typify the beginning of the Jugendstil movement (Hamann 855–61).

Depictions of women tended to show them as languishing, delicate, elegant, cultured, and often sickly, unable to cope with the demands of a healthy and robust life. In its emphasis on the aesthetic and exclusive, Jugendstil soon became the prerogative of the leisure class. Georg Simmel called these connoisseurs "gate-keepers of inwardness," and Mann spoke of an inwardness protected by the establishment (qtd. in Hermand, *Jugendstil: Forschungsbericht* 41).

The movement was marked by other paradoxes as well. It suggested reforms in furniture and clothing to liberate people from the choking decor of the Wilhelmian age, yet it became stuffy itself by virtue of an overabundance of decoration. In the applied arts it often turned into kitsch (Theodoretta Rosenplüh, qtd. in Mathes, *Prosa* 111–14). What had begun as an enthusiastic movement to renew all aspects of life soon degenerated into frivolous superficiality, out of touch with everyday realities. In contrast, expressionism, its successor, focused on these realities.

These developments contributed to the rapid downfall of Jugendstil. Satirized by Mann, it was held in contempt up to 1918 and considered an exercise in bad taste until an earnest study of its features and the discovery of a literary Jugendstil, mainly after World War II, renewed an interest and appreciation for the movement (Hermand, *Jugendstil: Forschungsbericht* 2–5; Jost 1–3).

We can detect signs of Jugendstil in Mann's earliest writing, the brief sketch *Vision*, published by the eighteen-year-old author in the short-lived Lübeck student paper *Der Frühlingssturm*, edited by Mann himself. In fact, the program of this paper, as spelled out by Mann, reflects the protest of the Jugendstil movement, stating as its goal to "stir up with words and thoughts the mass of cobwebs in antiquated brains and the ignorance of narrow-minded, puffed up philistines" who opposed Mann and his generation (Mathes, *Theorie* 128). Clustered in the limited space of its two pages are an amazing number of Jugendstil features: a languid mood affected by the precocious narrator, cigar smoke that created undulating lines and arabesque designs, and a floral motif. Also prominent are the colors red and white, which characterized Jugendstil and appeared in later works by Mann, most strikingly in the last scene of *Tristan* in association with an ostentatious display of robust health in Anton Klöterjahn, Jr., and his buxom nurse.

The decorative qualities of umbelliferous plants and clusters of flowers and fruits were not only favorites of such Jugendstil illustrators as Josef Maria Auchentaller, Koloman Moser, Fernand Khnopff, Heinrich Vogeler, and Josef Hoffmann, they also play a role in Mann's more ambitious second attempt at literature, his *Rahmennovelle* ("frame story") *Gefallen*, published in *Die Gesellschaft*. A lilac bush with its fragrant blossoms in its earliest spring bloom becomes, as it were, a silent and sympathetic witness to the narrator's first blissful love but also the object of his wild, destructive rage at his rude awakening from his sentimental dream at discovering his sweetheart's deceit (8: 23, 35, 40, 42).

His tale of bliss and disillusion, naïveté and cynicism, set in a bright and sunny spring, stands in sharp contrast to the dark, exotic atmosphere of the home in which the narration takes place (11–14). The fragrance of freshly cut lilacs compels the narrator, ten years older now, to tell this episode from his youth; even now his memory is so fresh that he savagely reaches for the lilac bouquet as if still wanting to use the flowers as a scapegoat for his disappointed love (42). The theme of women's emancipation, by the way, is essential to this story.

The two short novels *Little Herr Friedemann* and *The Joker*, published in rapid succession in the *Neue Deutsche Rundschau* in May and September 1897, show a certain similarity in their heroes, both of whom lead relaxed, partly inactive lives of leisure, of an aesthetic connoisseurship made possible by their financial independence. They are excellent examples of the pensioner's existence satirized by both Georg Simmel and Mann. One obvious difference, however, is that Herr Friedemann, forced by his physical handicap to suppress his desire for a normal life, resigns himself to the cultivation of his aesthetic sensibilities, whereas the Joker's decision to indulge in a leisurely life-style is voluntary. The Joker opts for his empty, nonproductive life the minute an inheritance assures him a modest but comfortable income. Both are failures. Herr Friedemann's emotional and sexual needs reassert themselves under the influence of Gerda von Rinnlingen's provocative presence; the Joker's dilettante existence has made him a man of no consequence. He realizes that he no longer counts and consequently loses all self-respect. In "Herr Friedemann" there is a subtle play on the preferred red and white Jugendstil color contrast, created by the silvery full moon, a starlit night, a white gravel path, and Gerda's reddish-blond hair. In addition, the fragrance of "all the flower beds" (25) and Gerda's inviting gesture to Herr Friedemann to follow her to a secluded spot for an intimate talk work their magic. It leads to the breakdown of Friedemann's reserve and, on Gerda's cruel rejection, to his bizarre suicide by forced self-immersion.

Gerda's role in this short work and her effect on Friedemann's life call for further elaboration. In literary Jugendstil two types of women frequently occur, the femme fatale and the femme fragile. Gerda von Rinnlingen clearly belongs to the first. She is elegant, independent, detached, cold, calculating, and unpredictable, with a hint of frequent illnesses and uncontrollable moods. Her striking appearance, with heavy red hair flashing like gold under the light (18), and her provocative air are unsettling to men and give her a strange power over them, especially vulnerable ones, whom she delights in exploiting. Like a predatory animal she lies in wait and pounces on her victim when ready for the kill. Her relationship with her husband and the response of the women in her society reveal some of these characteristics (9–10). Little Herr Friedemann experiences their full effect. His first distant sight of her as she drives past leaves him strangely disturbed, and his subsequent encounter, sitting next to her in the box at the opera—her white arm resting on the red plush—leaves him overcome with emotion and his carefully cultivated "happiness" in tatters. Helpless, he can only murmur to himself "Oh my God! my God!" (14–15). With all his defenses down, under the influence of Gerda's scrutinizing gaze, cynical voice, and cruel mockery (19–20), Herr Friedemann relinquishes his will to live and becomes her easy victim.

In "The Wardrobe," written in 1898 and published in the *Neue Deutsche Rundschau* in 1899, the hero, Albrecht van der Qualen (whose very surname bespeaks his torment), lives on the threshold between life and death, in an imaginary place out of time. His antirealistic and antinaturalistic story has fairy-tale aspects, and as Mann said, it is a narrative full of riddles. Its antinaturalism is emphasized by the appearance of a beautiful, nude young girl appearing and disappearing to the hero in the mysterious wardrobe, telling him stories as long as he keeps his distance. She is the spirit of poetry that has to remain separated from the real world, just as Albrecht van der Qualen is isolated from this world. Again Mann uses the favorite Jugendstil red and white color contrast. Qualen's room resembles the bachelor apartment Mann then occupied in Schwabing.

The close relationship, as well as the sharp contrast, between life and death is central to *The Road to the Churchyard*, but it is life that prevails in the figure of the youthful, provocative, and slightly cocky bicyclist, called simply Life (Leben). He and Lobgott Piepsam take the same road to the churchyard, but Piepsam's walk leads to his death. His sad life as an outsider, both in appearance and circumstances, gives us cause for concern and elicits our sympathy. But the ironic tone and the grotesque description of Piepsam let us take the story as it was meant to be, a burlesque, and enable us to sympathize with the bicyclist, with Life.

The bicyclist, a representative of a sport just then becoming exceedingly popular, reflects Mann as an aficionado. He writes in his *Sketch of My*

Life: "In those years I was such a passionate bicyclist that I hardly ever went by foot, and even in pouring rain, in rain boots and Loden cape I did all my traveling on this vehicle" (11: 107). There is plenty of other evidence for the popularity of the bike at this time, including Richard Dehmel's poem "Radlers Seligkeit" (Schutte and Sprengel 346–47), Oskar Bie's "Fahrrad-Aesthetik" (Mathes, *Theorie* 65–68), and many illustrations, among them Bruno Paul's title page of *Jugend* 1, 1896 (Mathes, *Prosa* 225) and E. Kneiss's "Zukunftsstrassenbild," in another 1896 issue of *Jugend* (*Du* 530).

In the works discussed so far, references to Jugendstil either were of secondary importance or were a straight comment on the movement. In *Tristan* (1903), Mann's short novel par excellence, Jugendstil elements dominate, mostly as satire. Except for Gabriele, a pure representative of the delicate and weak Jugendstil femme fragile, the characters display grotesque aspects of Jugendstil features. Whereas Gabriele's precarious state of health is viewed sympathetically, Spinell's weak disposition has earned him the nickname "the putrefied infant" ("der verweste Säugling") (99). Spinell is ridiculed not only for his self-indulgent, affectedly soft behavior but also for his deliberate pretentiousness when admiring beautiful persons or objects. A contemporary of Mann's, Peter Altenberg, in his short sketch *In München*, suggests that one should pay special attention to beautiful objects, treating them as old friends and greeting them when one enters a room (Mathes, *Prosa* 178–81). Detlev Spinell turns such a suggestion into a ridiculously grotesque scene. " 'What beauty!' " he exclaims, "tilting his head to one side, raising his shoulders, spreading out his hands and curling back his nose and lips," even losing his balance in this emotional display and "blindly falling upon the neck of no matter who might be at hand, whatever their status or sex" (99–100).

In the overly delicate and effeminate behavior of Spinell, Mann draws heavily on characteristics of Altenberg and another writer of the times, Arthur Holitscher, as has been pointed out by Vaget (*Kommentar* 85–86) and Hermand ("Peter Spinell"). The importance for Spinell of the interior decoration of his rooms in the Einfried sanitorium, his leisurely if not downright lazy life, his meager literary output, indicating his lack of vitality—all make him a grotesque antithesis of what Jugendstil set out to be. That forceful, vibrant, youthful rebellion has now turned into a movement of flabby and lethargic connoisseurs, mere consumers of art protected by their comfortable financial circumstances.

Only vicarious enjoyment, not participation in life, is left for Spinell, who ironically identifies himself most closely with the figure of Wagner's Tristan. Mann caricatures modish Jugendstil illustrations in his description of Spinell's book as a "novel of moderate length with a completely baffling cover design, printed on the kind of paper one might use for filtering coffee, in elaborate typography with every letter looking like a Gothic cathedral"

(100). Artists such as Melchior Lechter, the creator of Stefan George's letter types as well as of many illustrations for his books (Soergel and Hohoff 1: 399, 402, 412), Heinrich Vogeler's illustrations for the early Hofmannsthal (Soergel and Hohoff 1: 469) and title pages for the periodical *Die Insel* (Mathes, *Theorie* 24– 25), the letters designed by Otto Eckmann (Selz and Constantine 43), and illustrations by Peter Behrend, especially his famous color woodcut *The Kiss* (*Du* 521), are a few examples of the art caricatured by Mann's description.

Spinell's counterpart, Anton Klöterjahn, Sr., is as grotesque a contrast to a Jugendstil motif as Spinell is himself. That vulgar send-up of a healthy physique and an appetite for life is miles removed from the jolly and enthusiastic bicyclist called Life in *The Road to the Churchyard*. His son, Anton, promises to become a worthy successor to his father. What Spinell lacks, Klöterjahn has in abundance, and vice versa. What the two have in common is a selfish insensitivity to Gabriele's delicate constitution. The husband wants her cured, even though he has no intention of changing his ways; Spinell prefers to see her die rather than have her beauty defiled by the vulgarity of a continued life with Klöterjahn. In the end, hardly to our surprise, it is not the robust Klöterjahn but the impotent Spinell who indirectly causes Gabriele's death. Their verbal duel brings their confrontation to a climax, exposing to ridicule both the preciosity of Spinell's style and the blundering crudeness of Klöterjahn's. As noted earlier, Gabriele, the object of the duel, displays the typical attributes of the Jugendstil femme fragile: she is delicate and sensitive, beautiful and languishing, too vulnerable for life's physical demands and therefore doomed to an early death (see Thomalla).

Gabriele and her girlfriends in the garden scene represent a prominent Jugendstil motif: the fountain surrounded by irises at its border, and the old walnut tree, all set in a garden (108). This is also a motif recurring in many of Mann's writings. The scene symbolizes her secure and sheltered youth before her marriage, an atmosphere that she left at her peril to follow Klöterjahn—to fulfill her duty as woman, wife, and, eventually, mother. A glance at the works of Eckmann's many versions of irises (Mathes, *Prosa* 28), Auchentaller's stylized irises (Nebehay 74), and Walter Tiemann's illustration of a fountain for Rilke's *Das Stundenbuch* (Soergel and Hohoff 1: 610) confirm the popularity of this Jugendstil motif. Spinell's vision of Gabriele as a queen amid her maiden attendants also brings to mind the popular depiction of the Paradise Garden in the fifteenth century, as painted by the Master of the Frankfurt Paradise Garden. Although no claim is made that Mann was influenced by this well-known rendition, its similarity to the scene he describes deserves mention (Hamann 460–61).

Resplendent Munich at the turn of the century, the setting of *Gladius Dei*, is accorded a sympathetic and slightly bemused treatment by Mann— not, however, without some implied criticism. In addition to the obvious comparison with Savonarola's Renaissance Florence, there are many references to Jugendstil features around 1900 in Mann's descriptions of the architecture, bookbinding, and art objects. It is not the Renaissance-style architecture of Ludwigstrasse but rather buildings like the Elvira Studio or the Jugendstil houses by Helbig and Haiger, in the Ainmillerstrasse in Schwabing, that Mann evokes:

> Often, in a row of dull solid buildings, some artistic edifice stands out, the work of some young and imaginative architect: wide-fronted, with shallow arches and bizarre decorative motifs, full of style and inventive wit. Or suddenly, in some very boring facade, one door is framed by a saucy improvisation of flowing lines and luminous colors, bacchantes, water nymphs and rose-pink nudes. (76)

Herr Blüthenzweig's art shop at Odeonsplatz—his name both in its irony and in its straightforward meaning encompasses a whole aspect of the Jugendstil program—is stocked with "bronze nudes and fragile ornamental glassware; tall earthenware vases which have emerged from baths of metal vapor clad in iridescent colors; volumes in exquisite bindings, triumphs of fine modern book production, lavish luxury editions of the works of fashionable lyric poets" (76). Oskar Bie's description of the bibliophile products of the Insel Publishing House applies here too:

> Its books are ornaments for the bookcase, high sensations for the hand, exquisite for the mind, a subscription for cultivated souls, fingers, and purses. Not many can buy, much less understand how to touch, these delicate leatherbound volumes.
> (Hermand, *Jugendstil: Forschungsbericht* 41)

In Hieronymus's eyes, this art—appealing mainly to the senses—is devoid of any moral message or spiritual enrichment. Despite the young man's fanaticism—however grotesque and objectionable—his protest might also imply Mann's reservations about and rejection of the contemporaneous art that included Jugendstil (Wich, "*Gladius Dei*" 398).

Mann always had a much closer relationship to music than to art, as he himself declared in the Princeton University lecture about *The Magic Mountain*: "I must consider myself a musician among the poets. The novel has always been for me a symphony, a work of contrapuntal structure, a texture of themes, in which ideas play the role of musical motifs" (qtd. in von Gronicka, *Profile* 137; cf. 11: 611). It should be noted, however, that there was one artist among his contemporaries whom he admired very much: Ludwig von Hofmann, who also contributed significant paintings in the Jugendstil motif. In his 27 June 1914 letter to Hofmann, Mann describes the great impression Hofmann's painting *Die Quelle* had made on him and declares his desire to acquire it: "I am writing about a picture of yours which I fell madly in love with this winter." Indeed, Mann submits a plan that would enable him to buy the painting, which shows three youthful male nudes in a timeless landscape centered on a mountain spring. As Richard and Clara Winston point out, Mann acquired this painting and " . . . contrived to save it when he went into exile. It is now in the Thomas Mann Archives in Zurich, along with the entire contents of his study" (*Letters*, 1971 ed., 68).

It seems that *Tristan* can be interpreted as a satire of Jugendstil themes and *Gladius Dei* as a criticism of its arts. *Tonio Kröger* takes up another Jugendstil problem, that of dilettantism and the distinction between the dilettante and the serious artist. This issue had already arisen in *The Joker*, whose hero lacked the discipline and the will to develop his talents, remaining a dilettante all his life. Tonio, in his lengthy discussion with Lisaweta about the role of the artist, deliberately distances himself from the coffeehouse literati, from the writers who are not single-mindedly committed to their art (Vaget, *Kommentar* 114–16). He objects to Adalbert, the short-story writer who considers literature "that remote and sublime sphere in which one is incapable of grosser thoughts" (154), as well as to the lieutenant who writes about "music and love" (163); he is unhappy about the banker with a criminal record that enabled him to be a writer (158). For "a real artist is not one who has taken up art as his profession, but a man predestined and foredoomed to it" (157). Tonio, despite his obsession with being a writer and his efforts to stay aloof from literati like Adalbert, must confess that he cannot hermetically seal himself off from life and be only a cold-blooded observer. Because of his bourgeois conscience, he has fallen "foolishly in love with simplicity and naiveté, with the delightfully normal, the respectable and mediocre" (191).

Tonio Kröger is not Mann's last short fiction of this period with Jugendstil features. Three short novels with Jugendstil influences, written from 1903 to 1905 and translated in *Stories of Three Decades*, should especially be mentioned: *Das Wunderkind* (1903), *Beim Propheten* (1904), and *Wälsungenblut* (1905, published in 1921). The third work contains the most exciting concentration of Jugendstil features. The Aarenhold villa in Berlin Tiergarten W, with its exquisite objets d'art and the Aarenholds' meticulously planned and highly cultured life-style, expresses an aestheticism made possible by their wealth. The nineteen-year-old Aarenhold twins, Siegmund and Sieglind, particularly Siegmund, display a studied aestheticism combined with narcissicism, snobbery, and a self-centered isolation that exemplifies the extent to which Jugendstil could degenerate. Siegmund, despite his riches, leads an empty life so dominated by the display of wealth that there is hardly room left for life itself. Even the twins' love—they are inseparable and love each other for the sake of their "exquisite uselessness"—depends wholly on the material fortune that supports this idleness. Protected and isolated from the trivial world by their wealth, they can surround themselves with the most beautiful objects, while indulging in an unhealthy sensuality. Despite their aestheticism, their life represents a soulless existence.

Introducing students to these works by Mann is a challenge in itself. But having the opportunity to acquaint them with the study of an important art movement increases the challenge and heightens the learning experience for teacher and student alike. The indisputable Jugendstil elements in Mann's writing enable the instructor to take an interdisciplinary approach to teaching Mann's early short fiction. Not only do the works show Jugendstil features but the thematic importance of these elements permits us to think of them in terms of a literary Jugendstil.[1]

NOTE

[1]For further reading, see Bauer; J. M. Fischer, *Fin de siècle*; Hajek; Hermand, *Literaturwissenschaft* and *Lyrik*; Madsen; Requadt; and Wich, "Erzählungen."

Death in Venice and the Tradition
of European Decadence

Naomi Ritter

Teaching *Death in Venice* in a world literature or great-books course means fitting it into the context of European culture on the eve of the First World War. Hence, the teacher must illumine at least some of the portentous significance of Michael Hamburger's annus mirabilis, 1912 (263). Not pandering to students' craving for "isms," I do not talk about expressionism or futurism; only classicism seems indispensable in addressing both the style and the philosophical locus of Mann's story. Naturally, a discussion of his neoclassicism here—Homeric epithets, imitated dactylic meters—invites a consideration of their opposite: the problematic concept of decadence.

After reading Richard Gilman's *Decadence*, an imposing attempt to define the word out of existence, one doubts that this word best captures the tenor of that time. Moreover, one hesitates to clutter students' sparse vocabulary with such a questionable term. However, critics have dwelled so intensely on *their* idea of decadence that we seem to be stuck with the word. Perhaps William Rubin gives the only possible solution to the problem of the similarly controversial word *primitive*: he simply insists on the quotation marks in the title of his massive catalogue for a recent Museum of Modern Art show, *"Primitivism" in Twentieth Century Art*.

Assuming, then, that we must deal with *decadence*, I briefly outline what the word has come to mean and which errors these usages, often mere clichés, encourage. One example, especially familiar to our students, is that we cannot equate the "decadence" of figures in popular culture—the immorality of *Dynasty's* Alexis Colby, the excesses of Leona Helmsley—with the traits that Aschenbach develops. True, the taint of moral corruption attaches to all three characters. But the former two have no history of exemplary behavior from which to decline, for they appear as mere caricatures of the affluent society.

As for valid past and current meanings of *decadence*, I save lecture and discussion time by distributing a rough outline as a class handout.

1. *Inherited meaning.* Edward Gibbon the main source, definition espoused by most dictionaries: a falling off from classic norms, usually associated with moral corruption. Indignant overtones accrue particularly since the infamous harangue by Max Nordau, *Entartung (Degeneration)* (1895).

2. *Historical meanings.* Outgrowth of Romanticism, signals transition from nineteenth to twentieth century, often considered part of fin de siècle culture. Contains idea of the end—of a period, a movement, an ideal. The "last man" overlaps with Mann's "marked man" (Aschenbach's heightened sensitivity to climate, plague). Eschatology merges with fatalism. Main cause: postrevolutionary disillusion.

3. *Psychological meanings.* Radical imbalance of opposing drives. One extreme leads inevitably to its opposite: from asceticism to debauchery, denial to excess, anorexia to bulimia. For Aschenbach specifically: from public hero to private degenerate. His ideal that denies life brings death. Schopenhauer: decadence as collapse of overstrained (Prussian) will. Tendency to depict extreme states, violence. Example: Delacroix's *Death of Sardanapalus*.

4. *Aestheticism.* Cult of art, in compensation for progressive failure of sociopolitical ideals in nineteenth century, result of *épater les bourgeois*. Dandy as product of artist's isolation, sense of superiority.

5. *Against nature.* Especially since Baudelaire, the revulsion against both physical and human nature, preference for the artificial. Baudelaire, *Mon coeur mis à nu*: "Woman is *natural*, that is, abominable" (1: 677; my translation). Fear of overwhelming physical nature goes back to Romantics (Tieck, Shelley) and eighteenth century: Rousseau, crossing Alps with carriage shades drawn. Major "decadent" text is Huysmans's (*A rebours*). "Decadence" often, but not always, includes what convention considers antinatural: homosexuality.

6. *Death wish.* Forbidden love as seduction of death: *Liebestod* (love-death). Willed self-destruction; in Nietzsche's terms, Dionysian abandon overcomes Apollonian rationality. Soft core: love of ruins, decay; also starts in Romanticism.

7. *Narcissism.* Nineteenth-century literature focuses on conflict between individual and society; that of twentieth century goes inward to explore the self—often the author's own psyche. In general, the self becomes increasingly problematic in modern culture, artist especially so as art and society become more and more estranged. Reflexivity of all art in twentieth century an outgrowth of Romantic Promethean ideal, the Great Individual. Best example of narcissist "decadent" text: Wilde, *Picture of Dorian Gray*.

Naturally one could pursue further the intricacies of definition, comparing the strongly evaluative overtones of *decadence* with the objective sense usually contained in "classical" or "Romantic." In this discussion, one might start with Gibbon and his dubious legacy; as Gilman notes, we know from Livy and Juvenal that Rome was already corrupt when the barbarians arrived. Perhaps we can best summarize the failings of this inherited concept of decadence by questioning the hallowed analogy between the observed process of decay in the human body and the morphology of human societies.

In both undergraduate and graduate classes, one must discuss the antidecadent position already implied in the dialectic of decadence. A good historical example to introduce is Goethe's dictum that classical art is healthy, while Romantic art is sick (*Maximen* 487; my translation). Mann himself referred to the psychological need to *overcome* the sense of decline among his contemporaries—in particular Maurice Barrès, whom he cites in chapter 6 of *Reflections of a Nonpolitical Man* (1918). Indeed, Mann's own famous dualisms, ruthlessly overworked in the criticism, may testify to the same kind of dialectic contained in the writers' dual manifestation of decadence and their urge to counter it.

Also, because students may understand a phenomenon by studying its opposite, it helps to discuss the Faustian notion of striving for progress as the counterpole to decadence. Especially if the class has had some contact with Faust and his Promethean lineage, one can use the text directly. The crucial early image of Aschenbach specifically as a clenched fist ("eine geballte *Faust*"), combined with its counterimage of collapse at the end of chapter 3, lets us see the work as depicting a tragically failed heroic struggle against moral relativity (201). Here one can refer to item 3 above, Schopenhauerian collapse of the overstrained will.

Thus armed with both a scholarly caution toward decadence and an awareness of its corollary, the class can confront this text as a climactic example of the decadent tradition. I divide the story's participation in this literature into three thematic categories: the cult of art, forbidden love and death, and Venice. Indeed, I first simplistically define the story as Aschenbach's journey from his sheltered aesthetic realm through the perils of illicit love to death. (Items 4, 5, and 6 above may help to start discussion, plus a blackboard diagram: art→homosexuality→death.) To tackle these categories, we start at the logical point for most literary works, the title. Barely noted by many students, this particular title gives important clues for the quest into the work itself. It is never too soon to show students that the dense economy of the title characterizes not only the genius of Mann but also much that we admire in all art. Better than almost any other modernist work, this story demonstrates that there are no accidents in great writing.

Mann's title, giving equal weight to its two major concepts, also inextricably links them. Hence these two words already imply the inevitability of the imitated Greek mythic material that punctuates the story. Furthermore, like a genetic chord containing all the harmony developed in a musical piece, the title encapsulates the fated relation between the particular demise of Aschenbach and the larger significance of the plague that attacks Venice. This man, the symbol of heroic European achievement menaced from within, could die only in this specific place, for it too symbolizes magnificent yet decaying European culture in all the shimmering ambiguity that pervades the work. Noting these facets of the binary title right away, we launch the discussion of the themes it implies.

The problems of aestheticism, the cult of art, emerge summarily in chapter 2, the intellectual biography of Aschenbach, and in the Platonic "dialogues" (actually monologues) that induce the final cadence of the story

(200–06, 235, 261). I may slight Plato in revising Lord Acton's observation "Power corrupts, absolute power corrupts absolutely" into "Beauty corrupts, art corrupts absolutely." But this formula quickly captures that pessimistic view of the artist that Mann conveys with the Socrates-Phaedrus image. When we compare Aschenbach's aesthetics with that of "decadent" literary peers, Schopenhauer looms the largest: from him comes Mann's equating of life with health and art with death. August von Platen also exemplifies Mann's classicizing attitude, which students may appreciate in a handout of the exemplary Venetian sonnet of 1824, "Tristan": "Wer die Schönheit angeschaut mit Augen / Ist dem Tode schon anheimgegeben. . . ." 'He who has beheld beauty / Already belongs to death . . .' (my translation).

Wilde's *Picture of Dorian Gray* offers a more massive exploration of the dangers of aestheticism. The effete dandy, obsessed by his own image, relates only to Aschenbach's last bathetic days, but his stretto of Dionysian self-abandon parallels that of the increasingly criminal Dorian Gray. And students may contrast the two works as Faustian and anti-Faustian warning tales. Ultimately Mann's neo-Platonic pessimism toward the passion that art must contain differs basically from Wilde's denial of any emotion in art. Yet striking similarities in these texts show parallels in their contemporary yet diverse cultures. For instance, both stories depend on a particular city as a fateful locus: students may want to write papers comparing the novels of the "decadent" cities Venice, London, Paris (Zola's *Nana*), Saint Petersburg (Bely's *Petersburg*).

Other points of contact are the narcissistic male double; the dominating role of autobiography; the crucial problem of aging, not only for the homosexual but also in the aging century itself. Indeed, one might explore a suggestive link between the narcissism of homosexual love and the hypnotic self-love of European regimes in the age of empire. (See item 7 above and Freud's classic essay of 1914 linking narcissism and homosexuality, "On Narcissism.") With such a political interpretation, suggested already in the first sentence of *Death in Venice* and critically sanctioned by Heinrich Mann, we find in the inevitable demise of the failed Faustian artist the impending fall of the overblown state (see Vaget, *Kommentar* 185, 187, 194). Mann implies the end for Bismarck's Germany; Wilde portends the collapse of the no less exhausted Victorian empire.

Thus we arrive at my second focal area, forbidden love and death, which may mean most to students who first assess the significance of homosexuality. Here current culture helps, for few people now lack strong opinions on this topic. Without polemics for or against, the teacher can use this text to discuss the divergent values illumined by homoerotic attitudes. First students need to understand the positive side of the classical ideal, which Mann incorporates in the spiritualized ideal espoused in Aschenbach's monologues. Second, students should see, on the subliminal level of

Aschenbach's subconscious, his stifled homosexuality as a metaphoric, repressed protest against those very "heroic" middle-class values he has always exemplified. Both art and homoerotic culture implicitly attack the philistine; hence the congruence of the homosexual artist.

Students of German literature in particular may grasp the timeliness of Aschenbach's homosexuality in noting a maxim of Goethe relevant in this context: "The greatest people are always linked to their century by a weakness" (*Maximen* 378; my translation). Students should realize that this "weakness"—in the eyes of the traditional bourgeois—marked many great artists in the Modernist era. Rimbaud, Verlaine, Gide, Wilde, Cocteau, Diaghilev, Auden, Osbert Sitwell, Mann's own son Klaus appear among only the most famous names. And Mann's recently published diaries tell us that he, too, despite an "ideal" marriage and six children, suffered from long-repressed homoerotic urges. This subject brings up the autobiographical overtones of the text, as well as the antidecadent attitude of *overcoming* the sense of decline by writing one's way out of it.

Here the class may benefit by comparing the attitudes of Mann, Gide, and Wilde. Among these three, Gide explores most deeply the manifold conflicts raised by homosexuality. In *The Immoralist*, his protagonist Michel says, "I no longer know, now, the dark god I serve" (163). Aschenbach does not even contemplate the savage god until it is too late; perhaps Michel's brave wrestling with his conflicted sexuality allows him to survive the book. As for *The Picture of Dorian Gray*, the major role it played in Wilde's trial shows a tragic outcome for the conflict of art and morality.

More generally, of course, one must treat the tradition of the *Liebestod* that dates from Novalis. I have students analyze in class a handout of the sixth *Hymn to the Night*; for those familiar with English literature, Keats's "La Belle Dame sans Merci" makes an apposite comparison. (This link may also show the common roots of German and English Romanticism.) One might also note the femme fatale figure and explore the cultural significance of men creating images of woman as death. Surrender to her wiles amounts to invoking the seductive death wish of item 6 above. Baudelaire, Platen, Rimbaud, and Huysmans all treat the deathly erotic urge as an expression of the suicidal disillusion of the *mal du siècle*. A handout of Rimbaud's "Le bateau ivre" may illustrate the poet's fascination with the self-willed death.

My third rubric, Venice, symbolizes both a major historical and an aesthetic locus of the decadent tradition and the fated site of Aschenbach's demise. As for Venice itself, slides of the city as painted or photographed may help students sense its particular magic. The Visconti film also expands their awareness, although the teacher must caution against seeing it as a faithful film version of the text. I focus not so much on Venetian history as on centuries of artists' *perception* of this "Byzantine" city, associated with both a heroic human battle against nature (Marco Polo, civilization against the sea) and such symbols of artifice as glass and lace. Aschenbach and his fate merge perfectly with this background, for he also considers himself a champion over his own sickly nature, and he finally succumbs to the urge for cosmetics.

Another crucial tie to Aschenbach lies in the tendency of non-Italian writers, from Shakespeare onward, to link Venice with moral corruption. And the idea of a plague as divine punishment for mysterious sins goes back to Oedipus. Mann's plague penetrates Venice from the east, just as the cult of Dionysus invaded Greece. Here one might explore the Western racist-imperialist attitudes that see danger in the exotic. Highlighting the complex of art, foreignness, and sex, I quote Wallace Fowlie: "The exotic connotes the erotic" (18). As for "decadent" views of Venice, Platen, Wagner, and Nietzsche are the devotees most accessible to average students; those who welcome challenge may want to sample the further riches of Otway (1652–85), Byron (1788–1824), Henry James (1843–1916), Barrès (1862–1923), D'Annunzio (1863–1938), and Hofmannsthal (1874–1929).

Finally, we must leave students with some idea of the meaning of this text. Considering Mann's own pervasive ambivalence toward his text, class discussion should embrace various shades of negative and positive interpretation. Accordingly, I close with a caveat about finding a clear judgment on Aschenbach from the ironic German. The antididactic attitude that I try to instill toward all art emerges eloquently from Gide's preface to the second edition of *The Immoralist*. Again, a brief handout suffices:

> I wanted to write this book neither as an indictment nor as an apology, and I have taken care not to pass judgment. Today's public no longer forgives an author for failing, after the action he describes, to give his verdict; indeed in the very course of the drama he is told to take sides, to declare himself for Alceste or Philinte, for Hamlet or Ophelia, . . . for Adam or Jehovah. I do not claim that . . . neutrality is a sign of a great mind; but I do believe that many great minds have been greatly disinclined to . . . conclude—and that to state a problem properly is not to suppose it solved in advance. . . . Be that as it may, I have tried to prove nothing, but to paint my picture well and light it properly.   (xiii, xv)

If students know *Madame Bovary*, one may well compare Flaubert's trial as an example of worldly obtuseness on this point. And one may invoke Lawrence, Ginsberg, Rushdie, or other recent victims of the philistine notion of art as mimetic morality. If the discussion veers into the problem of realism itself, I quote a classic antirealist definition of art from Stendhal: "The work of art is a mirror being walked down a road" (60). It seems

appropriate to end our discussion of Mann with such far-reaching aesthet
ics, for students may thereby see how much he implies in this summary
text.[1]

NOTE

[1]For further reading, please see Dowling; Foster; Gibbon; Gilman; Girard; Kop-
pen, *Dekadenter Wagnerismus*; Pierrot; T. J. Reed, *Mann, Der Tod in Venedig:
Text* and *Mann: The Uses of Tradition*; Spackman; Spengler; Stern; and Vaget,
Mann: Kommentar.

Mann and the Modernist Tradition

Gerald Gillespie

I address this essay to those instructors who teach Mann in English translation as a world author but whose primary interests lie in his emergence
and original appeal as a modernist writer. Bridging the period between his
great early novels *The Buddenbrooks* and *The Magic Mountain*, *Tonio
Kröger* and *Death in Venice* are eminently suited for exploring German
and European cultural issues from the fin de siècle to the eve of World
War I: the modern artist problem, the struggle against decadence, the influence of Wagner (Koppen, "Vom Décadent"; Scher, "Kreativität") and
Nietzsche (Pütz, *Kunst*; Foster), and the sense of needing a new humanism. The stories exhibit the potential of that later Mann who, as essayist
and novelist, increasingly acted as a cultural and political commentator.
Mann's long residence in the United States as an anti-Nazi exile reinforced
the positive reception of his fiction that was already underway in the 1920s
in the English-speaking world (Gillespie, "Thomas Mann in komparatistischer Sicht"), and after World War II he entered the larger canon of
twentieth-century literature taught at American universities.

Mann fits well in a great many courses because he is one of the founda-
tional modernists, an artist concerned about the experience of modernity.
As the historical distance to World War II widens, his particular role as a
channel for German cultural awareness is less evident to untutored students. They are far more likely to have read Nietzsche than Goethe in
some other course: a Nietzsche who is presented as a philosopher relevant
for the twentieth century at large. Many come to Mann because they have
encountered his name in connection with novelists of the early twentieth
century such as Joyce, Gide, and Hesse. Thus *Tonio Kröger* and *Death in
Venice* can be integrated in modernist courses that, while not aimed primarily at German majors, often serve to attract future majors. For example, I have found that undergraduates like a combination of stories and
novels by Hesse, Kafka, and Mann from 1900 to 1930. I introduce each
artist by sketching his biography and ideas. As Beverley Driver Eddy rec-
ommends in her essay in this volume, I use pictures from each writer's life
and world and some pertinent quotations from letters or diaries as bridges
to the works. Students readily point out certain connections—they recognize that each of the three authors thematizes in his fictions a particular
sense of being culturally marked as different. Advanced undergraduates
and graduate students find it exciting to study Mann in any specialized
sequence that treats key themes and new waves of artistic experimentalism
in European culture from the late nineteenth century to modernism. One
of my own favorite combinations, bearing the title Literature of Decadence, starts in the 1880s with J.-K. Huysmans, Nietzsche, and others and
culminates with *Death in Venice*. This course explores coeval and correlative developments in the arts, technology, and the human sciences. The

potential list of viable syllabi is so extensive that these two instances must suffice to suggest the full range.

Coping with the European dimensions of *Tonio Kröger* and *Death in Venice* involves more than encouraging students to garner the works' thematic wealth and, when needed, supplying certain connections, such as key allusions—all certainly indispensable classroom activities. Instructors should go beyond identifying content and discuss formal configurations of content (see Gillespie, "Educational Experiment" 362–63). The shift in the traditional short novel form that occurs in *Tonio Kröger* and *Death in Venice* resembles narrative experiment in other nations. For example, Mitchell Morse notes analogies between exposition of the artist crisis, symbolic suggestion, and epiphanies in *Tonio Kröger* and in Joyce's *Dubliners* collection and *Portrait*; E. L. Marson points out that Joyce's *Ulysses* provides apter comparisons for the kinds of mythological fragmentation and condensation already practiced in *Death in Venice*.

Many students, of course, advance with surer footing from an inventory of contents to a consideration of structure. But the opposite strategy can be successful pedagogically since formal experiment is central to modernist aesthetics. Students who read Joyce, Eliot, and Woolf do not find it difficult to grasp that the mode of narration or of referentiality itself implicitly constitutes a master statement. Vaget discerns two fundamental Mannian story types: type A bundles motifs and focuses them through a principal incident or event, such as a musical evening; type B concerns itself with a chief protagonist's life line and concentrates on a final stage of definition. Looser type B, to which he assigns both *Tonio Kröger* and *Death in Venice* (*Kommentar* 45), can incorporate schemata of type A as subdivisions. Criticism has been too timid about accounting for Mann's belief that his stories of the early twentieth century were "lyrical," when they are often essayistic and shot through with irony. If, however, students are given excerpts from Huysmans's call, in *A rebours* (see *Against Nature* 195–99), for a concentrated symbolist fiction that is like a montage of prose poems, they will readily see how Mann's innovation fits logically as one realization of a fundamentally antirealist tendency in European modernism.

Tonio Kröger

Elizabeth Mary Wilkinson's introduction in English to *Tonio Kröger* (originally to her 1944 text edition of the work) is still one of the finest contextualizing analyses available ("Interpretation"). A progression from "genetic" and "final" to "formal" aspects of *Tonio Kröger* might flow somewhat as follows. Teachers would initially remind the class of biographical elements that Mann lifts, as if in a hidden self-portrayal, from his own parental home in Lübeck and his experience of moving to the artistic capital Munich after his father's death. That approach straightaway enables discussion

of how Mann establishes a sense of dissonance through the two tempera-
ments associated with the northern father and southern mother, appearing
in the protagonist's name and personal traits and other motifs. It is worth-
while for the teacher to mention in outline how Mann puts these same
motifs through symphonic variation in *The Buddenbrooks*, in which a
sense of "epical irony" conducts the "music" distributed across a whole
family and society. The author penetrates and critiques any apparent fixed
reality in the novel through the perspectival shifting of narrative voice (Petersen), and this feature is even more pronounced two years later in *Tonio
Kröger*. Students mindful of Joyce's combination of irony and musicality
quickly recognize that in *Tonio Kröger* (as again in *Death in Venice*) Mann's
art too depends on epiphanic resolutions, not on an older realist code
(Gillespie, "Epiphany").

In sociological terms, as the cumulative evidence of the story shows, Tonio's problem is that of a conscious outsider exiled from bourgeois nor-
malcy. In metaphysical terms, his dislocation as an artist, isolation, and
estrangement in the midst of life indicate a profound disturbance of existence. Tonio's boyhood walk with and parting from Hans Hansen in chapter 1 can be analyzed to reveal how Mann in effect composes an overture
stating the ground theme simultaneously on several levels. Although Tonio's calling is to be a communicator, the type he embodies is challenged
by early recognition that there is no adequate language; thus, in the double optic of the story, the artist as lead figure serves as a medium for
plumbing the tragedy of modern humanity. Herbert Lehnert ("Tonio
Kröger and Georg Bendemann") compares the epochal experience of alienation in *Tonio Kröger* and Kafka's *Metamorphosis*; more immediately communicable is comparison with the anguish and drives of the artist-elect
Stephen in Joyce's *Portrait* and later *Ulysses*.

One of the best ways for teachers to demonstrate Mann's break with
nineteenth-century realism in *Tonio Kröger* is to follow the exposition of
this ground theme section by section and observe the cumulative subversion of the usual rules of positivistic certainty that might have governed.
Chapter 1 opens in medias res as a narrating voice, deceptively similar to
the authoritative, omniscient historian from nineteenth-century fiction,
eavesdrops on Tonio's attempt to cultivate the friendship of the pure Nordic type, Hans Hansen. His efforts are thwarted by the intrusion of the
suburban banker's son, Erwin Jimmerthal. By his solid, old-fashioned (medieval) first name, Erwin, this representative of ruling bourgeois institutions suggests some deeper cultural heritage and clearly functions, by the
power of his family name, as an agent-herald of Tonio's deflection onto the
path of tribulation and spiritual values. (The fusing of the noun *Jammer*
'lamentation, grief, wretchedness' and the adverb *immer* 'always, forever'
in *Jimmerthal* suggests "vale of woe" and "vale of eternity.") In chapter 2,
the Inge episode, Tonio loses his sexual identity and will in the dance, and

tastes bitter existential defeat and disgrace. Suddenly chapter 3 shifts to a report by an objective narrator looking from outside at Tonio, over the course of his career, as a figure in a strict epic. Under compression, the "life" appears as a typical pattern, not a unique Romantic destiny. Chapter 4 is a virtual monologue through which the mature Tonio emerges strongly as a dramatic character. In the next chapter, Lisaweta's balancing stability helps Tonio reach his crucial decision to revisit his northern Hamletic homeland. The interrogation by the police at his former hometown, in chapter 6, underscores the question about Tonio's deeper identity. Definition by negation attains a climactic peak in chapter 7 as Tonio encounters a healthy, naive, simple world of communication in its "alien" purity in Denmark. The depictions of Tonio absorbed in the night storm on board ship and solitary on the beach, turned toward the endless sea, are the extreme point of nirvana. The climax of chapter 8, the longest section of the story, arrives as Tonio witnesses the reenactment of childhood longing and trauma at a dance in Denmark. The two pages making up chapter 9, Tonio's letter to Lisaweta, are in effect a compact essay interpreting his own life. To the extent his confession exhibits sympathetic transcendence, Tonio approximates the Schopenhauerian ideal for the artist—as much at least as Conrad's narrator-persona Marlow does in *Heart of Darkness* (1902).

In terms of narrative art, the first-person voice dominating the summary in chapter 9 fuses the subjective and objective realms of the story. The ending is undoubtedly the most positive outcome for an artist figure in Mann's early work, because in choosing to love ordinary life and beauty, Tonio grasps for communicable substance and thereby brings the "contrasting [Apollonian and Dionysian] elements into a union within himself" (Lesér 120). Despite differences of placement and scale, one can point out a broad analogy between Proust's changes of temporal, psychological, and narrational point of view in *Swann's Way* and the rapid internal genre shifts in *Tonio Kröger*. Proust's work starts with an overture in which a narrating voice brings forth substance out of tormented dreaming; this leads to the initially first-person story of a young boy's election to artisthood ("Combray" section); but that story is suddenly displaced by a jewel-like demonstration of the capacity of art to view the human dilemma, the third-person section "Swann in Love"; and eventually the first-person tale recommences ("Place-Names: The Name"). Students familiar with Proust's middle-aged, burned-out narrator Marcel, who experiences reconnection with the vital truths of his lost past as a redemptive breakthrough, recognize his spiritual affinity with Tonio. Tonio's artistic reconciliation with ordinary life and Stephen's ultimately sympathetic attunement to Bloom in *Ulysses* evidence the even closer thematic resemblance between Mann and Joyce (see Sultan).

Instructors will find that some of the most profitable class discussions spring from an effort to remind—or inform—students of key themes of symbolist and modernist aestheticism that appear in *Tonio Kröger* as they do in Joyce's *Ulysses*, most notably the Hamlet problem (Gillespie, "Afterthoughts"). As with *Ulysses*, it is the narrative structure that determines how we experience the context of Tonio's life. No solution arrives from the external world of history, nor does psychological growth occur according to external norms; instead, an illumination manifests itself from within. Were Mann's form of irony not such an uncharacteristic departure in tone (Neumeister 97), we might otherwise associate the manner of Tonio's arrival at his final confession with Jugendstil in general. That is, the way *Tonio Kröger* pursues the thematics of ambivalent modern sickness, distance from life, and spiritual longing, and the way it uses synaesthesia, interweaving, and transformation of forms and aesthetic-ethical mirrorings, would fit the gentle mode of Jugendstil as a then-contemporary answer to fears of decadence. The use of leitmotifs, tonal color, quotation, and other devices (Basilius) is only one level of the "musical" composition. Beneath the Jugendstil surface, Mann practices an abstract art that proceeds from a premise and employs hermetic figuration. By not relying on any fixed reality, and by superimposing relativistic analytical slices in several generic modes, Mann indeed seems in some measure close to the spirit of modern painting, notably to cubism and expressionism. Just as a set world does not exist but is produced by assemblage beyond impressionism, so in *Tonio Kröger* the artwork is a fluctuating process of creation from within.

I find that students are motivated to step back and try to see as a total construct the work that has just gripped them. At this stage in class discussions, a simplified model of the whole tends to enhance their enjoyment. The ground movement in chapters 1 (Hans), 2 (Inge), and 3 (Italy) can be described as a progressive narrative distancing in the pseudoepical mode, whereby concomitantly a threatening loss of the "inner" truth is revealed. The core section, chapters 6 and 7 (monologic conversation and medial coda), announcing a turning back to origins and depths, virtually restores the individual voice in a narrative close-up. Tonio's return home (6), his symbolic counterjourneying (7), and Danish epiphany (8) prepare the coda (9) in which the story mirrors itself and returns into its own beginning. The final sentence written by Tonio, "In it there is longing, and sad envy, and just a touch of contempt, and a whole world of innocent delight" (192), repeats as self-confession what first appears as an objective statement by the omniscient narrator closing chapter 1: "His heart was alive in those days; in it there was longing, and sad envy, and just a touch of contempt, and a whole world of innocent delight" (143). Outlining the structure in such broad terms is an effective way to underscore the surprising fact hidden beneath the seemingly traditional setting with which the short novel initially entices the reader. *Tonio Kröger* converts the "realism" into a subject matter subordinated to a successor worldview that, after Nietzsche, Bergson, and others, regards history as a psychological dynamic. The Mannian dialectic interplay of terms results in epiphanic moments of completion, but these occur within the inherent circularity of the work of art, a circularity allied to that governing the novels of Joyce and Proust.

Death in Venice

Edward Timms's essay in this volume furnishes crucial geopolitical references of the crisis felt by Mann as World War I approached. Here I shall pass over the historical context and sources of motivic material—which other essays in this book discuss in some detail—and concentrate on the problematics of "form" as a central modernist concern in *Death in Venice*. Mann clearly links the question of form with the threat of a breakdown of Europe in this "psychohistory." The short novel is relentless in producing a dubious perfection, an ambivalent self-contained beauty out of the relationships of its own materials; no detail whatsoever is independent of the work's relational construct. From the opening intimation of a crisis threatening Europe, the historian Aschenbach, who has sung Frederick the Great's triumph in creating a world through sheer will and discipline, represents, in his fateful attraction to the Byzantine mortuary in chapter 1, not an individual, as in older sentimental literature, but the mystery of the attraction itself.

The centrality of death is overwhelming; it is the disturbing discovery and creative conundrum (P. Heller, *"Der Tod"*). However, rather than cite only Freud's pronouncements, the literary generalist can explain Mann's daring probe into the closeness of the death urge and the life urge in the contemporaneous terms of Mann's day by reference to their juxtaposition in symbolist literature and in Joyce's *Ulysses* (Carpenter). When through Aschenbach, in chapter 3, we enter into "a dreamlike alienation" (209) on crossing to Venice, his recollection of the nineteenth-century poet's "measured music"—August von Platen's Venetian sonnets and other lyrics (Nicklas 37–39)—also prompts our deeper questioning of "his grave and weary heart" and the entire "adventure of the emotions" that is unfolding (210). The paradox is that Mann's tale both releases the dangerous music and contains it. *Death in Venice* witnesses the impossibility of dignity for the order-shaping artist, who ineluctably is ravished by passion, and transforms this tragedy itself into an artistic order.

Asking the students to recall the shifts in narrative point of view in *Tonio Kröger* usually jogs them into more immediate awareness of the extent of the modulations through which Mann conducts us in *Death in Venice*. I encourage the class to pinpoint the actual moves by the narrative voice, as it recedes, becomes intrusive, changes the focus, or adds ironic color. Having students try to identify subgenres or styles (e.g., quasi-official biography, interior monologue, hymnic evocation) that are associated with these narrative shifts is a first step. A second step is to have the students discriminate passages or levels within passages that are primarily visual or declarative and others that are primarily musical and suggestive. A third step is to show how the stylistic flux functions the way passages do in a symphonic composition. A fourth step is to note that the recurrence of Mannian leitmotifs from work to work bears analogy to Wagnerian musical "ideas" that are reexplored in newer compositions (e.g., the "mixed" parentage of Hanno in *The Buddenbrooks*, of Tonio Kröger, and of Aschenbach as variations).

A good illustration of the role of irony as a kind of counterpointing or disturbance that affects the musical-rhythmic properties would be the long sentence opening chapter 2. By its own disproportions, it undermines the neoclassical achievements it seems at first to put on parade (P. Heller, *"Der Tod"* 69–70). Alerting the class to a few such "microcosmic" details stimulates individual closer reading for further clues that often reflect the "macrocosmic" issues or processes of the story. By its knotted enumeration of achievements, the compound-complex sentence suggests a fall from grace into anguish and implicitly announces a major theme: Aschenbach's career exemplifies the pathway toward Nietzsche's "theoretical man," the post-Socratic extreme dessication of vitality that provokes a dangerous resurgence of animality, regression to barbarism (Foster 97–98, 157–58). Form so ennobled that it has become fragile and cannot bear itself craves for barbaric energy. Yet, although the short novel uses the Nietzschean idea of an Apollonian-Dionysian bipolarity in probing the ambivalence of European cultural achievement, it does not simply side with Nietzsche.

Instructors are likely to encounter an understandable human trait in many beginning and even some advanced students, sometimes induced by their experiences in social science or humanities courses that simplify complex works into partisan tracts. Many will want to identify what Mann is "for" or "against" in black and white terms. In the present cultural climate (replete with anti-European preachments), some of my students invariably construe that for Mann the Apollonian principle is "bad" and the Dionysian "good." To curb such reductionist urges, I inform the class of complicating factors we know from the author's own spiritual biography. Two are of special importance: Mann's rediscovery of Schopenhauer in 1899, which has carried over beyond *The Buddenbrooks* and *Tonio Kröger*, and his growing fascination with Goethe as a cultural model during the first decade of the twentieth century. It is best to come prepared with capsule statements about Schopenhauer and Goethe and the larger significance of each. The key lesson, which most students appreciate, is that such hidden "subtexts" provide Mann with considerable distance from the two most influential followers of Schopenhauer: from Wagner (teacher of the revolutionary musical principle of composition) and from Nietzsche (teacher of the bipolar paradigm and of a new cultural anthropology fusing myth and psychology). Such distance is in no way gainsaid by the equally important fact that Wagner and Nietzsche are tacitly present as twinned phenomena characteristic of Aschenbach's moment and situation. Once again, capsule statements about the influence of Wagner and Nietzsche are in order to fill in those significant points that one fails to elicit from the students.

In *Death in Venice* a perfected form, a fanatically shaped existence, what Aschenbach has striven to assert to the extreme point, is broken and dissolved. The loss of will and the cultural collapse consequent on imbalance and overdevelopment surface in Aschenbach's inability to stay at home writing in safety. Venice—the (decaying medieval and Renaissance) bridge between east and west, the sole European city in which human habitation is built on the water, the place celebrated by so many Romantic poets, and the site of Wagner's death—exemplifies the bottomless form made out of a void, a kind of magic or enchantment. Metaphorically, Venice both represents the Western achievement and reveals its darker underside, deeper roots, and foreign face. The eruption of the memory of the Dionysian orgy in chapter 5 is, effectively, a dream of the crumbling of the walls of civilization.

Mann's montage technique can be illustrated to advantage by discussing the significance of *unnamed* Mount Cithaeron—a reference that is "recollected" on many levels. Aschenbach thinks of his own summer retreat in the mountains while the frenzied horde with their music arrive in his dream (256). Thus a recessed biographical fact (Mann's summer house in Upper Bavaria) and a widely known historical fact (Nietzsche's habitual retreat to his house in Graubünden) become interpenetrated by the mystery of the sacred mountain where, as recounted in Euripides's *Bacchae*, Pentheus's kinsfolk hideously sacrifice him to his cousin Dionysus, who has returned from the east. If no student volunteers the pertinent mythological information, I find that reading some lines of the horrific ending of Euripides's play jolts the class wide awake. It is a reliable rule that whenever the instructor elaborates on some of Mann's cultural references, the artist's twin fascination with past cultural achievements and concern over potentially dangerous forces gain depth for the students. Before this orgiastic climax in *Death in Venice*, the buildup of overlaid allusions already includes, implicitly, Goethe's entire work *Elective Affinities* as a stylistic model of tragic narration and the "classic" Goethe as against the now suspect late Romantic Wagner (Vaget, " 'Goethe oder Wagner' " 54–55). Traces of Goethean vocabulary that lend a touch of preciosity to the protagonist are interspersed amid the more evident pieces of Greek discourses and stories that Aschenbach thinks of as early as chapter 3 on encountering Tadzio (217–24). For example, the term *shape* (217) echoes Goethe's favorite term *Gestalt* for the natural perfection of privileged creatures in his works. Luke is doubtlessly correct that the final paragraph of

Death in Venice ironically recapitulates the chilling naturalistic coda to Goethe's novel *The Sorrows of Young Werther* (xliv). It is usually necessary to inform students, because, save for the infrequent German major, they seldom recognize this particular allusiveness.

But the classical Greek references provide a surer anchor for illustrating Mannian irony. While in his waking thoughts Aschenbach combines classical sources in his mind to create a noble role as a modern Socrates smitten by beauty (235), he is unaware that he himself is an endangered Pentheus, an avatar of the doubleness manifested in the Wagner-Nietzsche complex of his own times. The devastating Dionysian dream realizes the warning "seizure" and "vision" of chapter 1 when Aschenbach, as a latter-day Pentheus, fails to acknowledge the heraldic "crouching tiger" in the "tropical swampland" that prefigures Venice (197). Dionysus remains recessed as in Aschenbach's fleeting thought of the myth of Semele (235), and, like his sacred mountain, the god is never directly named. However, the reader is privileged to participate in the unifying authorial irony that establishes the montage of deeper identities. Mann's art here bears analogy to the filmic techniques—the rhythmic cross-cutting of images from differing space and time and the fusing of composite images to evoke a general theme—that appear in D. W. Griffith's *Intolerance* (1913) and that are perfected in Sergei Eisenstein's *Potemkin* (1925) (see Gillespie, "Cinematic Narration").

In drawing on his own experience of emotional attachment to a male friend, as well as on Goethe's heterosexual Marienbad experience (Vaget, " 'Goethe oder Wagner' "), Mann is not attacking homosexuality but fathoming secret implications of a kind of fanaticism at the root of art that is related to the absolute law of passion. The grim joke of the love story is that no communication with the beloved occurs or can be realized in *Death in Venice*. As in mathematics, the conditions of the passion are never situated anywhere except in the artist's surrendering mind. Homoerotic love is pure form, an abstraction from any possible materiality, here a degeneration into the theoretical, remote from productive natural love, lacking vitality. If some students are acquainted with *The Magic Mountain*, the instructor can point out that Mann renews his exploration of linkages among homoeroticism, artistic hermeticism, and death in that great novel (Renner, *Das Ich* 92–109). Once captive in Venice, Aschenbach ultimately gives up communication with the world; his excessively Apollonian heroics, his Frederican motto *"durchhalten!"* (201), devolves into the complicitous attitude: "I shall say nothing!" (255). In the midst of this guilty silence, reminiscences are woven in his mind, intermingled quotations and imitations of Platonic dialogue, slowly nurturing a classical form. The force of the original Greek discovery of the attractive power radiates through the dubious instrument in which it still resonates—and Mann by no means rejects the validity of the original experience. This is a complex instance of what Dorrit Cohn designates as narrative transparency. Yet, ironically, it is dialogue in name only, since no actual conversation takes place; the ghostly form occurs, not the substance of exchange with a partner. The irony is doubled because beauty nonetheless overwhelms Aschenbach.

Irony is, as it were, tripled through the cool narrative stance, in contrast to the eventual catastrophe that is reported. Students rapidly catch on to the repetition of the death heralds whom Aschenbach encounters. They have something uncanny about them, much like the balloon seller in Flaubert's *Madame Bovary*, and particular suggestive attributes can be identified (e.g., Dionysus's staff). More immediately reminiscent of the grotesque figures in the paintings of George Grosz and James Ensor (Kaufmann 47), the heralds reinforce the spectral quality of the ephemeral beauty that Aschenbach glimpses in Tadzio. The sudden switch to virtually scannable hymnics at the start of chapter 4, which render the exhilarating feel of plunging into a Mediterranean world such as the Greeks might have perceived it, compels the reader to participate even while sensing that the prose is parodic. The radicality of the intense poetic vision as if in ancient times, a vision ambiguously attributable both to Aschenbach's and to some part of the narrating mind (as well as to the whole neoclassical tradition since humanism), is accompanied by grotesque deformation of behavior on the level of plot. Aschenbach loses his shape as a disciplined burgher, sinks into the mindless laughter of the lower orders, symbolically wills formlessness in yearning to reach Tadzio. The final image of the crumbling of form on the inherently empty boundary zone of the beach is virtually that captured by a camera. The remoteness of the omniscient narrator in the final lines strangely suggests a degree of affinity with Aschenbach as an eye with nothing more to see. This kind of eye seems capable of recording without reciprocity, as if there is only an emptiness, a becoming-meaningless, after a spiritual burnout.

It is helpful to lead students very early to consider the manner in which the total structure of this "bifocal" short novel (Gronicka, "Myth plus Psychology") mimics the play of forces and counterforces that are its subject matter. Like *Tonio Kröger*, *Death in Venice* opens with an in medias res episode, a story in its own right, that contains the ground pattern of the voyage toward death, first as a restless stroll to a mortuary. Chapter 2 of *Death in Venice* withdraws more demonstrably to the perspective of history and is more distinctly a closed form, whereas chapter 3 of *Tonio Kröger* is psychologically interpretive. Chapters 1 and 2 of *Death in Venice* are self-contained units, essentially land-bound in setting and motifs, and reaching back into the protagonist's past. The next two chapters are essentially water-girt, more open, terminating climactically. By moving into the immensity of the sea, which is associated with the timelessness and formlessness of the unconscious, chapter 5 ambiguously links the threat of chaos and the promise of life (Nicklas 39–42). Yet the final, terse paragraph of chapter 5, a neutral physical description of Aschenbach's collapse

and capsule report of the world's reaction, reasserts—in counterpoint—
the authoritative historical voice of chapter 2. In that chapter Mann re-
frames the story in terms of the objective, distanced genre of biography,
but rapidly undercuts the norms; just as the first paragraph of chapter 2
ends with a physical description (200) that qualitatively shifts from the
grounds of a neutral "official" curriculum vitae listing important works and
honors, so the last paragraph ends with an interpretive pathological analysis of the protagonist (206). Here the tension between an older naturalistic-
positivistic and a newer symbolist literary code reaches a modernist
resolution through an abstract logic based on myth. Myth furnishes an alternative timeless paradigm, a mirror for the European present. As in *Tonio Kröger*, the bipolarity in Aschenbach is depicted as a conflict between
the native paternal and foreign maternal inheritance. Any reader of *The
Buddenbrooks* or *Tonio Kröger* will instantly recognize the Dionysian
strain entering in *Death in Venice* "with the writer's mother, the daughter
of a director of music from Bohemia" (200).

Venice represents the boundary of realms (Nicklas 32–42), and the story
culminates in a final passing beyond a boundary as Aschenbach dies fixed
on Tadzio as Hermes the "soul-guide" (Gillespie, "Ways"). The encounter
with Tadzio brings out two kinds of perfection that are secretly wedded
(this, too, is a major theme that recurs in *The Magic Mountain*): pure form
and absolute formlessness, the void. The final image of Tadzio, vertical and
finite, moving into the sea, horizontal and endless, demonstrates (as an
inversion of the birth of Venus) the mystery that love for form is simultaneously a secret attraction to death and oblivion. Pivotal therefore is the
connection established between the charm of Tadzio's name, with "its
long-drawn-out u-sound" (223), and the inarticulate signal made by the *va-
poretto*'s whistle, which erupts in the orgiastic dream as the music of the
Dionysiacs (256). Readers sense that it is a symptomatic warning sign when
Aschenbach succumbs to the "jangling tones" of popular entertainment on
again encountering herald figures (247–49) of *"the stranger-god"* (256)
whom finally he cannot evade in dreams. The reader views his infatuation
with the beautiful boy in an ironic light, once the narrator reveals Aschenbach's early notice of Tadzio's poor teeth and sickliness and eventual conscious "feeling of satisfaction or relief" at the thought of his death (225).
Marson explores in detail how the other repressed Greek truth, prefigured
in Euripides's *Bacchae*, breaks forth from underneath the Platonic mask
(see Gillespie, "Ways").

Typically, Mann takes us beneath the surface of Aschenbach's final neoclassical achievement (see Berlin's essay in this volume) in setting "free
from the marble mass of language that slender form . . . as a model
and mirror of intellectual beauty" (234). The reader is privileged to learn
that his subsequently much-admired "brief essay" (236) was written "with
the music of [Tadzio's] voice in his ears" (236). Hence even the hymnic

experience of the Mediterranean day (238–39), recapitulating centuries of Western imagining of Apollonian splendor (Gillespie, "Ways"), acquires a double character: it is both gloriously spellbinding and ominously hypertrophic. When the narrator observes the events in Aschenbach's mind virtually as would a Joycean demiurgic creator, Mann at the end of *Death in Venice* deliberately reopens the wound and terror experienced by the modern artist.

Psychoanalysis, Freud, and Thomas Mann

Jeffrey B. Berlin

Almost all students recognize, from the opening paragraph of *Death in Venice*, the manifest psychological issues this work presents. Thus after the initial reading of this classic, students are never at a loss for words when asked to summarize their first thoughts about the overall topic "Thomas Mann, *Death in Venice*, psychoanalysis, and Freud." Several students are always anxious to place Gustav von Aschenbach on a couch and hear about his "*motus animi continuus*" (195), "fatigue" (195), "perfectionistic fastidiousness" (199), "duty to achieve" (201), "defiant despite" (202), "elegant self-control" (203), "taste" (237), "infatuation" (244)—in short, his inner struggle. Is his response to life, they ask, a midlife crisis? Is it depression? Is more than the artistic will exerting itself? Some students relate Aschenbach's ecstasy and torment to Mann's own response to life. These are typical student answers, all of which could lead to interesting discussions. However, I actually defer commentary about their responses until a later time, indicating that certain caveats must first be considered and that there is more to be learned than a strict "case study" approach might reveal.

In fact, as I explain to the class, our primary objective is to establish through our study of his self-commentary and *Death in Venice* Mann's early attitude toward, and the ways he was influenced by, psychoanalysis, psychology, and Freud. In so doing, we also want to clarify the psychoanalytic *Zeitgeist*, with special attention to some of Freud's ideas. Furthermore, such discussion permits the opportunity to delineate the meaning and implications of psychoanalytic literary interpretations, for which *Death in Venice* of course functions as our primary source of investigation. Such an approach clarifies Mann's position on this important topic and introduces students to him as a writer and a thinker. At the same time, such commentary allows students to grasp some fundamental ideas in *Death in Venice*. It also enables the class to understand certain aspects of the psychoanalytic *Zeitgeist* and, in particular, Freud's revolutionary theories and ideas, as well as the equally intriguing field of literature and psychology.

These lectures and discussions take place over several classes and adhere to the following general thematic order: (1) the validity of self-commentary, (2) the psychoanalytic *Zeitgeist*, (3) psychoanalytic analyses of literary works, (4) Freud's influence on early Mann, (5) Mann's early attitude toward psychoanalysis, and (6) beyond psychoanalysis and psychology: Mann and neoclassicism.

One of the problems hidden behind this series of topics, however, is that most of Mann's direct statements about Freud were made after *Death in Venice* was written (July 1911–July 1912). It is therefore important for students to note carefully the dates of Mann's remarks. Additionally, there is a certain ambiguity in Mann's comments with which we must contend. To what degree this latter point is related to Mann's growing appreciation of Freud over time is also important to consider.

Attention is directed to Mann's self-commentary and pronouncements about psychoanalysis and Freud, the most significant of which I have collected and distribute on a handout. These statements, proffered in letters and elsewhere, familiarize us with and clarify Mann's thought as well as help explain important aspects of *Death in Venice*. They provide provocative and stimulating topics for discussion. Because students find Mann's pronouncements enticing and exciting, they are eager to learn more of his ideas and their implications. The instructor has a wide range of observations from which to choose (cf. *Dichter über ihre Dichtungen* 1: 393–449). More specifically, Mann's self-commentary about psychoanalysis and Freud especially makes clear, as we will later discuss, his response to the " 'indecent psychologism' of the past epoch" (12: 28), which directly leads to his contact with the neoclassical movement and its subsequent effect on *Death in Venice*.

Before we scrutinize Mann's self-commentary, we should clarify the notion of an author as self-commentator. A related issue is whether a literary work must ultimately be judged on its own merits. This subject intrigues students, especially when they consider the following statement in *Death in Venice*:

> It is as well that the world knows only a fine piece of work and not also its origins, the conditions under which it came into being; for knowledge of the sources of an artist's inspiration would often confuse readers and shock them, and the excellence of the writing would be of no avail. (236)

The dual nature of this remark is evident: it focuses on both literary theory and psychology. There are many ways to approach the topic of the author as critic, as well as the issue of the author's intention. The beginning instructor is referred to the arguments of Frank Cioffi; Monroe Beardsley and W. K. Wimsatt, Jr.; P. D. Juhl; Joseph Margolis (*Art* and *Philosophy*); and René Wellek.

While Herbert Lehnert aptly illustrates that Mann's self-commentary is not always reliable ("Mann's Interpretations"), Hans Rudolf Vaget claims (*Kommentar* 9) that often it is even "interpretationsbedürftig" ("in need of interpretation"). Furthermore, according to T. J. Reed, Mann's "statements are a subcategory of creation itself, aimed at adjusting and altering the import of past productions in the light of the new positions from which they are regarded" ("Thomas Mann, Heine" 48). In a subsequent passage Reed comments: "What he says of himself has the function not of describing a state of affairs, but of prescribing the state of mind in which the public will approach his work" (49). More than once Mann also cautions us that he is not the most competent critic of his own works (see, e.g., Mann, letters of 6 September 1915 to E. Zimmer [*Letters*, 1971 ed., 76], 10 September 1915 to Paul Amann, and the essay "The Making of *The Magic Mountain*"), but this precaution does not debunk the methodology recommended here. If used with discretion, the self-commentary is instructive and challenging.

It is also interesting to consider the individuals to whom Mann's comments are directed. What is it about these people that conditions Mann's remarks? Does Mann use certain people to spread his ideas? Does he sometimes use opportunities as a self-incitement to understand what he is doing and to help others, while in other instances he attempts to persuade and nudge them around to a correct view of his ideas? Is Mann writing as an essayist who shapes and influences his culture? How do we evaluate an author's remarks in retrospect? In sum, Mann's pronouncements permit many interesting aspects to be considered.

I focus discussion on the psychoanalytic *Zeitgeist* by citing Mann's letter of 28 February 1951 to Joyce Morgan:

> [S]ince *The Little Herr Friedemann* . . . psychoanalytic writers have been interested in my problems, and evidently I have always had an affinity with this sphere. Besides, very soon the atmosphere was rife with psychoanalytic theories, and people absorbed them without expressly studying them. I cannot swear that even before writing *Death in Venice* I had not read some psychoanalytic writings that derived from Freud and had been sent to me by their authors. . . . Schopenhauer and later Nietzsche had already prepared me for Freud's teachings—yet it was not these alone, but my literary education in general, for psychoanalysis has the closest connections to great literature generally. (*Dichter über ihre Dichtungen* 1: 446)

(Because several of the key quotations in this essay are not readily available in translation or are even unavailable in translation, I have provided the necessary ones at length, thus allowing the instructor to employ the suggestions here.)

This reflective statement to Morgan, the content of which Mann expressed on several other occasions, directs students to Mann's early association with the prevalent atmosphere of psychoanalytic thought. This requires attention to Vienna, the home of Freud and psychoanalysis. Classes demonstrate much interest in the general reception of Freud and his theories, the "years of isolation and ostracism" (*Letters*, 1971 ed., 173), as Mann refers to it in his letter of 3 January 1930 to Freud. While the instructor has numerous sources available, Peter Gay's recent *Freud: A Life for Our Time* and his edition *The Freud Reader* are particularly useful. (The beginning instructor also might turn to the basic and valuable works by Cremerius; Crick; Curtius; Janik and Toulmin; Johnston; Leupold-Löwenthal; Noble; Ruitenbeek [*Freud* and *Psychoanalysis*]; Schick; and Zweig, *Briefwechsel* [with Freud].) Especially appropriate when examining Freud's reception, however, is Norman Kiell's *Freud without Hindsight: Reviews of His Work, 1893–1939*, which provides, along with commentary, a judicious selection of 172 of the 800 such reviews that have been located. In particular, I discuss the revolutionary aspects of Freud's discoveries, with special attention given to *The Interpretation of Dreams* (1900), *Three Essays on the Theory of Sexuality* (1905), and the essay "The Relation of the Poet to Day-Dreaming" (1908). During a later lecture I focus on Freud's "Delusions and Dreams in Jensen's *Gradiva*" (1907), which represents his first lengthy published analysis of a work of literature, excluding, of course, the remarks about *Oedipus Rex* and *Hamlet* in *The Interpretation of Dreams*. The reviews and opinions of Freud's contemporaries bring an added element of immediacy to the class.

Our discussion also concentrates on some key points in Mann's 1925 "After-Dinner Speech at the Vienna Pen Club" and his 1926 "My Relationship to Vienna" (11: 400): "I don't believe," Mann said, "that a product like *Death in Venice* has had such good readers in any German-speaking country or anywhere else as it has here . . . [in Vienna]." He added: "The difference [between Munich and Vienna] is that Munich's zest for living knows nothing of death, while Vienna does. It seems to me that only the kind which is acquainted with death has full intellectual value" (11: 369–71). Not to be forgotten, however, is that in Mann's statement to Morgan, cited above, the close kinship of Schopenhauer and Nietzsche to Freud is made evident. In this regard, I summarize and elaborate on the similarities and explanations that Mann provides about them in the essays "Freud and the Future" (1936) and "Schopenhauer" (1938).

Especially "Freud and the Future," which Mann presented on 9 May 1936 as a speech in Vienna on the occasion of Freud's eightieth birthday, advances the discussion and permits the relationship between literature and psychology to be pursued further. At one point in this important essay, Mann says:

> For some time both men [myself and Freud] have been aware of the close relationship between literature and psychoanalysis. However, I feel that what is festive about this hour resides, at least in my view, in what is probably the first public encounter of the two spheres in the manifestation of this awareness and in the demonstrative acknowledgment of it.   (11: 479)

And yet, succinctly stated, the discipline of psychology and literature or, perhaps the psychoanalytic interpretations of literary works, has been plagued by much controversy. Critics who have not been professionally certified in psychoanalysis have sometimes been called amateurs treading in unfamiliar areas where they do not belong. And the professional psychoanalyst in the literary arena does not always make it clear that a valid psychoanalysis cannot be done on a fictional character. Even though various speculations and observations may be noted, the fictitious character cannot respond to stimuli or answer questions, which are important activities in analysis. These problems are not the only ones that exist in the area of psychology and literature (for other aspects, see Brooks; Holland; Schwartz and Willbern; Trilling, "Art" and "Freud"; and Wellek and Warren). Who, we must ask, is being psychoanalyzed: the fictional character in the literary work or the author of this work? I relate Mann's letter of 10 September 1915 to Paul Amann, where, speaking of the critical response to *Death in Venice*, he says:

> . . . I have almost universally been misunderstood in the crudest fashion. What was most painful to me was that the "hieratic atmosphere" was taken as a personal claim on my part—whereas it was nothing but caricature. The cultural Hellenism, too, was taken literally, whereas it was only an expedient and an intellectual refuge for the character. . . . When I deal with an artist, or even a master, I do not mean "me," I am not asserting that I am a master or even only an artist. I am merely saying that I *know* something about the nature of the artist and master. (*Letters to Amann* 46–47; cf. 12: 105)

We examine the issues of the justification of critics who view Mann's works as quasi depictions of his personal beliefs. That the relationship between the author and the fictional persona troubled Mann is evident from his remarks above and elsewhere. And yet there is a relationship between Mann and Aschenbach. His statement in *A Sketch of My Life* (1930) that "nothing is invented in *Death in Venice*" (11: 124) contains much truth. In this regard, the discussions by Erich Heller ("Autobiography"), Helmut Jendreiek, Esther Lesér, and T. J. Reed (*Uses of Tradition* and "Introduction" to *Death in Venice*) are valuable as student assignments.

However the critic pursues the path of interpretation, psychology may aid, provided that—as I have indicated—certain caveats are kept in mind. These include an awareness of the intentions and limitations of psychoanalysis, the various methods by which its principles may be applied, and an understanding of oneself. The last statement relates to a conscious awareness that some literary writings that appeal to us are sometimes reflections of our own frustrations and desires.

At this point I direct attention to Freud's "Delusions and Dreams in Jensen's *Gradiva*," which, as I noted earlier, represents Freud's first published literary analysis. Reviews of Freud's "Delusions and Dreams" essay are available in Kiell's *Freud without Hindsight*. Since a bit of additional orientation is necessary here, the Ernest Jones and Peter Gay Freud biographies are helpful (see also the commentary in the Freud edition of *Der Wahn*). As I tell students, Freud's "Delusions and Dreams" essay is valuable in two ways: first in terms of its approach, which we examine; and second, as our later discussion shows, because of its prominent role in the making of *Death in Venice*.

Next we consider aspects of *Death in Venice* itself. Indeed, after we examine Hanns Sachs's 1914 article in the important Viennese literary-psychoanalytic journal *Imago* (begun in 1912), we study five other psychological or psychoanalytic analyses of *Death in Venice*: by Leah Davidson, Jean Jofen, Heinz Kohut, Harry Slochower, and Raymond Tarbox, all of which are assigned reading. Though all are instructive and some are better than others, their "perceptive" observations still sometimes make students skeptical. Nevertheless, this discussion enlightens students about the mechanics (and mistakes!) of such approaches and, equally important, suggests several key ideas and elements in *Death in Venice*. Of course, the strict psychoanalytic interpretation often does not clarify Mann's whole concept of "myth plus psychology," which plays an important role in *Death in Venice* (cf. Gronicka). This idea, more elaborately developed in the *Joseph and His Brothers* stories, later highlights Mann's powerful sense of duty, summarized well in his 7 September 1941 remarks to Karl Kerényi: "This cooperative labor of mythology plus psychology is a most gratifying phenomenon! It is essential that myth be taken away from intellectual Fascism and transmitted for humane ends. I have for a long time done nothing else" (*Mythology and Humanism* 103). However, I return to the "myth plus psychology" concept later.

Of central concern remains the important issue of the degree to which Freud and psychoanalysis influenced the early Mann. Certainly Mann knew about psychoanalytic thought and tendencies through books, newspapers, and periodicals of the day, aside from his own literary circle, friends, and intuition. Indeed, later in "Freud and the Future," Mann stated:

> [I]f someone decides to appoint a creative writer as the eulogist of a brilliant researcher, this says something about both of these and is revealing about both. It reveals that the person to be celebrated has a special relationship to the world of literature and also that there is a singular relationship of the writer to the field of knowledge of which the world regards the researcher as the founder and master. . . . [W]hat is special and remarkable about this mutual relationship and mutual closeness is that these remained for a long time in the "unconscious" of both men [myself and Freud]—thus in the psychic realm whose investigation, illumination, and conquest for humaneness is the real mission of this percipient spirit/intellect.   (11: 479)

But to what extent had he engaged himself in Freud's works? In the various statements cited above, Mann is vague. However, in a now controversial 1925 interview in Milan, Mann clearly encourages examination of Freudian undertones in *Death in Venice*:

> As regards myself, at least one of my works, the novella *Death in Venice*, came into being under the direct influence of Freud. Without Freud I would never have thought of treating this erotic motif, or I would surely have handled it differently. If I may use a military expression, I would say that Sigmund Freud's thesis constitutes a sort of general offensive against the unconscious with the aim of conquering it. To be sure, as an artist I must confess that I am not at all satisfied with Freudian ideas; rather, I feel perturbed and diminished by them. After all, an artist is probed by Freud's ideas as by X-rays to the point of violating the secret of his creative act.
>
> (qtd. in German in Michael, "Mann auf dem Wege" 166)

Critics have long deliberated the dating of Mann's intensive reading of Freud. The argument focuses on whether Mann carefully read Freud after or before the writing of *Death in Venice* (1911–12). The first mention of Freud in Mann's notebooks is dated 1916. Some critics, such as Manfred Dierks (*Studien*), argued that 1925–26, the preparation period for the *Joseph* novels, was the time of Mann's intensive Freud study; others, such as Frederick Beharriell (esp. " 'Never without Freud' "), claim that the reading came earlier. Mann's 3 January 1930 letter to Freud is imprecise: "I came to you shamefully late" (*Letters*, 1971 ed., 174). Clearly Freud's *Three Essays on the Theory of Sexuality* was used as early as 1915 for the "Analysis" chapter of *The Magic Mountain*, a work that, among other things, parodies the psychoanalyst in the figure of Dr. Krokowski. However, in a pioneering later article ("Der Wahn und die Träume"), Dierks altered his earlier position because his research permitted the conclusion that *Death in Venice* was influenced by Freud's ideas. Dierks's argument rests on a careful reading of *Death in Venice* and Freud's analysis of Jensen's *Gradiva*. Just as Mann borrowed various phrases and ideas from other works, which he freely incorporated into *Death of Venice*, so too, as Dierks shows, did Mann make use of *Gradiva* and Freud's essay on it. But, as Dierks says in "Der Wahn":

> The adoption of psychoanalytical knowledge around 1911 was no mere assimilation of ideas or montage of thoughts, so frequent elsewhere with Thomas Mann. His acquaintance with psychoanalysis met an existential need, and in this situation it stood the test both for himself and for his literary work—if a distinction between them can in fact be made. . . . Sigmund Freud's interpretation of *Gradiva* and

Thomas Mann's *Death in Venice* signify one of the many occasions in the first half of the century when the concepts of "literature" and "psychoanalysis" fall together. Now psychoanalysis, having learned so much from literature, exerts in turn its influence on the latter. (266)

Significantly, Dierks also offers a credible explanation as to why Mann was attracted to Freud and Jensen. In short, Dierks focuses on the role and meaning of dreams, as well as the concept of repression, as expressed in Jensen's fiction and Freud's theory. As Dierks indicates, in May 1911, when Mann saw Tadzio—or, rather, the Tadzio figure—during a visit to Venice, his latent homosexual emotions were aroused. Around this same time, Dierks suggests, Mann also read Freud and Jensen, which not only helped him understand himself but also suggested a structure and the thematic means to write about his feelings. These experiences, then, led to the composition of *Death in Venice*.

More specifically, Dierks says:

In 1911 now he [Mann] gets to know Freud's concept of the return of that which is repressed—more powerfully explained and more differentiated. How appropriate this was for integrating the conflict of instinctive drives is shown at the level of his aesthetic-semantic treatment: beyond Freud's concept and Jensen's narrative structures, a figure is created that for *Death in Venice* retained a quite extraordinary power of integration and made possible Thomas Mann's semantically densest text. His idea of the work correspondingly expresses the process of conflict integration and thereby for a while conflict balance: he speaks of the "feeling of a certain absolute change, a certain sovereign serenity I had never known before." (265)

Of course in the text of Dierks the whole argument rests on "structured identities and above all the unequivocal adoption of content and formulations" (264). Dierks has no evidence that in 1911 Mann actually read either *Gradiva* or Freud's interpretation thereof; he admits that Mann's *Notizen* have no reference to them at all but says, "that need not worry us, there isn't anything on Euripides either" (247). Nevertheless, the argument by Dierks is certainly persuasive, from the similarities between *Death in Venice* and *Gradiva* as well as from the theme of *Verdrängung* ("repression"); and it is true that, while Mann in his article "My Relationship to Psychoanalysis" (to be considered later) says that for the writer it is not so much *Verdrängung* as *ein Aufsichberuhenlassen* ("leaving things alone"), this could in fact be true of *Death in Venice*—Mann would rather let it lie than awaken interest in his homoerotic tendencies. The only actual evidence that Freud was an influence in 1911 is Mann's 1925 statement to an Italian reporter. But, as Dierks says, almost no one believed this now famous *La Stampa* interview until recently; and yet it is strange that, after such a public comment, Mann could write in the same year on his reaction to psychoanalysis without mentioning the interview.

At this point I ask students to ponder a number of issues, all of which need to be evaluated with regard to Dierks's most recent findings. To what degree should *Death in Venice* be seen as a creative work participating in the culture of the time? Is it that Mann wanted to be in tune with the new thought of psychoanalysis? Was not Mann also on the same track as Freud in investigating the psyche? Why does Mann move only slowly to acknowledge Freud—is it because Freud is a "cultural hero"? Is not Mann constantly shifting, adjusting, and growing? Was Mann toying with his readers? Is Mann's widening interest in Freud politically motivated? With regard to this last point, a fundamental fact about Mann's concept of "myth plus psychology" in *Joseph and His Brothers* already has been noted. And about this work Richard Winston proffers: "That he chose the Semitic world of ancient Palestine for his setting was an unobtrusive but firm response to the increasingly racist tone of German society and political life in the period between the wars." Even more important, Winston observes: "Perhaps a similar motive, conscious or unconscious, underlay his preoccupation with Sigmund Freud" (*Letters*, 1971 ed., xxiv). Dierks suggests, however, that

> Mann's path to antiquity and to myth in *Death in Venice* stems from the ideas of Jensen and Freud. The equation "human history = personal archaeology of the soul" comes in 1911 from Freud's interpretation of *Gradiva*. It will recur in Thomas Mann's later motto "myth plus psychology."
>
> (264; see also Dierks, "Mythologie" and "Tiefenpsychologie")

The ambiguity of many of Mann's remarks is tantalizing. While there are some polemical and unresolved issues here, instructors and students should consult, in addition to Dierks's various studies, those by Frederick Beharriell, Jean Finck, Frederick Hoffman, Herbert Lehmann, Wolfgang Michael, Caroline Newton, and Hans Wysling ("Thomas Manns Rezeption der Psychoanalyse"). Dierks's "Traumzeit und Verdichtung" is especially useful, as is Bernd Urban's *Thomas Mann, Freud und die Psychoanalyse.* Students should know that although Mann expressed dissatisfaction with "the conquering of the unconscious," he later altered his position: the essays "Freud's Position in the History of Modern Thought" (1929) and "Freud and the Future" acknowledge the value of Freud's medical and therapeutic teachings that will bring a "free and conscious humanity" (10: 280). What Mann may be suggesting by the title "Freud and the *Future*" also is a good topic for consideration.

Although there are many perspectives, we might summarize Mann's attitude with the comments he made about psychoanalysis in the summer of 1925:

> My relationship to psychoanalysis is as complex as it deserves. In psychoanalysis, that peculiar product of the scientific and civilizatory spirit, one can rightly see something great and admirable, a daring discovery, a considerable advance in knowledge, and a surprising and even sensational expansion of our knowledge about human beings. On the other hand, one can find that if it is improperly popularized, it can turn into an instrument of malicious enlightenment, an obscurantist mania for exposure and discreditation; to have reservations about the latter need not signify mere sentimentality. Its nature is knowledge, *melancholy* knowledge, particularly as regards art and artistry, which apparently is its special concern. Well, that was nothing new to me when I encountered it for the first time. I had essentially experienced it in Nietzsche, especially his critique of Wagner, and as irony it had become an element of my intellectual make-up and my production—and it is undoubtedly due to the fact that my writings have always attracted a certain characteristic attention and critical predilection on the part of psychoanalytic scholarship. For good and sufficient reasons *Death in Venice* also received such attention. (11: 748)

Students like to compare Mann's observations about psychoanalysis with the arguments of his contemporaries. While such discussion proves beneficial, it does not elucidate the full issue. Among other factors, Mann's early position is related to two bitter disputes—no doubt the "malicious enlightenment" and "obscurantist mania for exposure and discreditation" noted above—that he endured at the hands of two critics, first in 1910 from Theodor Lessing and again in 1912 from Alfred Kerr. Since the documents detailing Lessing's malicious scorn against another critic, Samuel Lublinski, and Mann's defense against these hostile attacks and allegations are available (cf. Hansen, *Manns Heine-Rezeption*; Mendelssohn, *Der Zauberer* [Teil 1]; Schröter, *Urteil*; Vaget, "Thomas Mann und die Neuklassik"; Winston, *Making*; and Wysling, "Ein Elender"), it is not necessary to repeat them here. The class is often surprised at the events: most students never entertain the notion that a preeminent figure like Mann would be exposed to such venom. Certainly Lessing's viciousness had poisoned Mann's already suspicious view about psychology when, two years later, he found himself embroiled in a similar dispute with Kerr.

The Lessing and Kerr episodes served to intensify Mann's skeptical view of psychology. Indeed, Mann's letter of 30 January 1913 to Ernst Bertram relates his intent to write a story entitled *Ein Elender (A Study in Abjec-*

tion), noting, "Have *I* made studies!! It could really be a good character novella" (*Thomas Mann an Bertram* 15). The "studies" refer to Lessing and Kerr, and in *Death in Venice* this "famous short story," *Ein Elender*, is attributed to Aschenbach's pen. The work is described as "an outbreak of disgust against an age indecently undermined by psychology and represented by the figure of that spiritless, witless semiscoundrel who cheats his way into a destiny of sorts . . ." (204). In "My Relationship to Psychoanalysis" Mann has commented on this passage. Regarding Aschenbach's decision to "repudiate knowledge," which "can paralyze the will, paralyze and discourage action and emotion and even passion, and rob all these of their dignity" (204), Mann remarks:

> This is a strong anti-analytic statement, but it has presumably been interpreted as a characteristic example of "repression," even though that which may make the artist-neurotic audacious enough to do his own thing despite all analytic revelations should be characterized not so much as repression as, more aptly though less scientifically, leaving things alone. (11: 749)

It is instructive to see that Mann misuses the term *repression*. Apparently other writers "accused" Mann of this terrible sin, and he accepts the word in the same opprobrious sense. Actually, when Mann felt offended by psychoanalytic interpretations of his writing and chose to disregard them, he—like Aschenbach, who "repudiates knowledge"—was not *repressing* (an unconscious process occurring when an individual cannot tolerate a particular thought, feeling, or idea and then, without the person's awareness, it becomes inaccessible to consciousness); he was *suppressing* (also an ordinary mental process, wherein the individual finds an idea or feeling unpleasant, unacceptable, or uncongenial and *chooses* to push it from awareness). Interestingly enough, these distinctions (along with the related concepts of "resistance" and "inhibition") were not clear even to Freud in his earliest writings but evolved as his theories, particularly that of metapsychology, were developed. The point to emphasize is that repression is not something that one must explain away or apologize for, as Mann is doing. Mann's attitude toward psychoanalysis admittedly appears largely ambivalent. Also, the concept of repression had figured prominently in Freud's essay on Jensen's *Gradiva*, and this aspect should not be overlooked. Mann's response, however, continues:

> That certainly does not mean simple animosity, for as the phenomenon Nietzsche shows, *Erkenntnis* ["knowledge"], which is not productive as a principle, can have a great deal to do with art and an artist can have an excellent relationship with it. It means anything but the delusion that the world could ever "get around"—to put it in

popular terms—the research results of Freud and his followers by
closing its eyes to them. It certainly will not get around, and art will
not do so either.   (11: 749)

Mann's suspicious view of psychology and psychoanalysis and the prevalent philosophy of "tout comprendre c'est tout pardonner" (cf. 204) is
reminiscent of Nietzsche, whose dictum in the epilogue of *Nietzsche contra Wagner*, for example, states, "Tout comprendre—c'est tout mépriser"
(682). The prologue of Mann's *Reflections of a Nonpolitical Man*, written
in February 1918, after the completion of the other chapters—the volume
itself was begun in 1915—exclaims:

> . . . in what respect I have something to do with the new and to
> what extent I, too, harbor some of that "resoluteness," that rejection
> of the "indecent psychologism" of the past epoch and its lax and ir-
> regular *"tout comprendre"*—that is, a will that may be called anti-
> naturalistic, anti-impressionistic, and anti-relativistic, but which has
> in any case been, in art as in morality, a will and not mere submis-
> siveness.   (12: 28)

Mann speculates in a similar sense in "On Belief," the tenth chapter of
Reflections:

> The longing, striving, and seeking of our time, which certainly does
> *not* aim for freedom but represents a desire for an "inner tyrant," for
> "absolute codes of values," for constraints, for moral rootedness, is a
> striving for *culture*, dignity, bearing, and form—and I have a right to
> speak of this, for I knew about it earlier than many others, watched
> for it, and attempted to portray it. . . .   (12: 516–17)

After giving some consideration to how, in *Death in Venice*, Mann provides
a seismograph (11: 240) of the *Zeitgeist* (cf. the essays by Stackelberg and
Timms in this volume), we continue by considering Mann's further statement in "On Belief":

> In a story [*Death in Venice*] I experimented with the rejection of the
> psychologism and relativism of the era coming to an end; I had a
> representative of art bid farewell to "knowledge for its own sake,"
> deny sympathy for the "abyss," and turn toward the will, to the judg-
> ment of values, toward intolerance, toward "resoluteness." I gave all
> this a catastrophic, that is, a skeptical-pessimistic, outcome. I cast
> doubt on whether an artist can gain *dignity*. I had my hero, who had
> attempted it, experience and confess that it is not possible. I am well
> aware that the "new will" that I made fail would certainly not have

become a problem for me or the object of my artistic urge if I did not share it, for in the realm of art there is no objective knowledge but only an intuitive and lyrical one. (12: 517)

Although *Death in Venice* provides psychoanalytically oriented critics with a gold mine, the story itself, in keeping with Mann's attitude, sharply repudiates psychoanalysis: "The hero, Aschenbach, is an artistic spirit," Mann says in a letter to Agnes E. Meyer on 30 May 1938, "who deserves, as an escape from the psychologism and relativism of the fin de siècle, a new beauty, a simplification of the soul, a new resoluteness, a rejection of the abyss, and a new human dignity beyond analysis and even knowledge" (*Dichter über ihre Dichtungen* 1: 437). The "escape from the psychologism and relativism of the fin de siècle," the "anti-naturalistic, anti-impressionistic, and anti-relativistic" tendencies, the "new beauty"—in short, the new times—echo Mann's attraction to the movement of neoclassicism that was supported and advanced by Samuel Lublinski, Paul Ernst, Georg Lukács, Wilhelm von Scholz, Rudolf Pannwitz, and others. The "shrewd commentator" of Aschenbach's work, cited in chapter 2 of *Death in Venice* (202), is in fact Lublinski, whose *Bilanz der Moderne* (1904) and *Ausgang der Moderne* (1908) impressed Mann. Lublinski's works delineate the *Zeitgeist*, which, according to him, represents a movement away from naturalism and neo-Romanticism and a trend toward neoclassicism. Vaget perceptively argues that "without contact with the neoclassical movement *Death in Venice* would not have been written" ("Thomas Mann und die Neuklassik" 435; see also Jethro Bithell; André von Gronicka, *Profile*; Hermann Kurzke, *Thomas Mann: Epoche*; Karl Kutzbach; T. J. Reed, *Uses of Tradition* and "Introduction" to *Death in Venice*; and Andreas Wöhrmann). We might add, however, that without Freud's "Delusions and Dreams in Jensen's *Gradiva*," along with other influences like Goethe's *Elective Affinities* (cf. Atkins; Lillyman; Otto; Thomas; Vaget, *"Der Tod"*; and Žmegač), Mann's classic might not have taken the form it attained.

In short, Mann wanted to "escape from the psychologism . . . of the fin de siècle." And Gustav von Aschenbach—Mann's fictional counterpart in *Death in Venice*—responds to "life" in such a manner. To be sure, Aschenbach *is* founding this "new classicism" and *seems* to understand what he rejects (cf., for instance, 204). But I ask students to consider the consequences of Aschenbach's repudiation of knowledge, response to art and beauty, and desire to be a classicist ("gewollte Klassizität"). They lead, for Aschenbach, to the creation of a masterful essay—"that page and a half of exquisite prose"—for which he has "used Tadzio's beauty as a model" (236) and which is, in fact, recognized as Mann's July 1911 "Coming to Terms with Richard Wagner" (cf. Lehnert, *Fiktion* 99–108; Consigny). That essay concludes, "I believe *a new classicism must come*" (10: 842; emphasis added). But for Aschenbach the result, as Mann says in a crucial letter to

Carl Maria Weber on 4 July 1920, is "passion as confusion and as a stripping of dignity" (*Letters*, 1971 ed., 103). Students often view his downfall as "the tragedy of supreme achievement," as Mann relates to Elisabeth Zimmer on 6 September 1915 (*Letters*, 1971 ed., 76), and as a lesson about the conflict resulting from intoxication with passion and devotion to art and beauty, as well as perfection of form. Attention returns, then, to the text of *Death in Venice*. Many aspects about (neo)classicism (cf. Amory) remain to be discussed, such as its further representation in *Death in Venice* and even the degree to which Mann might have become interested in its tenets so that he (or his fictional Aschenbach) would be a representative writer for the Wilhelmian era (cf. Sokel; Dassanowsky-Harris). (Mann did not claim to be a part of any literary mode [11: 311].) But to elucidate these issues would take us beyond the purpose of this essay.

Our discussion, then, proceeds in a direction usually not anticipated by students, who frankly expected *only* a "case study" approach. Examination of Mann's thought, however, along with the psychoanalytic *Zeitgeist* and Freud's ideas, provides an interesting aura to the classroom and ample materials for good discussion. Similarly, students had not expected to learn about neoclassicism or Mann's (Aschenbach's) "escape from the psychologism . . . of the fin de siècle." Such an approach establishes the groundwork for consideration of these and other aspects of *Death in Venice* and for further study of Thomas Mann.

TEACHING INDIVIDUAL TEXTS

Teaching *Tonio Kröger* as Literature about Literature

Beverley Driver Eddy

For several years I have been using *Tonio Kröger* as the final reading selection in my Introduction to German Literature classes, because the work is a readable study of what literature is about and what it purports to be. In this short novel, which bore the working title *Litteratur*, Thomas Mann asks some fundamental questions, such as What is the purpose of literature? What is the proper role of a literary artist? By posing these queries within the context of a literary work, he blends literary allusion with autobiography to create a tight and unified whole.

Class begins with a quick study of Mann's early life—his boyhood in Lübeck, his stay in Italy, his residence in Munich, his journey back to his home, and his vacation trip to Aalsgard, on the northern coast of Zealand, in Denmark—so that students can see that *Tonio Kröger* has a strong autobiographical basis. I show photographs of Mann's distinguished German father and his less conventional Brazilian mother and pictures of his boyhood home, including the narrow streets of Lübeck, the school, and the harbor. We look at photographs of Munich and the successful young writer, who so closely resembles Tonio in chapter 4. The students also see pictures of Aalsgard, the hotel, and the glass veranda. For all these pictures I use Klaus Schröter's illustrated monograph, *Selbstzeugnissen*; the collection in the American edition of Mann's diaries, edited by Richard Winston and Clara Winston; and Jürgen Kolbe's *Heller Zauber*, supplemented by photographs I took on visits to the German and Danish settings. Along with these autobiographical details the students are given copies of quotations from Mann's essays, letters, and interviews in which they read, among other things, Mann's comments on the similarities and differences between his mother and Frau Kröger (11: 420–23), as well as his statement that the Russian painter, Lisaweta Iwanowna, was pure invention. While this information is of course well known to the Mann scholar, we should remember that, to the uninitiated student, such basics come as a surprise. The students discover that Mann's short novel differs from his autobiography in several important respects. Unlike Mann, Tonio has no brothers or sisters. Mann did not have an embarrassingly "foreign" first name. And "Ingeborg Holm" had brown hair, not blond (11: 100).

As we compare autobiographical detail with the work, the students see that Mann took facts and recast them to suit the purposes of his story. If Tonio had had brothers and sisters, for example, he possibly would not seem so isolated in his northern hometown, because he would not be the sole figure to inherit the artistic traits that isolate him from his classmates. If Inge had had brown hair, there would not be the neat "blond-haired, blue-eyed—dark-haired, brown-eyed" dichotomy that is so central to Mann's themes of life versus art, normality versus criminality, emotion versus intellect. Guided speculation on Mann's reasons for these changes allows the students to consider the north-south polarity, so strong throughout the short novel, as a metaphor that Mann sustains by altering details of his own biography.

Once my students understand that *Tonio Kröger* is an artistic rendering of Mann's life, they are more receptive to the literary allusions that underlie the plot. Mann's first discernible model is Goethe, for whom Mann had immense admiration and of whom he had written: "If I ask myself about the inherited origin of my talent I must think of Goethe's famous little verse" (11: 451–52). The students read these lines from "Zahme Xenien" about Goethe's literary inheritance—

> My father gave me force and frame,
> The moral life's foundation;
> The gay heart from my mother came,
> The high imagination.
>
> (Lewisohn 4.9)

—and compare them with Mann's description of Tonio's father and mother (138). They can then see that the Goethe poem suggests a literary reference for Mann, much as Theodor Storm's poem "Hyacinths," with the lines "I long to sleep, to sleep, but you must dance" (147–48), is a literary reference for Tonio, providing an allusion that changes its focus as he matures and accepts his role as a bourgeois-artist.

The question of literary allusion raises interesting class discussions about the role of literature. Students are usually quick to note that the young Tonio identifies with literary figures, with the first-person speaker in "Hyacinths," and with King Philip in Schiller's *Don Carlos*. Many of the students can relate to Tonio's self-identification with figures from literature; there is usually a student in class, for example, who has identified at some point in life with Jo March of *Little Women*. Students talk about the situations that are especially conducive to such identification with literary figures, and many recognize that it was a period during which they felt like outsiders either in their families or among classmates. We discuss Tonio's statements about literature as a "revenge on life" for those who are "always falling over when they dance" (162). Is this a valid view of literature? Does literature validate our personal condition by reflecting and glorifying it in a fictitious character? Does it then become a form of escapism from difficult situations in life?

Many of my students rebel at this view of literature. They reply that literature has positive aspects as well, that it broadens understanding by introducing characters and situations that readers do not meet in everyday life. Sometimes students in my classes have mentioned Raskolnikov in Dostoevsky's *Crime and Punishment* as an example of the kind of figure who, in a news report, would seem simply despicable, whereas, through his portrayal in the novel, they understand at least partially the reasons for his crime.

This discussion provides the class with a key to understanding the difficult fourth chapter of the Mann short novel (other perspectives of which are discussed elsewhere in this volume). Students now see that Tonio, by arguing that literature is escapism, believes that, instead of helping people understand life better, it alienates them even further from the life around them. Lisaweta, in contrast, sees literature as the key to understanding, purification, and forgiveness. The artist "heals" by giving readers insights that dissolve their passions (159).

Because of their differing views, Tonio thinks of the literary author as a "charlatan" and a "criminal," while Lisaweta regards the author as a "priest." Tonio, who now identifies with the wordy, immobilized Hamlet, can do nothing with Lisaweta's words of wisdom, even when she describes his condition as that of "a bourgeois who has taken the wrong turning, . . . a bourgeois manqué" (164). Yet he offers a remarkable confession, telling her, "You have a right to talk that way, . . . conferred upon you by your national literature, by the sublime writers of Russia; their work I will willingly worship as the sacred literature of which you speak" (159). Although he now regards literature as something that cripples people and hinders action, he admits that Russian literature does not do so. He acknowledges, in other words, that there are various kinds of literature that serve various purposes. (Mann's own interest in and use of Russian literature, especially his reading of Goncharov's *Oblomov* during his visit to Denmark, may form another area of investigation. See, e.g., Banuls, "Thomas Mann und die russische Literatur.")

Tonio had already tried using literature positively, as a bridge to intimacy and understanding. As a boy he tried in vain to persuade Hans to read Schiller's *Don Carlos*, thinking, "[T]hen they would have something in common, something they could talk about" (143). He soon learned, though, that the bourgeois citizens he longed to be with had no use for literature, that in fact literature was forbidden fruit for such carefree people. He had already said of Ingeborg, "Only people who do not read *Immensee* and never try to write anything like it can be as beautiful and lighthearted as you; that is the tragedy!" (148). Tonio now considers literature a curse that sets people apart from life. He proffers a litany of examples: the banker-novelist turned criminal, the actor who is nothing without his stage makeup, the lieutenant who becomes laughable when he writes poetry, and the papal castrati. Healthy people, he seems to say, don't need literature—it is something only for outcasts, outsiders, people who fall in the dance.

To resolve his inner conflicts, Tonio chooses not to go to Russia, in spite of his admission to Lisaweta that Russian literature has the power to heal and make one whole. Instead he seeks his remedy in Denmark, the land of Hamlet, his present figure of literary identification (see Heine; Marx; Matthias; Steffensen).

It is good to remind students here that Mann's favorite literary reference, Goethe, had gone south to Italy as a Sturm und Drang poet, and that while there he achieved the artistic harmony that made him a mature representative of German classicism. But Tonio goes north, to Denmark, because, representing his father's heritage, it brings him back to his roots. He goes too because he loves the names ("names like Ingeborg" [165]), the heavy food, the rough North Sea—and the literature. He tells Lisaweta, "[T]hink of the books they write up there in the north, Lisaveta, books of such depth and purity and humor—there's nothing like them, I love them" (164). While Tonio is searching for his own identity in the northern climate of his father, he is also seeking his roots in literature, for the sense of purpose he had lost during his wanderings in Italy and his association with other, different writers.

What exactly is the literature that draws Tonio to Denmark? To suggest an answer, I refer students to a letter Mann wrote to his friend Kurt Martens a year before the publication of *Tonio Kröger*: "I am continually reading Herman Bang now, to whom I feel deeply related. I urgently recommend 'Tine' to you!" (*Briefe* 1: 36). This letter and Tonio's comments to Lisaweta on northern literature suggest that Mann himself looked to Scandinavia for writers congenial to his art. I point out to the students that the works of Bang, Henrik Ibsen, Knut Hamsun, Bjørnstjerne Bjørnson, and Jens Peter Jacobsen profoundly influenced German and Austrian writers of this period, authors as disparate as Gerhart Hauptmann and Hugo von Hofmannsthal, Rainer Maria Rilke and Hermann Hesse, Franz Kafka and Richard Dehmel. I suggest that Tonio's pilgrimage to the north may be read as a parable of this period, as modern Germany's rejection of purely classical influences for the idealistic humanity of the great northern writers. The north-south polarities of the short novel are to be bridged only by reversing German tradition, as Tonio finds his inspiration not in the fragrant air of classical Italy but rather in the sharp, salty air of the north.

What does Tonio do in Denmark to achieve his epiphany as a mature artist? At first glance, it seems, very little. His overnight stay in his home town (Lübeck) only confirms his biases that life and literature have little or nothing to do with each other, especially after he sees that his home has been turned into a public library. The rough sea does stir him to begin the composition of a poem. But at his Danish resort he does little more than take long solitary walks and sit for hours "with a book on his knees, but reading not a word of it," experiencing "a profound forgetfulness, floating as if disembodied above space and time." "Thus," Mann writes, "many days passed; he could not have told how many, and had no desire to know. But then came one on which something happened; it happened when the sun was shining and many people were there, and Tonio Kröger did not even find it particularly surprising" (181).

What occurs, of course, is that Tonio relives his youth in the reenactment of the dance lesson. "Hans" is present, as are "Ingeborg" and "Magdalena Vermehren." He watches from a glass veranda and then steps in briefly to help the Danish "Magdalena" to her feet. That is all. Why is he transformed?

I suggest that students might better address the question of how Tonio is changed. At this point, I draw their attention to the master of ceremonies, the postal assistant, who is a clear Danish counterpart to François Knaak. Students immediately see the parallels, but Tonio's association is not with Knaak; it is with "a comic character straight out of a Danish novel" (185). I introduce a passage from Bang's short novel *Her Royal Highness*, one of the Danish novels Mann greatly admired and from which he often quoted. In this work, first published in German translation in 1887 in a volume entitled *Verfehltes Leben* (*A Failed Life*; later published in *Die vier Teufel*), there is an amusing dance instructor, Herr Pestalozzi, who teaches his clumsy royal pupil the steps of the quadrille:

> Her Highness the Duchess was present even at Princess Maria Carolina's dance and deportment lessons. The old teacher was a reject from the ballet, who performed many foreign ballet bows and murderous leaps. Princess Maria Carolina danced the quadrille with three chairs. The foreigner was sweating, fiddling the "Quadrille à la

cour" on his thin violin. Her Highness was in despair: Princess Maria Carolina possessed no grace at all!

"—En arrière—en avant—un, deux, trois, compliment—But one looks at one's partner. Over there—the gentleman à gauche." Princess Maria Carolina worked her way desperately through her three chairs.

The ballet dancer played and beat the rhythm with his whole body.

"There—over there—trois, your highness . . . the gentleman à droite—the red ribbon, the gentleman à droite (the red and the blue ribbons around the chairs supported Maria Carolina's ability to understand) . . . deux, trois, compliment."

The antiquated ballet dancer jumped like a harlequin at the pantomime, as he scratched on his violin.

"Good,—good, un, deux, trois, the gentleman à droite . . . "

"The wrists," exclaimed her Highness. "Mr. Pestalozzi—these angular movements! Oh, what a curtsey, this curtsey!" Her Highness the Duchess leapt up.

"Once again . . ."

Princess Maria Carolina curtseyed with a rounded back.

"This posture!—look at her back!—Once again . . ."

Her Highness sang along.

With fixed eyes Princess Maria Carolina curtseyed in front of the three chairs.

"A horrible curtsey—horrible!"

Her Highness was beside herself: "The princess is as round-shouldered as a water-carrier."

Mr. Pestalozzi dried his face with a handkerchief that was as clean as an old makeup rag; water was almost trickling down his face.

(*Die vier Teufel* 91–92)

Students enjoy the humor of the Bang selection, and they invariably point out that, just as Mr. Pestalozzi has something in common with the postal assistant and with Knaak, so the princess Maria Carolina appears to resemble Magdalena Vermehren. Because of her royalty and her isolation from other children, she even resembles Schiller's King Philip; and students are fascinated to learn that a hopeless love causes Bang's princess to weep as she reads *Don Carlos*. Furthermore, near the close of the short novel, the princess, like Magdalena Vermehren, crashes to the floor while dancing with a clumsy partner. I caution my students, however, not to force the identity between *Tonio Kröger* and this particular Bang work, just as they should not look for too much identity between Tonio and Goethe, or between Frau Kröger and Frau Mann. He is using certain aspects of this Bang tale symbolically, just as he used these other influences. The point to emphasize is not that characters similar to those in a specific Bang novel appear in Mann's work but rather why they appear there.

Students now see that the Danish figures are part of Tonio's healing process. During his lethargic days on the coast, a novel on his lap, Tonio has internalized the literature of which he had spoken admiringly to Lisaweta. He observes this literature embodied in the life around him, so that his self-pity is transformed into tolerant humanity. As a writer, too, Tonio is transformed; he accepts Lisaweta's assessment of his nature and of the higher, purifying purposes of art, because he, too, has been purified through literature. Knaak is no longer "a preposterous monkey" (146) as the young Tonio had once observed but has instead become the subject of gentle humor.

The ultimate irony of the work is that, by experiencing the people in the Danish setting as literature, Tonio is able to objectify his own life and understand himself in ways he never had before. Tonio writes to his Russian friend to tell her that he now realizes how correct her analysis of him had been. He promises her that he will write better literature. By closing the letter to Lisaweta with the words he had used to end chapter 1, Mann suggests that *Tonio Kröger* is itself the realization of that promise (Swales, *A Study* 33). At this point Mann and Tonio Kröger merge. This merging explains the striking passage in the second chapter, in which a mature Mann used a direct form of address to tell Ingeborg how much Tonio had loved her. It explains, too, the gentle irony and warm humor of the first chapters. It comes then as no surprise that the lesson Tonio learns in Denmark is one that Mann acknowledged in a 1924 Danish interview. When asked whether any Danish writer had a particular influence on his writing, he replied without hesitation: "Yes, Herman Bang. . . . I have read everything by him and learned a great deal from him" (Hansen and Heine 67). In *Tonio Kröger* Mann suggests that what he had learned is humanity. For him, at least, *Litteratur* has the power to transform.

Tonio Kröger's Conversation with Lisaweta Iwanowna: Difficulties and Solutions

Rodney Symington

When introducing *Tonio Kröger* to students, most teachers probably first present biographical background on Thomas Mann to show that the story is rooted in Mann's personal life and deals with concerns that were close to him as a writer. His parentage, his childhood and youth, his relation to his home town, Lübeck, his lifelong doubts about the writer's calling—these and other autobiographical elements have left their indelible mark on the story.

Students generally find few problems with the earlier sections of the work; indeed, they frequently find them so attractive that they go so far as to identify with the hero ("I am Tonio Kröger!"); it might even be necessary to warn against the interpretative dangers of narcissism. During the discussion of these early sections the peculiarities of Mann's style—particularly his use of the leitmotif as a structural device—can be demonstrated and elucidated. Teachers can ask students to find examples of the leitmotif to illustrate the fundamental dichotomy of the story (artist vs. bourgeois, Tonio vs. Kröger). Most students have little difficulty comprehending (and enjoying) the first three chapters.

But the central section of the short novel, with its complex discussion of the nature of the artist and the latter's role in society, often comes as a dash of cold water after the rather sentimental content of the episodes involving Hans Hansen and Ingeborg Holm, and most students need considerable help in understanding the arguments and in achieving clarity about the issues involved. I therefore find it useful to offer further biographical information that relates specifically to this section, so that it can be seen in context. This part of the story represents Mann's struggle with himself, and although the ideas contained in Tonio Kröger's conversation with Lisaweta Iwanowna transcend the narrow confines of Mann's own person, they are deeply rooted in his problems as an artist, not just at the time he began writing *Tonio Kröger* but for decades thereafter.

From the first conception of *Tonio Kröger*, in the fall of 1899, to its completion three years later, Mann was battling with the central issue of his life and work. That issue—we can even justifiably speak of a crisis at this time in Mann's life—was his view of himself as a writer who had come to doubt both the validity of the artist and the use of literature. Even more critical was the fact that his assessment of himself and of the ironic attitude he had adopted toward experience produced in him the depressing conclusion that to devote oneself to literature meant death as a sensitive, feeling human being. In a letter to his brother Heinrich (13 Feb. 1901), written at the very time when he was struggling to create the conversation between Tonio Kröger and Lisaweta Iwanowna, Mann confessed to having been depressed over the past winter to the point of entertaining serious thoughts of suicide. He had been saved by a new experience, his friendship with Paul Ehrenberg, which had shown him "that there is something sincere, warm, and good in me after all, and not just 'irony'; that after all everything in me is not blasted, overrefined, and corroded by the accursed scribbling. Ah, literature is death! I shall never understand how anyone can be dominated by it *without* bitterly hating it!" (*Letters*, 1971 ed., 23).

Mann's notebooks indicate that, from the start, the conversation about literature was both central and dominant in his conception of *Tonio Kröger* (Scherrer and Wysling 48–63). One might say that the idea of the essayistic central section was there first, and that the story (insofar as there is one) was written around it. When Mann reached Tonio's conversation with Lisaweta, he suddenly experienced difficulty in continuing: in fact, it took him several months to finish writing it (11: 115). At this time (February 1901), the theme of literature was so preeminent that the working title of the story was *Litteratur*. It was not until late 1902 that he was able to bring it to completion. This long gestation period is significant as an indication of the personal and artistic hurdles that Mann was struggling to overcome.

Just as Mann had to solve considerable problems in relation to Tonio's conversation with Lisaweta, the student is likewise faced with a number of interpretative dilemmas and difficulties. For example, it is helpful for the discussion of the conversation (ch. 4) if students can realize from the start that it is really not a conversation at all; to all intents and purposes it is a monologue, into which the mostly functional character of Lisaweta interjects the occasional comment to retain the fictional pretense of a dialogue. (When students are asked to work out the ratio of his words to hers, they find it is approximately eight to one.) If students are then invited to analyze the statements put into Lisaweta's mouth, they will quickly come to understand that her role (both here and at two other places in the short novel) is much like that of the confidante in French classical theater: it is a device that enables the author to reveal to us the innermost thoughts of his main character while holding to the tenet of verisimilitude. It is true that in the course of the conversation she does make some important comments (in that they reveal and represent Mann's own ironic self-criticism)—and indeed she makes the conclusive comment about Tonio Kröger's artistic nature—but for the main she is present only to act as a sounding board for his outpourings.

Furthermore, students can easily be guided to the conclusion that Tonio's "monologue" is itself a literary device, employed here by Mann to insert in his work what is quite obviously a statement of his personal concerns. It contains a fictional reflection of Mann's assessment of his own situation as an artist. He himself called this chapter the "lyric-essayistic central section" (11: 115). Students may well agree with the second part of Mann's hyphenated epithet, but we can also ask them to consider to what extent the conversation is, in fact, lyrical and not simply emotional. In contrast to an essay, furthermore, the arguments here are not presented logically; that is, one cannot follow a logical train of thought from beginning to end as one would expect from an essay. Rather, the arguments emerge piecemeal and in the wrong order, so to speak, so that students should be encouraged to unravel the thread of the argument for themselves. What we are presented with is a succession of thoughts—one might almost say random thoughts—that seem to occur to Tonio as he speaks. The ideas themselves, and particularly the manner in which they are delivered, indicate both a highly emotional state and a Tonio Kröger full of self-doubts.

An additional difficulty for students resides in the number of statements in the conversation that are either epigrammatic or ambiguous or, as so often in Mann's essays and fictional work, indicative of a whole complex of ideas. For example, Tonio in his conversation with Lisaweta makes several statements that sound as if they belong in a work by Oscar Wilde: "And only amateurs think that a creative artist can afford to have feelings" (155); "Literature isn't a profession at all . . . it is a curse" (157). Such terse and startling utterances need careful consideration and elucidation.

Furthermore, although the element of personal confession in *Tonio Kröger* is strong, students should be sensitive to the ubiquitous element of irony, which—as in all Mann's works—tends to relativize even apparently unequivocal statements. And, finally, not only is it hazardous for a critic to accept statements in Mann's fiction at their face value, but one needs to be skeptical of Mann's own comments about his work (as suggested in regard to his description of this section as "lyric-essayistic"). As a reader of his own works, Mann (like many other authors) is not always reliable, a point noted by several contributors to this volume.

Students can also be asked to compare the apparently loose structure of the conversation with that of the short novel as a whole. They usually find it surprising that, despite the length of time it took Mann to compose this conversation, it does not seem as tightly structured as one might expect of such a text from his pen. It is as if the intellectual and emotional confusion of the author has found its equivalent expression in the rather bewildering form of the conversation.

The following, then, emerge as some of the fundamental questions for students to think about:

1. What is Tonio's line of argument in his conversation with Lisaweta?
2. What does this conversation signify for Tonio's character and its development?
3. Considering the heavily autobiographical nature of the work, what does this conversation (and its function in the short novel) tell us about Mann's development as a writer?
4. Is the view of the writer presented here of more general validity, or does it remain a personal statement of confession by the author?

If the students are encouraged to rearrange Tonio Kröger's remarks into a logical argument, they might produce something like the following summary.

Artists are born with a personality that already sets them aside from other people at an early age. Even in youth, they are sensitive and perspicacious and soon see through the shams and facades of everyday life. Henceforth, because of this insight, artists adopt an ironic attitude to experience, and the chief aim, once they begin to write, is to mold experience into aesthetically pleasing form. In doing this, however, artists are aware that they are deliberately manipulating the raw material of existence; thus, in their view, both their own claims to be human and the validity of their artistic creations are thrown into doubt. Instead of simply living and experiencing, they are compelled by their artistic temperament to observe, to analyze, and to reshape experience into aesthetic form, a process that leads, or so they believe, into their freezing and killing it. They are, in their own harsh judgment, charlatans and frauds, with a nature closely allied to that of the criminal. Furthermore, Tonio's incessant insights into the nature of existence eventually produce in him a feeling of disgust, whereas other artists are only bored by or indifferent to them. Life, for its part, is indifferent to artists and their achievements, continuing its course no matter what they do.

Despite all the knowledge (and the nausea it brings), this artist at least still loves life—not the exaggerated manifestations of life as seen in extreme examples, but rather life as it is embodied in the everyday and the ordinary. All genuine artists cherish this longing for "innocence, simplicity and living warmth" (161). "Life" as thus defined is in eternal opposition to intellect and art—and never the twain shall meet. Artists should leave normal people, the "blue-eyed innocents" (162), alone, and normal people for their part should never attempt to stray from the straight and narrow path onto the rocky road of art.

It is always interesting to invite students, after they have read and analyzed this section, to pass judgment on the view of the artist that is being proposed here, which is striking in its mercilessness. If we are to believe Mann, the act of aesthetic creation requires that the artist be ruthless and calculating: form can be brought into being only by the conscious exercise of the artist's ability to cast material into form. This act is devoid of all feeling; it is a cold, rational process whose end is the production of something aesthetically pleasing. "All healthy emotion, all strong emotion lacks taste" (156), remarks Tonio epigrammatically. (One might ask the students to note, in passing, the irony of this statement: Tonio's remarks throughout this section are deeply heartfelt and emotional. Do they therefore lack taste?) Indeed, the emotion has first to be reworked—with no regard to its significance as *emotion*—into a form that gives aesthetic pleasure. Not *what* the material is, but *how* it is treated, is all-important (155).

What, I then ask my students, do we make of Tonio Kröger's view of art as valid only if it gives aesthetic pleasure? Clearly, in stating this view, he is subscribing to aestheticism as the function of art. (We learn too little about Tonio's own works, however, to judge whether they live up to his own prescription.) Other important questions for students to think about and discuss are these: If the form is all that matters in a work of art, and the content is largely irrelevant, where does that leave Mann's *Tonio Kröger*? And second, are we expected by the author to appreciate only the *form* of the story or also its content?

It seems obvious that students should be encouraged to conclude that, while *Tonio Kröger* provides us with considerable aesthetic pleasure, its content nevertheless is important; that is, the short novel clearly has a "message." Mann even indicated this when he criticized himself in a letter to Kurt Martens (28 Mar. 1906, *Letters*, 1971 ed., 48), claiming that his admission of a love of life in *Tonio Kröger* was so direct and unequivocal that it "verges on the inartistic." So despite the words that Mann puts into Tonio Kröger's mouth, content is important. We might even take the view that, since *Tonio Kröger* is both a personal analysis of, and a future program for, the artist Thomas Mann, its content is at least as significant as the aesthetic effect of the work.

Students should therefore be careful, throughout the conversation with Lisaweta, not to swallow Tonio Kröger's words uncritically, nor should they overlook the frequent hyperbole and the ironic tone. The example of the banker who began writing short stories in jail (158) is just such a case in point: while, on the surface, students might feel inclined to grant Tonio (and Mann) the comparison between the banker's fraudulent behavior and that of the artist, on closer scrutiny it can be made clear that whereas the banker hoodwinks customers against their will, the artist pulls the wool, so to speak, over the eyes of readers—with their permission and collusion. In other words, the artist's "victims" willingly suspend disbelief. The analogy with the banker is somewhat faulty.

According to Tonio, the "fraudulent" work of art has ambivalent effects on people. The example cited is that of Wagner's opera *Tristan and Isolde*, "a morbid, profoundly equivocal work" (158). At this point some explanation of Mann's relation to Wagner is probably necessary. In choosing Wagner as his example, Mann is grappling with a question that bothered him his whole life. Was Wagner a great artist who had something genuinely important to say and was able to express it brilliantly in magnificent form, or was he (as Nietzsche had finally concluded) merely a charlatan who knew how to exploit his talent and manipulate his audience in a thoroughly calculating manner? The "equivocal" nature of *Tristan and Isolde* lies precisely in this question: its powerful effect on a receptive audience is unquestionable, but is the work sincere? For Mann (through Tonio Kröger) the answer is clear: the sincerity of all artists is questionable, precisely because their art consists in the manipulation of their material (158). For them, the effect is more important than the integrity of the content.

The two objections made to Tonio's assertions by Lisaweta Iwanowna at this point are both significant, and I encourage students to analyze their implications in full. First, Lisaweta suggests that while Tonio Kröger professes to be talking about artists in general, he is, in fact, talking about himself (159). Thus through the mouth of Lisaweta, Mann is ironically admitting that he can claim no more than to be speaking *pro domo*.

Second, Lisaweta raises the persuasive objection that there is another possible view of literature: namely, that literature is uplifting and ennobling, the expression of all that is finest in human culture (159; students generally agree wholeheartedly with her). This objection is again a literary reflection of Mann talking to himself; in having Tonio Kröger recognize this function of art as manifested in Russian writers, Mann is paying homage to a literature and to writers he particularly admired. But as for the redeeming power of words so highly praised by Lisaweta, Tonio (and with him Mann) has come to believe just the opposite: that words freeze emotion, by converting it into a rigid form. The key word in this context is *eliminated* (in German, *erledigt*), and here it occurs no fewer than four times in the text in quick succession (160, 161). It is clearly a crucial word both in this conversation and in Tonio Kröger's/Thomas Mann's view of art: "Apply to a writer: the whole thing will be settled in a trice. He will analyze it for you, formulate it, name it, express it and make it articulate, and so far as you are concerned the entire affair will be eliminated once and for all: he will have turned it for you into a matter of total indifference" (160).

In so doing, the "artist" has performed a most ambiguous service—alleviating your burden, to be sure, but at the same time, by giving form to emotion, destroying its fundamental quality: its humanity. Tonio carries his rhetorical flourish to its logical conclusion: if artists were to express the human content of the entire world, the world "will have been eliminated, redeemed, abolished" (161). The choice of verbs here bespeaks a definite hint of Wagnerian Götterdämmerung; the redemption of the world through art would be a highly equivocal achievement, resulting in the suffocation of life. But it is meant, of course, only ironically, since such redemption will never be accomplished.

The next section of the conversation is probably the most difficult for students to grasp, because it is so laconic. Following his flood of self-criticism, Tonio's peroration is a somewhat startling confession: "I love life" (161). This statement also benefits from elucidation by the instructor, because, as Tonio quickly and forcefully asserts, his love of life is not the Nietzschean admiration for the powerful or the extraordinary: "Do not think of Cesare Borgia or of any drunken philosophy that makes him its hero!" (161). Mann (who, in questioning the role and nature of the artist, was strongly influenced by Nietzsche) is referring here to Nietzsche's glorification of the "Übermensch," represented by the figure of Cesare Borgia, a ruthless and immoral despot, who did not shrink from murdering his own relatives. In Mann's notes for *Tonio Kröger* we find the following passage: "Not, as Nietzsche claims, Cesare Borgia represents 'life'! But type X, life in its seductive banality!" (Scherrer and Wysling 53). The last phrase recurs here in the story, as Tonio affirms his love of ordinary existence and his "longing for the bliss of the commonplace" (161).

At the conclusion of the conversation, Mann puts into the mouth of Lisaweta his own ironic judgment of Tonio Kröger and himself—and, as we read, we assume an identity between author and hero that is questioned elsewhere in this volume. Tonio, she asserts, is, and always will be, a bourgeois (163). But he is a bourgeois with a difference: he is one who has strayed onto the wrong path, he is "a bourgeois manqué" (164)—a phrase that in both its content and its form summarizes the entire content of the brief novel. Tonio's reaction to this statement is both significant and ironic. He says: "Thank you, Lisaweta Iwanowna; now I can go home with a good conscience. *I have been eliminated*" (164). In other words, by using the identical phrase that he used to describe his own artistic process, Tonio is declaring that Lisaweta has turned him into form. She has done to him precisely what he does to the raw material he exploits: she has expressed his heartfelt but tasteless admissions in the appropriate form ("a bourgeois manqué") and thereby "eliminated" him once and for all. The artist has been turned into art! A lively discussion usually results from the invitation to interpret this conclusion. Indeed, elsewhere in this volume it is interpreted quite differently.

If students are asked to analyze the structure of *Tonio Kröger*, they find that each of the nine "chapters" represents a station in Tonio Kröger's life. The conversation with Lisaweta delineates therefore not a conclusion but a transition: it has been merely one more stage in Tonio's development as a writer. Tonio's conversation with Lisaweta has helped him in two ways: first, it has allowed him to speak and unburden his mind of its troubling thoughts and emotions; and second, in hearing Lisaweta Iwanowna's categorization of him as a "bourgeois manqué," he is brought face-to-face with his authentic form. His return to Lübeck and the ensuing trip to Denmark further crystallize his thoughts and help him achieve a fruitful synthesis of the two halves of his being. In his final letter to Lisaweta, he has come to realize, as did Mann, that the conflict that has brought him at times closer to despair has the potential for becoming a perhaps inexhaustible source of inspiration for his art. It is this love of live that saves the artist from falling into the trap of sheer aestheticism: the constant tension between the formal demands of art and the emotional warmth of human experience provides both a stimulus for the artist to grapple with the problem again and again and a safeguard against becoming nothing more than an aesthetic formalist. The significance of this tension can be gauged from the fact that almost everything Mann wrote or planned to write between *The Budden-brooks* and *The Magic Mountain* deals with the same issue (Reed, *Uses of Tradition* 92). And even though this theme was later often transmuted, it dominated Mann's creative efforts for the rest of his life.

Death in Venice as Psychohistory

Edward Timms

Death in Venice, published in 1912, is likely to interest students of history and psychology as well as of literature. It is a story saturated with the atmosphere of a historical moment. The psychological dimension of Mann's account of the death of the writer Gustav von Aschenbach is so complex that students may tend to ignore the historical setting, established in the opening sentence: "On a spring afternoon in 19—, the year in which for months on end so grave a threat seemed to hang over the peace of Europe . . ." (195). The aim of this presentation is to fill in the blanks suggested by that enigmatic date and to suggest that *Death in Venice* may be read in terms of the psychohistory of Europe on the eve of World War I.

Mann leaves the precise date of the action ambiguous. But for contemporary readers it was obvious that *Death in Venice* must be set in the summer of 1911 (the year when the story was conceived). That was the year when Western Europe, which had enjoyed forty years of peace and prosperity, was convulsed by a series of political crises. On 1 July 1911, during a dispute between Germany and France over territorial claims in Morocco, the German gunship *Panther* was dispatched to Agadir. For several months there ensued a battle of nerves that seemed likely to result in a European war, until Germany finally backed down. This is the war scare to which Mann alludes in this first sentence, which sets the story in an invisible political framework. The action of *Death in Venice* begins early in May, and Aschenbach's death occurs at the height of summer, probably in mid-July—the month of the Morocco crisis.

How significant is the implied link between the artist's death and the "threat [that] seemed to hang over the peace of Europe"? Why does Mann in the first chapter specifically associate Aschenbach with "the collective European psyche" (198)? The answer is provided in chapter 2, which shows that Aschenbach is not an isolated outsider, like Tonio Kröger. He is an establishment figure, respected and indeed recently ennobled by the state. His works include a monumental study of Frederick the Great, the eighteenth-century Prussian king who set Germany on the path toward political domination in Europe. Students may be tempted to skip this second chapter, which interrupts the action in order to summarize Aschenbach's literary achievements. But the ideological perspective established here is crucial to the full significance of the story. Aschenbach's career is modeled on the Prussian principles exemplified by Frederick: the achievement of "fame" through "the constant harnessing of his energies" (200–01). The key concepts are "discipline" ("Zucht," 201) and "composure" ("Haltung," 203). Aschenbach's art is based on "the same constancy of will and tenacity of purpose" that enabled the Prussian king to conquer Silesia during the Seven Years' War (202).

Aschenbach's achievement represents the artistic refinement of a military ethos. Those key Prussian concepts "Zucht" and "Haltung" signify "military discipline" and "standing to attention," as well as self-control and composure. The author has meditated on "the bloody inferno of the Seven Years War sick bays" and his book on Frederick the Great includes a "dialogue between Voltaire and the king on the subject of war" (206). The figures of his fictional world embody a "new hero-type" based on the overcoming of inner weaknesses. But Mann's narrative suggests that this "heroism of weakness" has a more problematic aspect: "elegant self-control concealing from the world's eyes until the very last moment a state of inner disintegration" (202–03).

When a writer becomes as famous as Aschenbach (we are told), "there must be a hidden affinity, indeed a congruence, between the personal destiny of the author and the wider destiny of his generation" (202). Here again there are hints of political symbolism—of the idea that Aschenbach's dilemma represents self-destructive tendencies within European society. Students who take up this suggestion may find it hard to reconcile such a political reading of the story with its psychological theme: Aschenbach's infatuation with Tadzio, the beautiful Polish boy. The homosexuality of the artist seems remote from that heroic ethos that Aschenbach claims to derive from Frederick the Great.

Once again the context is crucial. Traditionally Frederick the Great was regarded as the embodiment of manly virtue. He was celebrated in these terms by Thomas Carlyle in his *History of Frederick the Great* (1865), a book that Mann admired. In a letter of 5 December 1905 to his brother Heinrich, however, he explains that he cannot share Carlyle's conception of heroism. Mann's own aim would be "to portray a hero in a human, *all too* human way, with skepticism, with *malice*, with psychological radicalism and nevertheless positively, lyrically, from my own experience" (*Thomas Mann–Heinrich Mann: Briefwechsel* 44). Mann never completed the full-scale study of Frederick the Great that he planned. He wrote *Death in Venice* instead, grafting his psychologically radical view of Frederick onto Aschenbach. For Mann, Frederick is great not because he was manly in the conventional sense but because he was able to overcome disturbing inner impulses, including homosexual tendencies. In a letter analyzing the theme of homosexuality in *Death in Venice*, written on 4 July 1920 to Carl Maria Weber, Mann includes Frederick in his list of great men who had been erotically attracted to other males (*Briefe* 1: 178).

Only by taking account of this context will students of *Death in Venice* be able to decode the references to Frederick the Great. The story associates the Prussian ethos with a suppression of emotional impulses, which renders this "new hero-type" extremely vulnerable. But for Mann's readers in 1912 there was a further reason why homosexuality should be identified with the German political elite. During the years from 1907 to 1909 a series of court cases in Berlin and Munich exposed homosexual practices in aristocratic circles. This sensational affair involved a close friend of Kaiser Wilhelm II, the diplomat Philipp von Eulenburg. And the journalist who conducted the campaign against this clique of homosexuals was a friend of Mann's named Maximilian Harden. Mann's letters to his brother Heinrich in 1908 show that he followed the Eulenburg case closely. Eulenburg, who denied all homosexual activity, was publicly disgraced when a youth with whom he had once had an affair was persuaded to testify against him. Only the collapse of Eulenburg's health saved him from being imprisoned for perjury. But the affair seriously undermined the prestige of the German political establishment.

A study of this context may help students recognize that *Death in Venice* has both a personal and a political dimension. Through the figure of Aschenbach the story obliquely exposes the hollowness of the Protestant ethos of the German ruling class—"elegant self-control concealing . . . inner disintegration." But Mann does not share Harden's simplistic view that homosexuality is a form of decadence. Aschenbach's feelings for Tadzio represent a precarious equilibrium between aesthetic delight and emotional self-abandon. This may be linked with the fact that Mann was indeed writing from his "own experience." Before his marriage, in 1905, to Katia Pringsheim, he had undergone an intense homoerotic relationship with a painter named Paul Ehrenberg. And while on holiday in Venice in 1911, he had encountered a Polish boy who inspired similar feelings.

The character of Aschenbach is thus a synthesis of personal, psychological, and political elements. He represents that tension between feelings and facades that was so typical of European society before World War I. But can any of the secondary characters be fitted into this kind of psychohistorical reading? What of that old man masquerading as a youth whom Aschenbach encounters in chapter 3? Students are likely to spot the ironic parallel between Aschenbach's revulsion at the behavior of this foolish old man and his own attempt to rejuvenate himself later in the story. But might not the setting of the encounter with the grotesque old man also be significant? Aschenbach's experiences unfold on the frontiers between Austria-Hungary and Italy. His journey from his home in Munich takes him first to an island in the Adriatic, where he feels depressed by the "petit-bourgeois Austrian hotel clientele" (207). Then he takes a motor launch to Pola.

At this point it may be useful to consult a map showing the political frontiers of Europe before World War I. Pola, a port near Trieste, was situated in an Italian-speaking province of the Austro-Hungarian Empire. Territorial disputes had resulted in wars between Austria and Italy in 1859 and again in 1866 (when Italy regained control of Venice). Pola was the spearhead of Austrian power in the Adriatic on the eve of the war. It is specifically identified in *Death in Venice* as a "naval base" ("Kriegshafen," literally "war harbor," 207). The young men who share Aschenbach's journey from Pola to Venice are Italian-speaking subjects of the Hapsburg Empire. Their political sympathies are indicated by the fact that when the boat anchors off the shores of Venice, they feel "patriotically attracted by the military sound of bugle calls" (210). They are evidently Italian irredentists who would like Pola to be liberated from Austrian rule and united with Italy.

The old man masquerading as a youth is a more ambiguous figure. He is not one of those who respond to the Italian bugle music, and both his age and his foppish yellow suit may incline the reader to identify him with Austria-Hungary (black and yellow were the Hapsburg colors). The Hapsburg Empire was a decrepit political system desperately trying to rejuvenate itself, to prove that it was the equal of resurgent young Italy. As the boat crosses from Austrian into Italian waters, the old man becomes grotesquely drunk and completely loses self-control. Psychologically Aschenbach's revulsion at this spectacle seems connected with his fear of old age. But there are hints of a more fundamental unease when, contemplating the old man in yellow, he feels "that the world was undergoing a dreamlike alienation, becoming increasingly deranged and bizarre" (209).

These political undertones are made more explicit by the cosmopolitan atmosphere of Aschenbach's hotel in Venice. The story here anticipates the technique Mann was later to use in *The Magic Mountain*, where the inmates of a sanatorium represent the conflict of nationalities in Europe. The hotel guests in *Death in Venice* also form a cross-section of different nationalities: "Americans, many-membered Russian families, English ladies, German children with French nurses." Mann adds the observation that "the Slav component seemed to predominate" (216). Even this seemingly innocent observation acquires ideological undertones, if we recall that German political ambitions on the eve of World War I were overshadowed by fear of the Slavs, especially of the growing military power of Tsarist Russia.

Mann's own view of Russia was not shaped primarily by political considerations. But he too tended to portray the Slavs in terms of an East-West opposition: the profound irrationality of the East (exemplified by Dostoevsky) threatening the shallow enlightenment of the West (represented by Voltaire). The fact that Aschenbach becomes infatuated with a Polish youth fits the pattern of psychohistory. Germanic self-control succumbs to the lure of Slavonic sensuousness. These forces of irrationality are contrasted with Anglo-Saxon pragmatism, embodied by the English travel agent whom Aschenbach consults when he wants to discover the truth about Venice. British common sense offers an antidote to the self-destructive German delusion.

Venice thus symbolizes the precariousness of European civilization, while the sea contains the threat of some disruptive force, dimly apprehended, but not yet fully understood. At first Aschenbach is delighted to contemplate "the scene on the beach, the spectacle of civilization taking its carefree sensuous ease at the brink of the element" (220). But as he succumbs to his infatuation for Tadzio, so he comes to feel that the whole structure of civilized existence is threatened by what he sees in his final dream as a "delirium of annihilation" (257).

What is the force that brings death to Venice? The simple answer is an epidemic of cholera. But Mann's fundamental concern is with a sickness of a very different kind—hypocrisy and self-delusion. This theme is announced in chapter 2, where Aschenbach's mature achievements are linked with the decision to "repudiate knowledge" (204). Later, in a passage of heightened perception, Aschenbach concedes that "the magisterial poise of our style is a lie" (261). His art, like his conception of heroism, is based on a formal control that is morally ambivalent, involving the denial of more disturbing truths. It is not out of ignorance that Aschenbach exposes himself to the risk of cholera. His infatuation with Tadzio leads him to disregard the warning signs, the strange odors that he unconsciously associates with "squalor and wounds" (242).

This is not simply an individual aberration. The dishonesty of Mann's hero is linked with that of his environment: the hotel management, which tries to hush up rumors of an epidemic; the Italian authorities who issue official denials; and the newspapers that conspire to suppress the truth. *Death in Venice* portrays a whole social system inhibited from facing dangerous truths by polite convention and "cupidity" (245). It is symbolically appropriate that the first foreign visitor to die from the epidemic is an Austrian (253).

As Aschenbach himself succumbs to delusion and disease, the vulnerability of "the European psyche" is revealed. The last sentence of the story records that "the world was respectfully shocked to receive the news of his death" (263). But the reader has been shown the void behind the facade. And students may be asked to ponder the links between these final words and the opening sentence of *Death in Venice*, which synchronizes the tragedy of Aschenbach with that threat to "the peace of Europe." War, disease, and sexuality are conceived as atavistic forces, threatening to destroy a civilization governed by repression and the denial of knowledge.

These wider implications will scarcely be visible if we confine ourselves to a text-immanent approach. For *Death in Venice* is both a psychological study and a work of the historical imagination. At the time of writing, Mann may himself have been unaware of the full resonance of his story. His primary aim was certainly to explore the psychology of the artist; he was inspired partly by the death of Gustav Mahler, partly by an incident in the life of Goethe. It is not Goethe, however, but Frederick the Great whose ethos infuses the story, giving it inescapable political undertones. And in *Reflections of a Nonpolitical Man*, published in 1918, Mann acknowledges that *Death in Venice* is "located in a specific period, located in its tension of the will and its morbidity immediately before the war." The story, he adds, contains "sensitively seismographic elements" (152–53; my translation). In other words, *Death in Venice* can be read as psychohistory.

Plato and Nietzsche in *Death in Venice*

Susan von Rohr Scaff

Death in Venice is a relatively difficult text for students, and the task of engaging them in Mann's sophisticated themes can be daunting. One of the most challenging facets of the story is the web of classical allusions that culminates in Gustav Aschenbach's "Platonic" reveries on love. Although the references to Greek myth and philosophy may at first seem merely erudite to young readers, the ancient lore contributes to an aspect of the story that generally fascinates them: Aschenbach's twisted psychology. It is while the Apollonian and Dionysian elements of his psyche do battle that Aschenbach is driven to the most desperate rationalization of his passion for Tadzio, his invocation of Platonic beauty to dignify his homoerotic lust. The "Platonic" passages, along with the Dionysian nightmare that marks the depth of Aschenbach's demise, bring the psychological dynamic of the story to a climax. I have found it effective in teaching *Death in Venice*, therefore, to emphasize the human significance of Mann's classical allusions. Stressing the centrality of Platonic thought in the short novel and locating this philosophical element within the story's mythic frame facilitates my students' understanding of Mann's principal theme of psychological dissolution.

The opening passages of *Death in Venice* allow the teacher to ask the class simply to consider the protagonist's state of mind, evidenced vividly in the spontaneous "vision" of a faraway land in paragraph 6. This sets up the discussion in terms that are relatively familiar to American readers and therefore disarming. The class responds well to the categories of discipline, orderliness, stolidity, and repression, all readily discerned in the first five paragraphs, and relates these without difficulty to the opposing ideas of, and the craving for, corruption, irrationality, voluptuousness, and even terror (the crouching tiger [cf. Parkes]), betrayed in the rank and grotesque imagery of Aschenbach's "intensely passionate" swampland "seizure" (197). Once students feel comfortable with elucidating the polarities of Aschenbach's character, I introduce the (loosely) analogous Nietzschean categories of the Apollonian and the Dionysian, which are central in the classical orientation of *Death in Venice*.

Often several class members can recount the Apollo and Dionysus myths. With these before them, the students connect the regularity of the sun's course with Aschenbach's daily round in Munich, and the sensual yearning and terror of his fantasy with Dionysian ecstasy and debauch. I then talk about Nietzsche's philosophical appropriation of the myths, the Apollonian-Dionysian dichotomy that influenced Mann. Referring to *The Birth of Tragedy*, I explain the philosopher's association of Apollo with clarity, form, order, cognition, (scientific) knowledge, and, most important, individuation, or the sense of self. On the other side, I discuss Dionysian delirium: the ecstatic self-dissolution that is at once the wild joy of abandon and the deep suffering that accompanies the devastation of individual identity. For emphasis I describe the barbaric rites of Dionysus (the frenzied dancing, mob fury, and mutilation of the deity), which are the inspiration for Nietzschean epiphany. To demonstrate the power of the Dionysian for Aschenbach, I point again to his hallucination and sometimes even read in advance from his orgiastic dream near the end of the story (255–57).

The Nietzschean antithesis forms the basis of thoughtful classroom interpretations of Aschenbach's struggles to resist sensual temptation and maintain the discipline that preserves his civilized identity. In Mann's thought, a human being must participate in both the Apollonian and the Dionysian modes to resist rigidification, on the one hand, and disintegration (moral and physical), on the other. Having already considered the protagonist's mental state, the class is prepared to understand the psyche's need for balance as it is illustrated, for example, in Aschenbach's artworks. In his fiction as in his life, the artist has suppressed the life-giving forces that reinvigorate the psyche and inspire aesthetic creativity. Reduced to an arid regularity reflected in the symmetrical, or Apollonian, form of his art, he now hazards a destructive outbreak of Dionysian life forces; for "moral resoluteness," when simplified and made inflexible, risks "a resurgence of energies that are evil, forbidden, morally impossible" (204–05). He has pressed himself to the outer limits of Apollonian mastery and may fall victim to deep instincts beyond his control.

With Aschenbach's psychological debility in mind, I lead the class through the temptation scenes. We discuss the "tempter" figures—the red-haired stranger, the boatman, the grotesque old fop, and the gondolier—each of whom beckons the artist in some way to self-surrender; the sea, which lures him to self-forgetful oblivion; and the spreading plague, which tantalizes him with bodily dissolution. Because I am preparing the group to understand the significance of the Platonic form of beauty for Aschenbach's ultimate defense of himself, I stress the yearning for "formlessness" visible particularly in the pervasive sea imagery. I emphasize, for example, the seductiveness of the sea as a respite from the complexity of life's formalized tasks, the deep longing the waters inspire for "the unarticulated and immeasurable, for eternity, for nothingness" (221). I ask the class to consider the ocean's allure in connection with the fact that Aschenbach has lived like a closed fist; for even as a boy he put the duty to achieve first, ignoring the blandishments of "youth's idleness, its carefree negligent ways" (201). As we take up the four "seducers" to the psychic and mythic underworld—the realm of "death" in Venice—I suggest that Aschenbach's fist has now gone slack. The guiding principle behind the analyses of all the enticements is the artist's present susceptibility to relinquishing the "forms" of civilized life and, along with them, his mental and corporeal integrity.

Thinking about Aschenbach's psychological vulnerability prepares the class for the protagonist's self-justification in terms of Platonic love (234–35, 260–61). When Aschenbach speaks of Tadzio as an image of spiritual beauty and the very perfection of form, he is calling on Plato's theory of forms. When he paints the picture of an old man and a youth absorbed in conversation outside the Athenian wall, moreover, he invokes Socrates's ennobling encounter with Phaedrus and, in his association of love and beauty, Socrates's discourses on love in the *Phaedrus* and the *Symposium* (cf. Bridges, "Problem"; Kelley). At the lower-division level most students will not be familiar with the Greek texts, and a brief lecture on the rudiments of Platonism is usually necessary, preferably with contributions from those class members who have studied ancient thought in a humanities or Western philosophy course. Because they have already observed the strains on Aschenbach's psyche, however, and recognize his deep need to vindicate himself, students can approach the rhetoric of love and beauty with an appreciation for the self-exculpating function of Platonic ideas for Aschenbach. It is to protect his dignity and legitimize his ignoble behavior that Aschenbach counters his improper yearning to abandon conventional forms with the adulation of formal beauty.

The most telling Platonic allusions are in fact to Tadzio as the very image of loveliness. I ask the class, therefore, to think first about Aschenbach's calling the Polish boy "Beauty itself" and "Form as the thought of God," the "one and pure perfection" dwelling "in the spirit" and imaged in a human body for our devotion (234). I explain that Aschenbach is proclaiming the godlike youth a medium of Platonic beauty. For Plato everything has a true "form," or idea, and all earthly objects and beliefs are imperfect reflections of an eternal reality. The object of life is, ideally, to achieve rational perception of the immutable ideas in incremental recollections of an original absolute knowledge buried deep within the mind. The individual progresses through the mistaken belief that the apparent is real, to a recognition that true form stands behind the imperfect worldly image, to a perception of abstract or mathematical shapes, and finally (in rare cases and after much cognitive effort) to full apprehension of the fundamental ideas such as beauty, justice, and goodness. In these Platonic terms Aschenbach can claim Tadzio as an object of worship by declaring that the boy's image triggers innate memories of divine beauty. By professing his perception of essential loveliness through Tadzio, in other words, Aschenbach elevates himself to one of the higher stages of Platonic comprehension.

The enormity of Aschenbach's behavior toward Tadzio in itself renders the artist's learned rationalizations suspect. Despite his philosophizing, Aschenbach does not in practice distinguish spiritual beauty from its sensuous counterpart. Aschenbach wants to make Plato's argument that the soul in love is nobly inspired by the beloved's comeliness: "only with the help of a bodily form is the soul then still able to exalt itself to a higher vision" (234). He is alluding here to Socrates's speech in the *Symposium* on the "ladder" of love (sections 201d–212c) and in the *Phaedrus* on the nobility of love (244b–257b). The soul in love is charmed at first by the beauties of the body; but while the lover experiences physical enchantment, he immediately raises himself above that lowly attraction, appropriating sensual desire to rational apprehension of higher truths. In the *Symposium* he comes in stages to perceive the superiority of the beauty of the soul and, ultimately, to discern the very form of beauty (210b–211c). In the *Phaedrus* he sprouts wings as his beloved recalls him to perfect beauty, and he soars upward toward eternal being (249e). Aschenbach's passion, however, does not inspire such ascent. Students will see immediately that Aschenbach, unlike these true Platonic lovers, abandons the life of intellectual mastery, succumbing instead to Dionysian lust. As he trails Tadzio through the streets, his behavior is lascivious and despicable, not elevating and worthy.

Close reading of the Platonic passages reveals, moreover, that Aschenbach cunningly misrepresents Plato's text to justify his salaciousness. Aschenbach envisions Socrates telling Phaedrus that beauty is the only form "visible" to us—that is, accessible to the senses. What would happen, he asks, if reason, virtue, and truth were to make themselves manifest "sensuously"? We would perish just as Semele did when Zeus appeared to her in his overwhelming glory. Direct perception of beauty is endurable, however, because beauty alone is an experience of the senses. The lover smitten by beauty thus enjoys both divine perception and sensual pleasure (235). Aschenbach, however, is subtly revising Plato's thought here. In the *Phaedrus* Socrates does single out beauty as the only form manifest to the senses. But he quickly adds that the lover consumed by lust is too distracted to revere the revealed form (250d–e). The true lover will allow the better elements of his mind to lead him, in beauty's presence, to a life of ordered philosophical contemplation with his beloved. While the liberated pair will know the joys of lovemaking, their exalted life will exclude wanton desire (256b). Aschenbach is as duplicitous in calling Socrates a "sly wooer" as he is in having him make the non-Platonic claim that the lover "is more divine than the beloved" in whom beauty is housed (235). Aschenbach is distorting the Socrates of the *Phaedrus* to rationalize his own "sly" and anything-but-divine courtship.

By the end of the short novel, Aschenbach can barely keep up his pretense of Platonic love. Imagining himself one last time in the person of Socrates wooing Phaedrus, he puts words in Socrates's mouth that would shock Plato. Aschenbach, in fact, now shamelessly confounds formal beauty and Dionysian formlessness, an impossible philosophical combination, especially in view of Nietzsche's explicit refutation of Socratic thinking in *The Birth of Tragedy*. Invoking both Platonic and Nietzschean notions of desire nonetheless, Aschenbach characterizes the artist as one who treads the path toward beauty yet cannot advance without the company of Eros. The artist desires perfected spirit and at the same time lusts after the exalted yet debased "knowledge" of the Dionysian abyss. Not surprisingly, Aschenbach cannot maintain this unnatural alliance of form and degeneration. Acceding to the incompatibility of Platonic and Nietzschean ideas, he desperately claims the artist's noble determination to reject abysmal knowledge in order to pursue "Beauty alone." Aschenbach, however, must relinquish even this last self-defense. The artist, he admits, will "necessarily go astray." In fact, the artist can neither extol beauty and lust together nor depart the formless abyss in pursuit of pure form. By his very nature he will abandon beauty to sink, as Aschenbach has, into "dissolute emotional" adventures, the "terrible criminal emotions" of "self-debauchery" (261).

Having considered Aschenbach's descent to degeneracy through Platonic and Nietzschean categories, the class is equipped to understand the artist's death in sophisticated psychological and philosophical terms. Students will readily see in Tadzio's motion toward the sea the culminating moment in the artist's temptation to dissolution (263). Reflecting on the psychological dynamic of Aschenbach's assent to the gesture, they will attribute the artist's end to a fatal resurgence of long-repressed desires for love and life, dissolution and death, that "drowns" the civilized or Apollonian self in a Dionysian sea. Having considered Aschenbach's internal debate between the wisdoms of Plato and of Nietzsche, moreover, they will identify the artist's surrender at the philosophical level as a repudiation of form and a capitulation to the Dionysian void. They will probably be inclined, in addition, when offering both interpretations, to emphasize the moral dimension of Aschenbach's surrender. Aschenbach, as he admitted himself, has succumbed to "terrible criminal emotions," and students are usually quick to propose that he now suffers the rightful "punishment" of death.

The group may be reluctant, though, to consider the possibility (however cryptically Mann broaches it) that Aschenbach meets in death a symbolic "resurrection." The ambiguity of Mann's ending, I point out, shifts attention away from the moral justice of Aschenbach's death and may raise the story to a new level, that of mythic rebirth. Once the students are reminded of Mann's persistent association of Aschenbach with Dionysus and are asked to recall the myth's theme of dismemberment and resurrection, they become more receptive to the notion of archetypal renewal. I point to the words Mann chooses to describe Tadzio's gesticulation. The boy motions "outward, hovering ahead and onward, into an immensity rich with unutterable expectation" (263). This diction conveys the enormity and fear yet also the auspicious promise present in the somewhat darker endings of *The Magic Mountain* and *Doctor Faustus*. Only a rare student will have read these books, but mentioning the later works enables the class to read *Death in Venice* as one of Mann's several presentations in fiction of the uncertain fate of the modern age. Like Hans Castorp and Adrian

Leverkühn, Aschenbach epitomizes for Mann the fallibilities and probable fate of the contemporary world. But also like them he may take his place within an overarching "mythic" pattern of history that experiences self-dissolution and tragic death, Mann would like to believe, as the precursor of new times.

Visconti's Cinematic Version of *Death in Venice*

John Francis Fetzer

Ingmar Bergman makes an incisive observation about cinematic adaptations of literary masterworks: "Film has nothing to do with literature; the character and substance of the two art forms are usually in conflict" (xvii). Luchino Visconti's *Morte a Venezia* of 1971, based on Thomas Mann's short novel of 1912, has found a small coterie of apologists who feel that the film remains faithful to the spirit of the author's work while creating a unique cinematic idiom in its own right. Most critical voices, however, decry the infidelity with which the Italian director treats the tightly knit structure of the original prose text. Along with transforming the protagonist, Gustav von Aschenbach, from a successful, classically disciplined writer into a controversial, avant-garde composer modeled closely on Gustav Mahler (a case of "cinematic license" that permits Visconti to interpolate elements from Mann's *Doctor Faustus* novel of 1947, such as the brothel scene with the prostitute Hetæra Esmeralda), the director finds it necessary to eliminate other sections completely. These include the Munich background, with the appearance of the mysterious stranger, and the vision of the primeval jungle as well as its later counterpart, the Dionysian dream sequence, which marks the surrender of the Apollonian master of artistic control to the forces of chaos. In view of the deletion of such key scenes, which Mann enthusiasts feel are indispensable, and of the distortion of other essential fictional premises, is there any merit in using this film for classroom instruction in conjunction with the text?

The undeniable power of Visconti's visual imagery evokes a sense of Venice's seductive atmosphere and provides tangible actualizations of such provocative figures as the young-old dandy on board the steamer, the brash Venetian gondolier, and the impertinent street singer, whose ensemble performs the haunting ditty with the bloodcurdling laugh refrain. There are, however, two seminal scenes in the original text with a common frame of reference that the cinematic rendition retains virtually intact. These vignettes capture a quintessential aspect of the short novel and, moreover, enhance its verbal message through the media of sight and sound, a kind of visual and aural reinforcement of the written text. The parallel scenes embody, in objective-correlative fashion, what could be termed the thematic thrust of the novel, and they involve "threshold situations."

The first of these key moments occurs when Aschenbach, having finally ensconced himself in his Lido residence, sits awaiting dinner in the plush lobby of the hotel, while an orchestra plays entertaining, light melodies in the background. At this point Aschenbach first catches sight of the beautiful Polish lad Tadzio; as the boy and his all-female entourage move toward the dining room, we read: "For some reason or other he [Tadzio] turned round before crossing the *threshold*, and as there was now no one else in the hall, his strangely twilight-gray eyes met those of Aschenbach, who with his paper in his lap, lost in contemplation, had been watching the group leave" (218). The second passage is found near the close of the work, when Aschenbach, now the broken artist and a dying man slumped in his beach chair on shore, watches his idol, with the wide expanse of the Adriatic at his back, stride out into the water:

> Once more he [Tadzio] stopped to survey the scene. And suddenly, as if prompted by a memory, by an impulse, he turned at the waist, one hand on his hip, with an enchanting twist of the body, and looked back over his shoulder at the beach. There the watcher sat, as he had sat once before when those twilight-gray eyes, looking back at him then from that other *threshold*, had for the first time met his.
>   (263; emphasis added in both passages)

In their verbal and visual formats these two scenes serve as frames, since they come at the beginning and the end of Aschenbach's fateful association with Tadzio, the embodiment of beauty for the writer. In addition, they constitute "threshold" situations in both the literal and metaphoric senses of that term, as the following analysis demonstrates (see also Cook).

The threshold, like windows, porticos, and gateways, marks the line of demarcation or the transition point between two otherwise disparate realms (the rooms of a house) or regions (inside and outside worlds) that can be regarded as either independent or interdependent. The threshold itself consists of a kind of limbo territory or liminal terrain, a frontier between entities that ultimately stand in some sort of reciprocal or dialectical relationship with each other. Standing on the threshold, consequently, implies a state of "betweenness"; a sense of hovering or a straddling stance prevails. Joseph Campbell, in his study *The Hero with a Thousand Faces*, has shown that the act of crossing one of life's thresholds occupies a key position in tribal initiation rites, in religious cults, in mythic and popular lore (one thinks of the Lares and Penates, Roman guardians of the domestic threshold). Therefore, it is reasonable to postulate that a meticulous crafter of prose fiction such as Mann would ascribe to two scenes involving literal and figurative thresholds an importance above and beyond mere scenic decor or descriptive repetition for its own sake. This is evident from the second passage, in which the author almost challenges his reader to recall the earlier scene by such phrases as "had sat once before," "that other threshold," and "for the first time." Even the recapitulation of the "twilight-gray eyes" of the lad incorporates threshold components from both the temporal sphere and the color spectrum. "Twilight" signifies the transitional time between daytime and darkness (the word itself implies "two types of light"), while the gray zone of the color palette results from the fusion of all hues (white) and the absence of any color whatsoever (black).

Even though a "threshold" potential may be established on several levels for these two scenes, the key question that one should raise with students is the following: What application does this have to Mann's short novel per se? The answer, at least with regard to the first scenic portrayal, seems to lie in the precarious duality confronting the writer Aschenbach. He finds himself poised on the frontier (or perhaps "precipice" would be a more appropriate term) between his Apollonian past and his Dionysian future; years of devotion to creative order, self-imposed discipline, and clarity of design are soon to be superseded by euphoric moments of disarray, licentiousness, and confusion. A similar condition might be charted for all of Europe itself at the time of the work's creation, for the continent hovered on the brink of a cataclysmic war, which would shake the old order to its foundations and lead to a fundamental restructuring of political and social life. Further, there already had been sweeping alterations in the concepts of the physical universe (Einstein's relativity theory) as well as in aesthetic theories and techniques (abstract art, atonal music).

The second scene, however, constitutes a point of intersection marking the transition from life to death (with the beach area serving as a frontier between confines of the land and the unbounded expanse of the sea). In both instances, one can draw the students' attention to the fact that Aschenbach finds himself wedged between dual potentialities. To this extent the visual threshold serves as an objective correlative for his spiritual quandary. Insofar as it constitutes a "twilight zone" between seemingly irreconcilable absolutes (the Apollonian and the Dionysian, life and death, the finite and the infinite), the threshold reflects the ambivalent nature of Aschenbach's state of "betweenness." Some philological asides of general interest might be pertinent for class discussion at this point. The word *ambivalent* implies validity on both sides and projects a sense of the coexistence of opposite or conflicting states. The term thus conveys doubt regarding either which of the paths to follow or how best to mediate the one faction by the force of the other. The English word *doubt* has its roots in *duo habere*, which also entails "twoness," or duality; in German the double aspect of the term can be seen in its stem *Zwei-fel*. Just as the beautiful boy served, at the outset, as the force that unleashed in the Apollonian artist the suppressed Dionysian side of his being (see Scaff's essay in this volume), so does Tadzio, as "psychogogos," or guide of the soul, function at the close as an intermediary or even mediator between life and death. It is the ultimate reciprocity of these ostensibly dichotomous realms that Mann seems to be underscoring in the repeated threshold images.

The word *underscore* in the previous paragraph brings to mind the musical underpinning that Visconti deploys to emphasize this sense of thresholdism. Since the director was apparently captivated by Mahler, it is not surprising to find that the composer's music in general, and the Adagietto from his Fifth Symphony in particular, dominate the musical substructure of the film. The Adagietto, which serves here as a kind of twentieth-century counterpart to Wagner's "Liebestod," is intoned at the beginning while the film's credits are still being shown. Indeed, it appears at key junctures throughout and then re-sounds at the close, acoustically uniting the whole. Aside from Visconti's personal fetish for Mahler, this movement embodies a musical coefficient to the "threshold" image of the verbal and visual spheres that may have induced the director—if only subconsciously—to make this selection.

There is another significant aspect to be discussed, and it does not mandate on the part of the instructor or student a total comprehension of music. Indeed, Leonard Bernstein, in his Harvard lecture series of 1971, subsequently published as *The Unanswered Question*, includes a chapter entitled "The Delights and Dangers of Ambiguity" in which the composer-conductor-musicologist defines his basic term *ambiguity* as something "capable of being understood in two possible senses" (195). Bernstein illustrates this premise with reference to the Adagietto from Mahler's Fifth, which, he claims, has had the world swooning ever since Visconti's film, because the composer, in his treatment of both tempo and tonality, hovers tantalizingly between viable alternatives, indicative in each case of dual resolution. For instance, the tonic triad of F major is initially suggested, but since the fundamental note and tonic root of this chord, F, is not actually sounded, a second possibility, A minor, is latent; by delaying a definitive resolution to this issue, the composer entices the listener into an aural limbo between potential resolutions. Could one, then, not argue that the musical ambiguity thus created corresponds to the Apollonian-Dionysian dichotomy latent in Aschenbach's nature and activated when he exchanges glances with Tadzio as the boy stands on the threshold in the hotel lobby? Their relationship culminates in the liminal life-death dialectic when the writer observes the statuesque lad for the final time wading into the water, between land and sea, silhouetted by the sun (Apollo) but beckoning the twilight of life (Dionysus) as Mahler's Adagietto echoes the scene with a striking enharmonic ambiguity.

Yet one apparent discrepancy disturbs the neat symmetry of this emerging visual-aural pattern: in the first of the two threshold scenes, silence rather than sound accompanies the meaningful exchange of glances between the man of letters and his idol incarnate. Before this moment, however, the salon orchestra had been performing light waltz tunes from Lehar's operetta *The Merry Widow*. Certainly it would have been inappropriate for such shallow music to accompany the decisive encounter of hearts and minds, even though one might argue for a kind of frivolous *coincidentia oppositorum* quality of the piece, involving both life ("merry") and death ("widow"). Nevertheless, silence, which may be said to occupy a place on the sound spectrum somewhere between music that is trivial (Lehar) and that which seems transcendental (Mahler), does provide a suitable acoustical ambience for this decisive moment. Silence constitutes the line of demarcation between the earlier inconsequential background music and music of consequence that moves ever more prominently into the foreground.

But even if the ambivalent aural component is absent at this initial meeting, the symbolic threshold quality of the situation is still undergirded by two pictorial facets of the portrayal, both of which have roots in the Romantic tradition. As a peripheral note—if the level of the class is suitable—a comment on Mann's relationship to Romanticism would be in order here (Eichner's work "Thomas Mann und die deutsche Romantik" is still quite useful). With regard to the two visual aspects of the film, the first involves the lush, overly large blue vases that form part of the lobby decor; the second is the pictorial juxtaposition of the principal figures, with Aschenbach from rear view facing Tadzio in frontal perspective. The gaudy azure hue of the vases is most striking, almost shocking, and it serves as a prefiguration of the bright blue skies that later displace the leaden, overcast horizon in Venice. This occurs following Aschenbach's halfhearted attempt to flee both the city and Tadzio because of the threat they might pose to his well-being. In this context the instructor might recall the blue flower of Romanticism, the blue-eyed beloveds or the azure distances that populate the pages of Romantic writers. It can be argued that, according to a color theory promulgated by Goethe and still in vogue around 1800, blue originated at the tangential intersection of white (light, day) and black (darkness, night)—in other words, at a key threshold point in the color spectrum. Likewise, the contrast of frontal prospect and rear-view perspective is an arch-Romantic iconographic device utilized extensively by such painters as Caspar David Friedrich. It becomes the virtual hallmark of his entire oeuvre; paintings such as *Monk by the Sea* (1808–09), the *Chalk Cliffs of Rügen* (1818), and *The Stages of Life* (1834), all readily available as slides or in book-illustration format, underscore this point. Friedrich's predilection for such *Rückenbilder* should be regarded as another modality of thresholdism, for the impression such a vantage point imparts to the viewer is that of a mediating agent, serving as an intercessor between diverse realms—near and far, land and sea, heights and depths, and, metaphorically speaking, the finite and the infinite.

A similar sense of the interdependence of ostensibly independent spheres arises from the numerous Janus-like juxtapositions in Visconti's camera technique. At least one such frontal and rear-view confrontation, involving a variation in the musical background as well as a much-debated literary interpolation on the part of Visconti, deserves mention. This scene occurs when Aschenbach happens to stroll into the lobby of the hotel and finds Tadzio sitting at the piano, playing the theme of Beethoven's familiar "Für Elise." Once again, the Janus-faced device is invoked as the boy turns around to look at his admirer while continuing the melody. Soon afterward we have a flashback to a bordello, where a Hetæra Esmeralda–like figure is heard playing "Für Elise" on a slightly out-of-tune instrument. She is depicted peering around the upright piano at her client (Aschenbach), who stands with his back to us while poised on the threshold of the establishment. Aside from the visual element involved here, linking homosexual and heterosexual eroticism through a common music theme, there is an aural ambivalence at play, for Beethoven's composition moves enharmonically between the keys of A minor and C major. Disparate tonal messages are transmitted by virtue of musical interplay with dual-directional potential in a composition, which is certainly not as subtle as Mahler's Adagietto but nevertheless indicative of the deep-seated ambivalence of Aschenbach's relationship to both the lad and the lady. Tadzio embodies the beauty of form, which Aschenbach, during his Apollonian years, had adored in the abstract and emulated in his "classical" works; now, however, his Dionysian infatuation with the purely physical manifestation of that beauty in a specific, alluring object holds only destruction for the creative artist, leading to his physical and spiritual demise. The paradox that the same object can function as a source of aesthetic inspiration and psychic or physical disintegration also comes to the fore in *Doctor Faustus* in the object of desire, Hetæra Esmeralda. The composer Adrian Leverkühn incorporates the prostitute into the thematic and harmonic texture of his music in a refrain consistently associated with her: "O dear girl, how evil thou art." The oxymoron embodied in this "dear-evil" figure indicates that Hetæra may cause "evil" (the physical demise of the artist) by infecting him with syphilis; yet she is also the ultimate source of his radically innovative musical idiom, through the alterations of the brain set in motion by the venereal affliction, thus making possible creativity of a new, modern stamp.

The preceding brief discussion has focused on two scenes that occur in both Mann's short novel and Visconti's film adaptation of that work. In comparing the fictional presentation with the cinematic re-presentation of these vignettes, instructors can highlight the scenes, threshold implications and the play and interplay of the verbal medium in literature, the visual dimension in the "moving picture," and the aural component in the form of music as background and foreground. Instructors can show that the common denominator is a persistent ambivalence or ambiguity resulting from the ubiquitous element of "twoness" involved. The roots of this duality can be traced to the period of Romanticism of around 1800. Like all ages of transition in which the old is "no more" and the new is "not yet," the Romanticists were aware of momentous changes on the horizon on the political, social, and aesthetic levels. They realized that they occupied an intermediary and, they hoped, mediating position. It is significant that the turn of the twentieth century saw a neo-Romantic revival that once again found ramifications in the political, social, and aesthetic spheres. Today, as we approach the year 2000 and the threshold of yet another "brave new world," we would do well to alert our students to those "delights and dangers of ambiguity" that Bernstein postulated for the dual message of music (194).

When reading Mann's short novel and viewing Visconti's film in tandem with Mahler's music, we are actually coping with a tripartite thresholdism appropriate to our age of ambiguity. This triple-layered alliance of ambivalence might be applied to the context of continuity amid change, of future prospects tempered by a retrospective glance at the past, of Apollonian form in the face of Dionysian formlessness, of life forces conditioned by an awareness of forces terminating life, and of a host of other dialectical polarities. From whichever vantage point the classroom discussion proceeds, we would teach an appreciation of the delights and, perhaps, an awareness of the dangers of that fragile, fascinating, all too human condition of "betweenness" to which we have fallen heir. But such a heritage is not without merit: as the American writer Mabel Dodge Luhan noted, "[W]e are just at the Threshold and nothing is ever so wonderful as the Threshold of things" (213).

CONTRIBUTORS AND SURVEY PARTICIPANTS

The following scholars and teachers generously agreed to participate in the survey of approaches to teaching Mann's short fiction that preceded preparation of this volume. Without their invaluable assistance, support, and suggestions, the volume would have remained incomplete.

Karen R. Achberger
Saint Olaf College

Dieter W. Adolphs
Michigan Technological
University

Leonard Ashley
Brooklyn College, City University of
New York

Michael Bachem
Miami University

Thomas I. Bacon
Texas Tech University

James R. Baker
San Diego State University

Dagmar Barnouw
University of Southern California

Thomas F. Barry
University of Southern California

Lawrence Bechtel
Virginia Polytechnic Institute and
State University

Jeffrey B. Berlin
Philadelphia College of Textiles and
Science

Arnd Bohm
Carleton University

George Bridges
University of Idaho

Joseph L. Brockington
Kalamazoo College

Elaine Brown
New York Institute of Technology

Steven R. Cerf
Bowdoin College

Jane S. Chew
Furman University

Edson Chick
Williams College

Christopher R. Clason
Duquesne University

Fritz G. Cohen
Purdue University

Adrian Del Caro
University of Colorado, Boulder

Manfred Dierks
Universität Oldenburg

Ulrich Dittmann
Ludwig-Maximilians-Universität,
München

David Dollenmayer
Worcester Polytechnic Institute

Christopher Dolmetsch
Marshall University

Eric Downing
Harvard University

Beverley Driver Eddy
Dickinson College

John Francis Fetzer
University of California, Davis

Kurt Fickert
Wittenberg University

Richard C. Figge
College of Wooster

Bruce E. Fleming
U.S. Naval Academy

Erich Frey
Occidental College

Ralf Frodermann
Braunschweig

Michael Gilbert
Wake Forest University

Gerald Gillespie
Stanford University

Ingeborg Glier
Yale University

Jutta Goheen
Carleton University

Heribert Gorzawski
Otto-Pankok-Schule, Mülheim-Ruhr

John L. Grigsby
Mississippi Valley State University

Christian W. Hallstein
Carnegie Mellon University

Volkmar Hansen
Heinrich-Heine-Universität,
Düsseldorf

James Hardin
University of South Carolina

Charles H. Helmetag
Villanova University

Hildburg Herbst
Rutgers University, New Brunswick

Peter Hertz-Ohmes
State University of New York,
Oswego

Roger Hillman
Australian National University,
Canberra

Sigfrid Hoefert
University of Waterloo

Werner Hoffmeister
Dartmouth College

Jean Jofen
Baruch College, City University of
New York

Ilsedore B. Jonas
Carnegie Mellon University

Klaus W. Jonas
University of Pittsburgh

Ernst Keller
Monash University

Christian B. Kulczytzky
Philadelphia College of Textiles and
Science

Alice Kuzniar
University of North Carolina,
Chapel Hill

Edward T. Larkin
University of New Hampshire

Richard H. Lawson
University of North Carolina,
Chapel Hill

Herbert Lehnert
University of California, Irvine

Esther H. Lesér
University of North Dakota

Hans-Ulrich Lindken
Heinrich-Heine-Universität,
Düsseldorf

David Luke
Oxford University

Robert K. Martin
Concordia University, Loyola
Campus

Harry Matter
Berlin

Regula A. Meier
Old Dominion University

Reed B. Merrill
Western Washington University

Joseph Mileck
University of California, Berkeley

Thomas R. Nadar
Auburn University

James Northcote-Bade
University of Auckland

Manfred Poitzsch
University of Wisconsin, Eau Claire

Edith Potter
Scripps College

Terrence James Reed
Oxford University

Rolf Günter Renner
Albert-Ludwigs-Universität, Freiburg

Ulrike S. Rettig
Wellesley College

Naomi Ritter
University of Missouri

Judith Ryan
Harvard University

Gert Sautermeister
Universität Bremen

Susan von Rohr Scaff
University of Arizona

Wendelin Schmidt-Dengler
Universität Wien

Rainer Schönhaar
Universität Stuttgart

David Scrase
University of Vermont

Roderick Stackelberg
Gonzaga University

Guy Stern
Wayne State University

Martin Swales
University College, London

Alan J. Swensen
Colgate University

Rodney Symington
University of Victoria

Martin Thunich
Leibnizschule-Gymnasium, Hannover

Edward Timms
Cambridge University

Hans Rudolf Vaget
Smith College

Edith Welliver
DePauw University

John Whiton
University of Waterloo

Ernest M. Wolf
San Diego State University

Les Wright
Hamilton College

William L. Zwiebel
College of the Holy Cross

WORKS CITED

Works by Thomas Mann

Mann, Thomas. *Aufsätze, Reden, Essays: 1893–1913, 1914–1918, 1919–1925.* Ed. Harry Matter. 3 vols. Berlin: Aufbau, 1983–86.

———. *Die Betrogene: Faksimile-Wiedergabe des Manuskripts.* Ed. Freunde des Schweizer Kinderdorfes "Kiriath Yeari." Lausanne: Werkstatt Frederic Wahli, 1953.

———. "Bilse und ich." *Gesammelte Werke* 10: 9–22.

———. *The Black Swan.* Trans. Willard R. Trask. Berkeley: U of California P, 1990.

———. *The Blood of the Walsungs.* Death in Venice *and Seven Other Stories* 292–319.

———. *Briefe.* Ed. Erika Mann. 3 vols. Frankfurt: Fischer, 1961–65.

———. *Briefwechsel mit seinem Verleger Gottfried Bermann-Fischer 1932–1955.* Ed. Peter de Mendelssohn. Frankfurt: Fischer, 1973.

———. "Briefwechsel Thomas Mann–Kurt Martens 1, 1899–1907." Ed. Hans Wysling, with Thomas Sprecher. *Thomas Mann Jahrbuch* 3 (1990): 175–247.

———. "Briefwechsel Thomas Mann–Kurt Martens 2, 1908–1935." Ed. Hans Wysling, with Thomas Sprecher. *Thomas Mann Jahrbuch* 4 (1991): 185–260.

———. "Coming to Terms with Richard Wagner." *Thomas Mann: Pro and contra Wagner* 45–48.

———. *Death in Venice.* Trans. Kenneth Burke. New York: Modern, 1970.

———. Death in Venice *and Other Stories by Thomas Mann.* Trans. and introd. David Luke. New York: Bantam, 1988.

———. Death in Venice *and Seven Other Stories.* Trans. H. T. Lowe-Porter. New York: Vintage-Random, 1954.

———. *Dichter über ihre Dichtungen: Thomas Mann.* Ed. Hans Wysling, with Marianne Fischer. 3 vols. München: Heimeran, 1975–81.

———. *Essays of Three Decades.* Trans. H. T. Lowe-Porter. New York: Knopf, 1947.

———. *An Exceptional Friendship: The Correspondence of Thomas Mann and Erich Kahler.* Trans. Richard Winston and Clara Winston. Ithaca: Cornell UP, 1975.

———. *Die Frankfurter Ausgabe der Gesammelten Werke.* Ed. Peter de Mendelssohn. Frankfurt: Fischer, 1980–86.

———. "Freud and the Future." *Essays* 411–28.

———. "Freud's Position in the History of Modern Thought." *Past Masters and Other Papers.* Trans. H. T. Lowe-Porter. 1933. Freeport: Books for Libraries, 1968. 167–98.

———. *Gesammelte Werke in dreizehn Bänden.* 1974. Ed. Hans Bürgin and Peter de Mendelssohn. 13 vols. Frankfurt: Fischer, 1990.

———— . *The Hesse-Mann Letters: The Correspondence of Hermann Hesse and Thomas Mann, 1910–1955.* Ed. Anni Carlsson and Volker Michels. Trans. Ralph Manheim. New York: Harper, 1975.

———— . *Letters of Thomas Mann.* Trans. Richard Winston and Clara Winston. New York: Knopf, 1971.

———— . *Letters of Thomas Mann: 1889–1955.* Trans. Richard Winston and Clara Winston. Abr. ed. Berkeley: U of California P, 1990.

———— . *Letters to Paul Amann.* Ed. Herbert Wegener. Trans. Richard Winston and Clara Winston. Middletown: Wesleyan UP, 1960.

———— . *Lotte in Weimar: The Beloved Returns.* Trans. H. T. Lowe-Porter. Berkeley: U of California P, 1990.

———— . "The Making of *The Magic Mountain*." *The Magic Mountain.* Trans. H. T. Lowe-Porter. 1953. New York: Vintage-Random, 1969. 717–27.

———— . "Mein Verhältnis zur Psychoanalyse" ("My Relationship to Psychoanalysis"). *Gesammelte Werke* 11: 748–49.

———— . *Meistererzählungen.* Zürich: Manesse, 1987.

———— . *Mythology and Humanism: The Correspondence of Thomas Mann and Karl Kerényi.* Trans. Alexander Gelley. Ithaca: Cornell UP, 1975.

———— . *Notizbücher 1–6.* Ed. Hans Wysling and Yvonne Schmidlin. Frankfurt: Fischer, 1991.

———— . " 'On Myself': Thomas Manns 'Doppellecture' vor den Studenten der Universität Princeton, 2.–3. Mai 1940." Wysling, *Dokumente und Untersuchungen* 67–100.

———— . "Platen." *Essays* 259–69.

———— . *Reflections of a Nonpolitical Man.* Trans. Walter D. Morris. New York: Ungar, 1983.

———— . "Richard Wagner and *Der Ring des Nibelungen*." *Gesammelte Werke* 9: 502–27.

———— . "Richtigstellung." *Gesammelte Werke* 11: 798–801.

———— . "Schopenhauer." *Essays* 372–410.

———— . *Schwere Stunde: Faksimile der Handschrift.* Ed. Bernhard Zeller. Stuttgart: Klett, 1975.

———— . *A Sketch of My Life.* Trans. H. T. Lowe-Porter. New York: Knopf, 1970.

———— . "The Sorrows and Grandeur of Richard Wagner." *Thomas Mann: Pro and contra Wagner* 91–148.

———— . *Stories of Three Decades.* Trans. H. T. Lowe-Porter. New York: Knopf, 1936.

———— . *Tagebücher: 1918–1921, 1933–1934, 1935–1936, 1937–1939, 1940–1943.* Ed. Peter de Mendelssohn. 5 vols. Frankfurt: Fischer, 1977–82.

———— . *Tagebücher: 1944–1946, 1946–1948, 1949–1950.* Ed. Inge Jens. 3 vols. Frankfurt: Fischer, 1986–91.

———— . *Thomas Mann an Ernst Bertram: Briefe aus den Jahren 1910–1955.* Ed. Inge Jens. Pfullingen: Neske, 1960.

———. *Thomas Mann: Briefwechsel mit Autoren.* Ed. Hans Wysling. Frankfurt: Fischer, 1988.

———. *Thomas Mann:* Der Tod in Venedig. Ed. A. W. Hornsey. Boston: Houghton, 1969.

———. *Thomas Mann:* Der Tod in Venedig. Ed. George E. Boyd and Henry M. Rosenwald. New York: Oxford UP, 1973.

———. *Thomas Mann:* Der Tod in Venedig. Ed. T. J. Reed. Oxford: Oxford UP, 1971.

———. *Thomas Mann: Diaries 1918–1939.* Ed. Hermann Kesten. Trans. Richard Winston and Clara Winston. New York: Abrams, 1982.

———. "Thomas Mann–Heinrich Mann: Briefwechsel: Neu aufgefundene Briefe 1933–1949." Ed. Hans Wysling, with Thomas Sprecher. *Thomas Mann Jahrbuch* 1 (1988): 167–230.

———. *Thomas Mann–Heinrich Mann: Briefwechsel: 1900–1949.* Ed. Hans Wysling. Frankfurt: Fischer, 1984.

———. *Thomas Mann: Pro and contra Wagner.* Ed. Patrick Carnegy. Trans. Allan Blunden. Introd. Erich Heller. Chicago: U of Chicago P, 1985.

———. *Thomas Mann's "Goethe and Tolstoy": Notes and Sources.* Ed. Clayton Koelb. Trans. Alcyone Scott and Clayton Koelb. University: U of Alabama P, 1984.

———. *Thomas Mann:* Tonio Kröger. Ed. Elizabeth M. Wilkinson. Oxford: Blackwell, 1968.

———. *Thomas Mann:* Tonio Kröger. Ed. John A. Kelly. New York: Appleton, 1959.

———. *Thomas Mann: Wagner und unsere Zeit: Aufsätze, Betrachtungen, Briefe.* Ed. Erika Mann. Frankfurt: Fischer, 1963.

———. "Tischrede im Wiener Pen-Club" ("After-Dinner Speech at the Vienna Pen Club"). *Gesammelte Werke* 11: 368–72.

———. Der Tod in Venedig: *Text, Materialien, Kommentar, mit den bisher unveröffentlichten Arbeitsnotizen Thomas Manns.* Ed. T. J. Reed. München: Hanser, 1983.

———. "Verhältnis zu Wien" ("My Relationship to Vienna"). *Gesammelte Werke* 11: 399–401.

———. "The Wardrobe." *Stories* 71–77.

———. "The Years of My Life." Trans. Heinz Norden and Ruth Norden. *Harper's* Oct. 1950: 250–60.

Books and Articles

Abrams, M. H. *A Glossary of Literary Terms.* 5th ed. New York: Holt, 1988.

Améry, Jean. "Venezianische Zaubereien: Luchino Visconti und sein *Der Tod in Venedig.*" *Merkur* 25 (1971): 808–12.

Amory, Frederic. "The Classical Style of *Der Tod in Venedig.*" *Modern Language Review* 59 (1964): 399–409.

Anchor, Robert. *Germany Confronts Modernization: German Culture and Society, 1790–1890.* Lexington: Heath, 1972.

Anger, Sigrid, ed. *Heinrich Mann 1871–1950: Werk und Leben in Dokumenten und Bildern.* 2nd ed. Berlin: Aufbau, 1977.

Arnold, Heinz Ludwig, ed. *Thomas Mann.* 2nd ed. München: Text und Kritik, 1982.

Atkins, Stuart. "*Die Wahlverwandtschaften*: Novel of German Classicism." *German Quarterly* 53 (1980): 1–45.

Aytac, Gürsel. "Thomas Mann in der Türkei." Papenfuss and Söring 189–96.

Baer, Lydia. *The Concept and Function of Death in the Works of Thomas Mann.* Freiburg: Waibel, 1932.

Bahr, Ehrhard, ed. *Thomas Mann: Der Tod in Venedig—Erläuterungen und Dokumente.* Stuttgart: Reclam, 1991.

Bance, Alan F. "*Der Tod in Venedig* and the Triadic Structure." *Forum for Modern Language Studies* 8 (1972): 148–61.

———, ed. *Weimar Germany: Writers and Politics.* Edinburgh: Scottish Academic, 1982.

Bang, Herman. *Verfehltes Leben.* Trans. Emil Jonas. Leipzig: Friedrich, 1887.

———. *Die vier Teufel und andere Novellen.* Berlin: Fischer, n.d.

Banuls, André. "Schopenhauer und Nietzsche in Thomas Manns Frühwerk." *Etudes Germaniques* 30 (1975): 129–47.

———. "Thomas Mann: Leben und Persönlichkeit." Koopmann, *Handbuch* 1–17.

———. "Thomas Mann und die russische Literatur." Bludau, Heftrich, and Koopmann 398–423.

Barnouw, Dagmar. *Weimar Intellectuals and the Threat of Modernity.* Bloomington: Indiana UP, 1988.

Baron, Frank. "Sensuality and Morality in Thomas Mann's *Tod in Venedig.*" *Germanic Review* 45 (1970): 115–25.

———. "Das Sokrates-Bild von Georg Lukács als Quelle für Thomas Manns *Tod in Venedig.*" *Im Dialog mit der Moderne.* Ed. Roland Jost and Hansgeorg Schmidt-Bergmann. Frankfurt: Athenäum, 1986. 96–105.

Basilius, H. A. "Thomas Mann's Use of Musical Structure and Techniques in *Tonio Kröger.*" *Germanic Review* 19 (1944): 284–308.

Baudelaire, Charles. *Œuvres complètes.* Ed. Claude Pichois. 2 vols. Paris: Gallimard, 1975.

Bauer, Roger, et al., eds. *Fin de siècle: Zu Literatur und Kunst der Jahrhundertwende.* Frankfurt: Klostermann, 1977.

Baumgart, Reinhard. *Das Ironische und die Ironie in den Werken Thomas Manns.* München: Hanser, 1964.

Beardsley, Monroe C., and W. K. Wimsatt, Jr. "The Intentional Fallacy." Margolis, *Philosophy Looks at the Arts* 367–80.

Beck, Götz. "Fiktives und Nicht-Fiktives: Bemerkungen zu neueren Tendenzen in der Thomas-Mann-Forschung." *Studi Germanici* 9 (1971): 447–76.

Beebe, Maurice. *Ivory Towers and Sacred Founts: The Artist as Hero in Fiction from Goethe to Joyce*. New York: New York UP, 1964.

Beharriell, Frederick J. " 'Never without Freud': Freud's Influence on Mann." K. Hughes 1–15.

———. "Psychology in the Early Works of Thomas Mann." *PMLA* 77 (1962): 148–55.

Bellmann, Werner. *Thomas Mann: Tonio Kröger—Erläuterungen und Dokumente*. Stuttgart: Reclam, 1983.

Bely, Andrei. *Petersburg*. Ed. and trans. Robert McGuire and John Malmstad. Bloomington: Indiana UP, 1978.

Berendsohn, Walter A. *Thomas Mann: Artist and Partisan in Troubled Times*. Trans. George C. Buck. University: U of Alabama P, 1975.

———. *Thomas Mann und die Seinen: Porträt einer literarischen Familie*. Bern: Francke, 1973.

Bergman, Ingmar. "Introduction: Bergman Discusses Film-making." *Four Screenplays of Ingmar Bergman*. Trans. Lars Malmström and David Kushner. New York: Simon, 1960. xiii–xxii.

Bergson, Henri. "Laughter." *Comedy*. Ed. Wylie Sypher. Garden City: Doubleday, 1956. 61–190.

Bergsten, Gunilla. "Thomas Mann in Schweden." Bludau, Heftrich, and Koopmann 424–33.

———. *Thomas Mann's Doctor Faustus: The Sources and Structure of the Novel*. Trans. Krishna Winston. Chicago: U of Chicago P, 1969.

Berlin, Jeffrey B. "In Exile: The Friendship and Unpublished Correspondence between Thomas Mann and Heinrich Eduard Jacob." *Deutsche Vierteljahrsschrift für Literaturwissenschaft und Geistesgeschichte* 64 (1990): 172–87.

———. "On the Making of *The Magic Mountain*: The Unpublished Correspondence between Thomas Mann, Alfred A. Knopf, and H. T. Lowe-Porter." *Seminar* 29 (1992): forthcoming.

———. "Thomas Mann." *Erstausgaben deutscher Dichtung: Eine Bibliographie zur deutschen Literatur 1600–1990*. 2nd ed. Ed. Gero von Wilpert and Adolf Gühring. Stuttgart: Kröner, forthcoming.

Berman, Russell A. "Montage as a Literary Technique: Thomas Mann's *Tristan* and T. S. Eliot's *The Waste Land*." *Selecta* 2 (1981): 20–23.

———. *The Rise of the Modern German Novel: Crisis and Charisma*. Cambridge: Harvard UP, 1986.

Bermann-Fischer, Gottfried. *Bedroht—bewahrt: Der Weg eines Verlegers*. 2nd ed. Frankfurt: Fischer, 1981.

———. "Bewegte Zeiten mit Thomas Mann." *Lebendige Gegenwart: Reden und Aufsätze*. Zürich: Classen, 1977. 74–91.

Bermann-Fischer, Gottfried, and Brigitte Bermann-Fischer. *Briefwechsel mit Autoren*. Ed. Reiner Stach. Frankfurt: Fischer, 1990.

Bernini, Cornelia, et al., eds. *Internationales Thomas-Mann-Kolloquium 1986 in Lübeck*. Bern: Francke, 1987.

Bernstein, Leonard. *The Unanswered Question: Six Talks at Harvard*. Cambridge: Harvard UP, 1976.

Bithell, Jethro. "Neo-Classicism." *Modern German Literature: 1880–1950*. London: Methuen, 1963. 251–78.

Bleicher, Thomas. "Zur Adaptation der Literatur durch den Film: Viscontis Metamorphose der Thomas Mann–Novelle *Tod in Venedig*." *Neophilologus* 64 (1980): 479–92.

Blissett, William. "Thomas Mann: The Last Wagnerite." *Germanic Review* 35 (1960): 50–76.

Bloom, Harold, ed. *Thomas Mann*. New York: Chelsea, 1986.

——, ed. *Thomas Mann's* The Magic Mountain. New York: Chelsea, 1986.

Bludau, Beatrix, Eckhard Heftrich, and Helmut Koopmann, eds. *Thomas Mann 1875–1975: Vorträge in München, Zürich, Lübeck*. Frankfurt: Fischer, 1977.

Blume, Bernhard. "Der Briefschreiber Thomas Mann." *Lebendige Form: Interpretationen zur deutschen Literatur: Festschrift für Heinrich E. K. Henel*. Ed. Jeffrey L. Sammons and Ernst Schürer. München: Fink, 1970. 277–89.

Böhm, Karl Werner. *Zwischen Selbstzucht und Verlangen: Thomas Mann und das Stigma Homosexualität*. Würzburg: Königshausen, 1991.

Bolduc, Stevie Anne. "A Study of Intertextuality: Thomas Mann's *Tristan* and Richard Wagner's *Tristan und Isolde*." *Rocky Mountain Review of Language and Literature* 37 (1983): 82–90.

Boschert, Bernhard, and Ulf Schramm. "Literatur und Literaturwissenschaft als Medium der Bearbeitung von Verdrängung: Beobachtungen an Thomas Manns *Der Tod in Venedig*—Ein Beitrag zur Germanistik als Friedens- und Konfliktforschung." *Politische Aufgaben und soziale Funktionen von Germanistik und Deutschunterricht*. Ed. Norbert Oellers. Tübingen: Niemeyer, 1988. 19–34.

Bradbury, Malcolm, and James McFarlane, eds. *Modernism 1890–1930*. New York: Penguin, 1978.

Bramsted, Ernst. *Aristocracy and the Middle Class in Germany*. Chicago: U of Chicago P, 1964.

Braverman, Albert, and Larry D. Nachman. "The Dialectic of Decadence: An Analysis of Thomas Mann's *Death in Venice*." *Germanic Review* 45 (1970): 289–98.

Brennan, Joseph G. *Thomas Mann's World*. New York: Russell, 1962.

Bridges, George. "The Almost Irresistible Appeal of Fascism; or, Is It Okay to Like Richard Wagner?" Rev. of *Thomas Mann: Pro and contra Wagner*, ed. Patrick Carnegy. *Germanic Review* 64 (1989): 42–48.

——. "The Problem of Pederastic Love in Thomas Mann's *Death in Venice* and Plato's *Phaedrus*." *Selecta: Journal of the Pacific Northwest Council on Foreign Languages* 7 (1986): 39–46.

Bronsen, D. "The Artist against Himself: Henrik Ibsen's *Masterbuilder* and Thomas Mann's *Death in Venice*." *Neohelicon* 11 (1984): 323–44.

Brooks, Peter, "The Idea of Psychoanalytic Literary Criticism." *The Trial(s) of "Psychoanalysis."* Ed. Françoise Meltzer. Chicago: U of Chicago P, 1988. 145–59.

Bruford, W. H. *The German Tradition of Self-Cultivation:* Bildung *from Humboldt to Thomas Mann.* London: Cambridge UP, 1975.

Bullivant, Keith. "Thomas Mann and Politics in the Weimar Republic." *Culture and Society in the Weimar Republic.* Totowa: Rowman, 1977. 24–38.

Burgard, Peter J. "From *Enttäuschung* to *Tristan:* The Devolution of a Language Crisis in Thomas Mann's Early Work." *German Quarterly* 59 (1986): 431–48.

Bürgin, Hans. *Das Werk Thomas Manns: Eine Bibliographie.* Frankfurt: Fischer, 1959.

Bürgin, Hans, and Hans-Otto Mayer. *Thomas Mann: A Chronicle of His Life.* Trans. Eugene Dobson. University: U of Alabama P, 1969.

Bürgin, Hans, Hans-Otto Mayer, et al., eds. *Die Briefe Thomas Manns: Regesten und Register.* 5 vols. Frankfurt: Fischer, 1977–87.

Burton, Richard. "Terminal Essay." 1885. Partially rpt. in *Sexual Heretics: Male Homosexuality in English Literature from 1850 to 1900.* Ed. Brian Reade. London: Routledge, 1970. 158–93.

Busch, Frank. *August Graf von Platen—Thomas Mann: Zeichen und Gefühle.* München: Fink, 1987.

Campbell, Joseph. *The Hero with a Thousand Faces.* Princeton: Princeton UP, 1968.

Carnegy, Patrick. *Faust as Musician: A Study of Thomas Mann's Novel* Doctor Faustus. New York: New Directions, 1973.

———. "The Novella Transformed: Thomas Mann as Opera." *Benjamin Britten: Death in Venice.* Ed. Donald Mitchell. New York: Cambridge UP, 1987. 168–77.

Carpenter, William. *Death and Marriage: Self-Reflective Images of Art in Joyce and Mallarmé.* New York: Garland, 1988.

Carstensen, Richard. *Thomas Mann sehr menschlich: Streiflichter—Schlaglichter.* 2nd ed. Lübeck: Weiland, 1975.

Cather, Willa. "Paul's Case." *The Troll Garden.* Lincoln: U of Nebraska P, 1983. 102–21.

Cerf, Steven R. "Benjamin Britten's *Death in Venice:* Operatic Stream of Consciousness." *Bucknell Review* (1988): 124–38.

———. "Mann and Myth: The Author's Response to the *Ring.*" *Opera News* 54 (1990): 18+.

———. Rev. of *Music, Love, Death, and Mann's* Doctor Faustus, by John F. Fetzer. *South Atlantic Review* 56 (1991): 158–60.

———. Rev. of *Narzissmus und illusionäre Existenzform,* by Hans Wysling. *German Quarterly* 57 (1984): 326–27.

———. "Thomas Mann und die englische Literatur." Koopmann, *Handbuch* 230–42.

Chrambach, Eva, and Ursula Hummel. *Klaus und Erika Mann: Bilder und Dokumente.* München: Spangenberg, 1990.

Church, Margaret. "*Death in Venice:* A Study of Creativity." *College English* 23 (1962): 648–51.

Cioffi, Frank. "Intention and Interpretation in Criticism." Margolis, *Philosophy Looks at the Arts* 381–99.

Cohn, Dorrit. "The Second Author of *Der Tod in Venedig*." Ezergailis, *Critical Essays* 124–43.

Conley, John. "Thomas Mann on the Sources of Two Passages in *Death in Venice*." *German Quarterly* 40 (1967): 152–55.

Consigny, Scott. "Aschenbach's 'Page and a Half of Choicest Prose': Mann's Rhetoric of Irony." *Studies in Short Fiction* 14 (1977): 359–67.

Cook, Albert. *Thresholds: Studies in the Romantic Experience*. Madison: U of Wisconsin P, 1985.

Corngold, Stanley. *The Fate of the Self: German Writers and French Theory*. New York: Columbia UP, 1986.

———. "Mann as a Reader of Nietzsche." *Fate of the Self* 129–59.

———. "The Mann Family." Corngold, Lange, and Ziolkowski 46–53.

———. "Thomas Mann and the German Philosophical Tradition: Two Essays on Nietzsche." Corngold, Lange, and Ziolkowski 9–16.

Corngold, Stanley, Victor Lange, and Theodore Ziolkowski, eds. *Thomas Mann: 1875–1955*. Princeton: Princeton UP, 1975.

Cox, Catherine. "Pater's 'Apollo in Picardy' and Mann's *Death in Venice*." *Anglia: Zeitschrift für englische Philologie* 86 (1968): 143–54.

Craig, Gordon A. *The Germans*. New York: Putnam, 1982.

Cremerius, Johannes. "Der Einfluss der Psychoanalyse auf die deutschsprachige Literatur." *Psyche* 41 (1987): 39–54.

Crick, Joyce. "Thomas Mann and Psycho-analysis: The Turning-Point." *Literature and Psychology* 10 (1960): 45–55.

Curtius, Mechthild. "Kreativität und Antizipation: Thomas Mann, Freud und das Schaffen des Künstlers." *Seminar: Theorien der künstlerischen Produktivität*. Ed. M. C. Böhmer and Ursula Böhmer. Frankfurt: Suhrkamp, 1976. 388–425.

Daemmrich, Horst S. "Mann's Portrait of the Artist: Archetypal Patterns." *Bucknell Review* 14 (1966): 27–43.

Dahrendorf, Ralf. *Society and Democracy in Germany*. Garden City: Doubleday, 1967.

Dassanowsky-Harris, Robert von. "Thomas Mann's *Der Tod in Venedig*: Unfulfilled 'Aufbruch' from the Wilhelminian World." *Germanic Notes* 18 (1987): 16–17.

Davidson, Leah. "Mid-life Crisis in Thomas Mann's *Death in Venice*." *Journal of the American Academy of Psychoanalysis* 4 (1976): 203–14.

Debon, Günther. "Thomas Mann und China." *Thomas Mann Jahrbuch* 3 (1990): 149–74.

Del Caro, Adrian. "The Political Apprentice: Thomas Mann's Reception of Nietzsche." *Studies in the Humanities* 12 (1985): 21–28.

———. "Reception and Impact: The First Decade of Nietzsche in Germany." *Orbis Litterarum* 37 (1982): 32–46.

———. "Towards a Genealogy of an Image: Nietzsche's Achievement according to Nietzsche." *University of Toronto Quarterly* 54 (1985): 234–50.

Del Caro, Adrian, and Renate Bialy. "Rückblick nach dem Exilerlebnis: Thomas Mann und Nietzsche." *Exil: Wirkung und Wertung*. Ed. Donald G. Daviau and Ludwig M. Fischer. Columbia: Camden, 1984. 149–59.

Dierks, Manfred. *Studien zu Mythos und Psychologie bei Thomas Mann: An seinem Nachlass orientierte Untersuchungen zum Tod in Venedig, zum Zauberberg und zur Joseph-Tetralogie*. Bern: Francke, 1972.

———. "Thomas Mann und die Mythologie." Koopmann, *Handbuch* 301–06.

———. "Thomas Mann und die Tiefenpsychologie." Koopmann, *Handbuch* 284–300.

———. "Traumzeit und Verdichtung. Der Einfluss der Psychoanalyse auf Thomas Manns Erzählweise." Heftrich and Koopmann 111–37.

———. "Der Wahn und die Träume in *Der Tod in Venedig*: Thomas Manns folgenreiche Freud-Lektüre im Jahr 1911." *Psyche* 44 (1990): 240–68.

Diersen, Inge. *Thomas Mann: Episches Werk, Weltanschauung, Leben*. Berlin: Aufbau, 1975.

Dietzel, Ulrich, and Gerda Weissenfels. *Aus den Familienpapieren der Manns: Dokumente zu den Buddenbrooks*. Berlin: Aufbau, 1965.

Dittmann, Ulrich, ed. *Thomas Mann: Tristan—Erläuterungen und Dokumente*. Stuttgart: Reclam, 1983.

Dover, K. J. *Greek Homosexuality*. New York: Vintage-Random, 1980.

Dowling, Linda. *Language and Decadence in the Victorian Fin de Siècle*. Princeton: Princeton UP, 1986.

Du: Kulturelle Monatsschrift 29: München um 1900. Zürich: Conzett, 1969.

Edel, Leon. *Writing Lives: Principia Biographica*. New York: Norton, 1984.

Eder, Jürgen. "Thomas Mann: Briefwechsel mit Schriftstellern." Koopmann, *Handbuch* 742–72.

Effe, Bernd. "Sokrates in Venedig: Thomas Mann und die 'platonische Liebe.' " *Antike und Abendland* 31 (1985): 153–66.

Eggenschwiler, David. "The Very Glance of Art: Ironic Narrative in Mann's *Novellen*." *Modern Language Quarterly* 48 (1987): 59–85.

Egri, Peter. "The Function of Dreams and Visions in *A Portrait* and *Death in Venice*." *James Joyce Quarterly* 5 (1968): 86–102.

Eichner, Hans. "Thomas Mann and Politics." Schulte and Chapple 5–19.

———. "Thomas Mann und die deutsche Romantik." *Das Nachleben der Romantik in der modernen deutschen Literatur: 2. Amherster Kolloquium*. Ed. Wolfgang Paulsen. Heidelberg: Stiehm, 1969. 152–73.

Evans, Tamara. " 'Ich werde Besseres machen . . .': Zu Thomas Manns Goethe-Nachfolge in *Tonio Kröger*." *Colloquia Germanica* 15 (1982): 84–97.

Ezergailis, Inta M., ed. *Critical Essays on Thomas Mann*. Boston: Hall, 1988.

———. *Male and Female: An Approach to Thomas Mann's Dialectic*. Hague: Nijhoff, 1975.

———. "Spinell's Letter: An Approach to Thomas Mann's *Tristan*." *German Life and Letters* 25 (1972): 377–82.

Farelly, David James. "Apollo and Dionysus Interpreted in Thomas Mann's *Der Tod in Venedig*." *New German Studies* 3 (1975): 1–15.

Faulstich, Werner, and Ingeborg Faulstich. *Modelle der Filmanalyse*. München: Fink, 1977.

Fetzer, John Francis. *Music, Love, Death, and Mann's* Doctor Faustus. Columbia: Camden, 1990.

Feuerlicht, Ignace. *Thomas Mann*. New York: Twayne, 1968.

———. "Thomas Mann and Homoeroticism." *Germanic Review* 57 (1982): 89–97.

Fickert, Kurt. "Truth and Fiction in *Der Tod in Venedig*." *Germanic Notes* 21 (1990): 25–31.

Finck, Jean. *Thomas Mann und die Psychoanalyse*. Paris: Belles Lettres, 1973.

Fischer, Brigitte B. *My European Heritage: Life among Great Men of Letters*. Trans. Harry Zohn. Boston: Branden, 1986.

Fischer, Jens Malte. "Deutsche Literatur zwischen Jahrhundertwende und Erstem Weltkrieg." *Jahrhundertende—Jahrhundertwende*. 2 Teil. Ed. Hans Hinter-häuser. Wiesbaden: Athenaion, 1976. 231–60.

———. *Fin de siècle: Kommentar zu einer Epoche*. München: Winkler, 1978.

Fischer, Kurt von. "Gustav Mahlers Adagietto und Luchino Viscontis Film *Morte a Venezia*." *Verlust und Ursprung: Festschrift für Werner Weber*. Ed. Angelika Maass and Bernhard Heinser. Zürich: Ammann, 1989. 44–52.

Fischer, Samuel, and Hedwig Fischer. *Briefwechsel mit Autoren*. Ed. Dierk Rodewald and Corinna Fiedler. Frankfurt: Fischer, 1990.

Fleissner, R. F. "The Balking Staircase and the Transparent Door: Prufrock and Kröger." *Comparatist* 8 (1984): 21–32.

Fletcher, Angus. "Music, Visconti, Mann, Nietzsche: *Death in Venice*." *Stanford Italian Review* 6 (1986): 301–12.

Forster, E. M. "The Classical Annex." *The Life to Come and Other Stories*. London: Arnold, 1972. 146–50.

———. *Maurice*. New York: Norton, 1971.

Foster, John Burt, Jr. *Heirs to Dionysus: A Nietzschean Current in Literary Modernism*. Princeton: Princeton UP, 1988.

Foucault, Michel. *Surveiller et punir: Naissance de la prison*. Paris: Gallimard, 1975.

———. *La volonté de savoir: Histoire de la Sexualité*. Vol. 1. Paris: Gallimard, 1976.

Fowlie, Wallace. *Climate of Violence*. New York: Macmillan, 1967.

Frank, Bernhard. "Mann's *Death in Venice*." *Explicator* 45 (1986): 31–32.

Franke, Peter Robert. *Thomas Mann: Unbekannte Dokumente aus seiner Jugend*. Saarbrücken: Universität Saarbrücken, 1991.

———. "Der Tod des Hans Hansen: Unbekanntes aus der Jugend Thomas Manns." *Musil-Forum* 10 (1984): 43–55.

Freud, Sigmund. "Delusions and Dreams in Jensen's *Gradiva*." *Standard Edition* 9: 3–95.

———. "Humor." *Standard Edition* 21: 161–66.

———. "On Narcissism: An Introduction." *Collected Papers*. Trans. Joan Rivière. Vol. 4. London: Hogarth, 1934. 30–59.

————. *The Standard Edition of the Complete Psychological Works of Sigmund Freud.* Ed. and trans. James Strachey, with Anna Freud. 24 vols. London: Hogarth, 1953–74.

————. *Der Wahn und die Träume in W. Jensens* Gradiva *mit dem Text der Erzählung von Wilhelm Jensen.* Ed. Bernd Urban and Johannes Cremerius. Frankfurt: Fischer, 1973.

Freund, J. Hellmut, ed. *Unterwegs: Peter de Mendelssohn zum 70. Geburtstag.* Frankfurt: Fischer, 1978.

Freund, J. Hellmut, et al. *Almanach 83: Bilder aus dem S. Fischer Verlag 1886–1914.* Frankfurt: Fischer, 1969.

Frey, Erich. "Thomas Mann." Spalek and Strelka 473–526.

Frey, John R. " 'Die stumme Begegnung': Beobachtungen zur Funktion des Blicks im *Tod in Venedig.*" *German Quarterly* 41 (1968): 177–95.

Furness, Raymond. *Wagner and Literature.* New York: St. Martin's, 1982.

Furst, Lilian R. "Thomas Mann's *Tonio Kröger:* A Critical Reconsideration." *Revue des langues vivantes* 27 (1961): 232–40.

Galerstein, Carolyn. "Images of Decadence in Visconti's *Death in Venice.*" *Literature and Film Quarterly* 13 (1985): 29–34.

Garland, Mary. *The Oxford Companion to German Literature.* 2nd ed. Oxford: Oxford UP, 1986.

Gattermann, Günter. *Katalog der Thomas-Mann-Sammlung der Universitätsbibliothek Düsseldorf.* 9 vols. München: Saur, 1991.

Gay, Peter. *Freud: A Life for Our Time.* New York: Norton, 1988.

————, ed. *The Freud Reader.* New York: Norton, 1989.

————. Rev. of *The Brothers Mann,* by Nigel Hamilton. *New York Times Book Review* 5 Aug. 1979: 7+.

————. Rev. of *Thomas Mann: The Making of an Artist 1875–1911,* by Richard Winston. *New York Times Book Review* 3 Jan. 1982: 9+.

————. *Weimar Culture: The Outsider as Insider.* New York: Harper, 1968.

Geerdts, Hans Jürgen. "Thomas Manns *Tristan* in der literarischen Tradition." Wenzel, *Betrachtungen* 190–206.

Geiser, Christoph. *Das geheime Fieber.* Zürich: Nagel, 1987.

Gesing, Fritz. "Symbolisierung, Voraussetzungen und Strategien: Ein Versuch am Beispiel von Thomas Manns *Der Tod in Venedig.*" *Freiburger literaturpsychologische Gespräche* 9 (1990): 226–53.

Gibbon, Edward. *The History of the Decline and Fall of the Roman Empire.* Ed. Hugh Trevor-Roper. New York: Twayne, 1963.

Gide, André. *The Immoralist.* Trans. Richard Howard. New York: Vintage-Random, 1970.

Gillespie, Gerald. "Afterthoughts of Hamlet: Goethe's Wilhelm, Joyce's Stephen." *Comparative Literary History as Discourse: In Honor of Anna Balakian.* Ed. Mario Valdés and Daniel Javitch. Bern: Lang, forthcoming.

————. "Cinematic Narration in the Modernist Novel." *Narration.* Ed. Amiya Dev. Forthcoming.

———. "Educational Experiment in Thomas Mann." *Reflection and Action: Essays on the Bildungsroman*. Ed. James N. Hardin. Columbia: Camden, 1991. 362–81.

———. "Epiphany: Notes on the Applicability of a Modernist Term." *Sensus Communis: Contemporary Trends in Comparative Literature: Festschrift für Henry Remak*. Ed. Peter Boerner et al. Tübingen: Narr, 1986. 255–66.

———. "Thomas Mann in komparatistischer Sicht: Die angloamerikanische Auffassung seiner weltliterarischen Geltung." *Deutsche Literatur in der Weltliteratur: Kulturnation statt politischer Nation?* Ed. Franz Norbert Mennemeier and Conrad Wiedemann. Tübingen: Niemeyer, 1986. 122–26.

———. "The Ways of Hermes in the Works of Thomas Mann." *Sinn und Symbol: Festschrift für Joseph P. Strelka zum 60. Geburtstag*. Ed. Karl Konrad Pohlheim. Bern: Lang, 1987. 371–85.

Gilman, Richard. *Decadence*. New York: Farrar, 1979.

Girard, René. "The Plague in Literature and Myth." *To Double Business Bound: Mimesis, Literature, and Anthropology*. Baltimore: Johns Hopkins UP, 1978. 136–54.

Glassco, David. "Films Out of Books: Bergman, Visconti and Mann." *Mosaic* 16 (1983): 165–73.

Gockel, Heinz. "Aschenbachs Tod in Venedig." Wolff 27–41.

Goethe, Johann Wolfgang von. *Elective Affinities*. Trans. R. J. Hollingdale. New York: Penguin, 1971.

———. "Ganymed." *Sämtliche Werke*. Vol. 1. Zürich: Artemis, 1977. 322.

———. *Goethes Werke. Hamburger Ausgabe in 14 Bänden*. Ed. Erich Trunz et al. 14 vols. Hamburg: Wegner, 1966.

———. *Maximen und Reflexionen*. Vol. 12 of *Werke*. Ed. Erich Trunz. München: Beck, 1981.

Goldman, Harvey. *Max Weber and Thomas Mann: Calling and the Shaping of the Self*. Berkeley: U of California P, 1988.

Good, Graham. "The Death of Language in *Death in Venice*." *Mosaic* 5 (1972): 43–52.

Gorzawski, Heribert. *Stundenblätter* Tonio Kröger. Stuttgart: Klett, 1984.

Gray, Ronald. *The German Tradition in Literature 1871–1945*. Cambridge: Cambridge UP, 1965.

Grerolin, Jürgen. "Briefe als Texte: Die Briefedition." *Deutsche Vierteljahrsschrift für Literaturwissenschaft und Geistesgeschichte* 64 (1990): 756–71.

Gronicka, André von. " 'Myth plus Psychology': A Style Analysis of *Death in Venice*." *Germanic Review* 31 (1956): 191–205.

———. *Thomas Mann: Profile and Perspectives*. New York: Random, 1970.

Grossvogel, David I. "Visconti and the Too, Too Solid Flesh." *Diacritics* 1 (1971): 52–55.

Gulia, Georgi. "Das Schaffen Thomas Manns in der Sowjetunion." Bludau, Heftrich, and Koopmann 447–52.

Gullette, Margaret M. "The Exile of Adulthood: Pedophilia in the Midlife Novel." *Novel: A Forum on Fiction* 17 (1984): 215–32.

Günther, Joachim. "*Der Tod in Venedig*: Randbemerkungen zu Film und Buch." *Neue Deutsche Hefte* 18 (1971): 89–99.

Gustafson, Lorraine. "Xenophon and *Der Tod in Venedig*." *Germanic Review* 21 (1946): 209–14.

Hajek, Edelgard. *Literarischer Jugendstil*. Düsseldorf: Bertelsmann, 1971.

Hamann, Richard. *Geschichte der Kunst*. Berlin: Knaur, 1933.

Hamann, Richard, and Jost Hermand. *Stilkunst um 1900*. Berlin: Akademie, 1967.

Hamburger, Michael. *Contraries: Studies in German Literature*. New York: Dutton, 1970.

Hamilton, Nigel. *The Brothers Mann: The Lives of Heinrich and Thomas Mann 1871–1950 and 1875–1955*. New Haven: Yale UP, 1979.

Hannum, Hunter G. "Archetypal Echoes in Mann's *Death in Venice*." *Psychological Perspectives: A Jungian Review* 5 (1974): 48–59.

Hansen, Volkmar. *Thomas Mann*. Stuttgart: Metzler, 1984.

———. *Thomas Manns Heine-Rezeption*. Hamburg: Hoffmann, 1975.

Hansen, Volkmar, and Gert Heine, eds. *Frage und Antwort: Interviews mit Thomas Mann 1909–1955*. Hamburg: Knaus, 1983.

Härle, Gerhard. *Die Gestalt des Schönen: Untersuchung zu Homosexualitätsthematik in Thomas Manns Roman Der Zauberberg*. Königstein: Hain, 1986.

———. *Männerweiblichkeit: Zur Homosexualität bei Klaus und Thomas Mann*. Frankfurt: Athenäum, 1988.

Harpham, Geoffrey. "Metaphor, Marginality, and Parody in *Death in Venice*." *On the Grotesque: Strategies of Contradiction in Art and Literature*. Princeton: Princeton UP, 1982. 122–45.

Harweg, Roland. "Präsuppositionen und Rekonstruktion: Zur Erzählsituation in Thomas Manns *Tristan* aus textlinguistischer Sicht." *Textgrammatik: Beiträge zum Problem der Textualität*. Ed. Michael Schecker and Peter Wunderli. Tübingen: Niemeyer, 1975. 166–85.

Hasselbach, Karlheinz. Rev. of *Thomas Mann: Epoche, Werk, Wirkung*, by Hermann Kurzke. *German Quarterly* 60 (1987): 494–97.

Hatfield, Henry. "The Achievement of Thomas Mann." *Germanic Review* 31 (1956): 206–14.

———. *From The Magic Mountain: Mann's Later Masterpieces*. Ithaca: Cornell UP, 1979.

———. Rev. of Death in Venice *and Other Stories by Thomas Mann*, trans. David Luke. *Die Unterrichtspraxis* 23.2 (1990): 192.

———. Rev. of *Thomas Mann*, by André von Gronicka. *Germanic Review* 47 (1972): 314–15.

———. *Thomas Mann*. New York: New Directions, 1962.

———, ed. *Thomas Mann: A Collection of Critical Essays*. Englewood Cliffs: Prentice, 1964.

———. "Thomas Mann and America." *The Legacy of the German Refugee Intellectuals.* Ed. Robert Boyers. New York: Schocken, 1972. 174–85.

———. "Thomas Mann's *Tristan*: A Revised View." *Vistas and Vectors: Essays Honoring the Memory of Helmut Rehder.* Ed. Lee B. Jennings and George Schulz-Behrend. Austin: U of Texas P, 1979. 157–63.

Haug, Hellmut. *Erkenntnisekel. Zum frühen Werk Thomas Manns.* Tübingen: Niemeyer, 1969.

Haupt, Jürgen. *Heinrich Mann.* Stuttgart: Metzler, 1980.

Hayes, James A. "A Method of Determining the Reliability of Literary Translations: Two Versions of Thomas Mann's *Der Tod in Venedig.*" Diss. U of Massachusetts, 1973.

Hayes, Tom, and Lee Quinby. "The Aporia of Bourgeois Art: Desire in Thomas Mann's *Death in Venice.*" *Criticism* 31 (1990): 159–77.

Heftrich, Eckhard. *Vom Verfall zur Apokalypse: Über Thomas Mann.* Vol. 2. Frankfurt: Klostermann, 1982.

Heftrich, Eckhard, and Helmut Koopmann, eds. *Thomas Mann und seine Quellen: Festschrift für Hans Wysling.* Frankfurt: Klostermann, 1991.

Heine, Gert. *Thomas Mann in Dänemark.* Lübeck: Ackermann, 1975.

Heller, Erich. "Autobiography and Literature." Mann, *Death in Venice* (Modern Library) 101–27.

———. *Thomas Mann: The Ironic German.* South Bend: Regnery, 1979.

Heller, Peter. "Thomas Mann's Conception of the Creative Writer." Ezergailis, *Critical Essays* 143–75.

———. "*Der Tod in Venedig* und Thomas Manns *Grund-Motiv.*" Schulte and Chapple 35–83.

Hepworth, James B. "Tadzio-Sabazios: Notes on *Death in Venice.*" *Western Humanities Review* 17 (1963): 172–75.

Hermand, Jost, ed. *Jugendstil.* Darmstadt: Wissenschaftliche, 1989.

———. *Jugendstil: Ein Forschungsbericht 1918–1964.* Stuttgart: Reclam, 1965.

———. *Literaturwissenschaft und Kunstwissenschaft.* Stuttgart: Reclam, 1971.

———, ed. *Lyrik des Jugendstils: Eine Anthologie.* Stuttgart: Reclam, 1964.

———. "Peter Spinell." *MLN* 79 (1964): 439–47.

Hermand, Jost, and Frank Trommler. *Die Kultur der Weimarer Republik.* München: Nymphenburger, 1978.

Hermes, Eberhard. "Thomas Mann: *Der Tod in Venedig* (1912): Anregungen zur Interpretation." *Deutschunterricht* 29 (1977): 59–86.

Hermsdorf, Klaus, et al., eds. *Das erzählerische Werk Thomas Manns: Entstehungsgeschichte, Quellen, Wirkung.* Berlin: Aufbau, 1976.

Hiesinger, Kathryn Bloom, ed. *Art Nouveau in Munich: Masters of Jugendstil.* Philadelphia: Philadelphia Museum of Art; Munich: Prestel, 1988.

Hilscher, Eberhard. *Thomas Mann: Leben und Werk.* Berlin: Europäische, 1983.

Hirschbach, Frank D. *The Arrow and the Lyre: A Study of the Role of Love in the Works of Thomas Mann.* Hague: Nijhoff, 1955.

Hoffer, Peter T. *Klaus Mann.* Boston: Hall, 1978.

Hoffman, Frederick J. *Freudianism and the Literary Mind*. Baton Rouge: Louisiana State UP, 1967.

Hohoff, Ulrich, and Gerhard Stumpf, eds. *Thomas Mann im amerikanischen Exil: 1938–1952*. Augsburg: Universität Augsburg–Hofmann, 1991.

Hoile, Christopher. "Lambert Strether and the Boaters—Tonio Kröger and the Dancers: Confrontation and Self-Acceptance." *Canadian Review of Comparative Literature* 2 (1975): 243–61.

Holland, Norman N. *Holland's Guide to Psychoanalytic Psychology and Literature-and-Psychology*. New York: Oxford UP, 1990.

Hollingdale, R. J. *Thomas Mann: A Critical Study*. Lewisburg: Bucknell UP, 1971.

Hübinger, Paul Egon. *Thomas Mann, die Universität Bonn und die Zeitgeschichte: Drei Kapitel deutscher Vergangenheit aus dem Leben des Dichters 1905–1955*. München: Oldenbourg, 1974.

Hughes, H. Stuart. *Consciousness and Society: The Reconstruction of European Social Thought, 1890–1930*. New York: Vintage-Random, 1958.

Hughes, Kenneth, ed. *Thomas Mann in Context: Papers of the Clark University Centennial Colloquium*. Worcester: Clark UP, 1978.

Hughes, William N. "Thomas Mann and the Platonic Adulterer." *Monatshefte* 51 (1959): 75–80.

Hutchison, Alexander. "Luchino Visconti's *Death in Venice*." *Literature and Film Quarterly* 2 (1974): 31–43.

Huysmans, J.-K. *A rebours*. 1884. Paris: Fasquelle, 1970. Trans. as *Against Nature*. Trans. Robert Baldick. Harmondsworth, Eng.: Penguin, 1959.

Janik, Allan, and Stephen Toulmin. *Wittgenstein's Vienna*. New York: Simon, 1973.

Jendreiek, Helmut. *Thomas Mann: Der demokratische Roman*. Düsseldorf: Bagel, 1977.

Jens, Inge. "Es kenne mich die Welt, auf dass sie mir verzeihe." *Thomas Mann in seinen Tagebüchern*. Frankfurt: Fischer, 1989.

Jens, Inge, and Walter Jens. "Die Tagebücher." Koopmann, *Handbuch* 721–41.

Jofen, Jean. "A Freudian Commentary on Thomas Mann's *Death in Venice*." *Journal of Evolutionary Psychology* 6 (1985): 238–47.

Johnston, William M. *The Austrian Mind: An Intellectual and Social History 1848–1938*. Berkeley: U of California P, 1972.

Jonas, Ilsedore B. " 'Ich sah ein kleines Wunder . . .': Porträts von Thomas Manns Lebensgefährtin." *Philobiblon* 26 (1982): 318–28.

———. "Klaus Mann." *Dictionary of Literary Biography: German Fiction Writers 1914–1945*. Ed. James Hardin. Vol. 56. Detroit: Gale, 1987. 196–206.

———. *Thomas Mann and Italy*. Trans. Betty Crouse. University: U of Alabama P, 1969.

Jonas, Klaus W. "Auf den Spuren Thomas Manns: Kleiner Wegweiser durch deutsche Forschungs- und Gedenkstätten." *Imprimatur* 14 (1991): 199–228.

———. "In Memoriam: Helen T. Porter Lowe 1876–1963." *Monatshefte* 55 (1963): 322–24.

————. "The Making of a Thomas-Mann-Bibliography (1949–1989)." *Deutsche Vierteljahrsschrift für Literaturwissenschaft und Geistesgeschichte* 64 (1990): 744–55.

————. Rev. of *Aufsätze, Reden, Essays,* by Thomas Mann. Ed. Harry Matter. *German Quarterly* 58 (1985): 624–26.

————. Rev. of *Die Briefe Thomas Manns: Regesten und Register,* ed. Hans Bürgin, Hans-Otto Mayer, et al. *Journal of English and Germanic Philology* 89 (1990): 103–05.

————. Rev. of *Die Literatur über Thomas Mann,* by Harry Matter. *Monatshefte* 66 (1974): 83–87.

————. *Die Thomas-Mann-Literatur: Bibliographie der Kritik.* Vol. 1: 1896–1955. Vol. 2: 1956–75. Berlin: Schmidt, 1972–79.

Jones, Ernest. *The Life and Work of Sigmund Freud.* 3 vols. New York: Basic, 1953–57.

Jones, James W. Rev. of *Männerweiblichkeit,* by Gerhard Härle. *German Quarterly* 63 (1990): 309–11.

Jost, Dominik. *Literarischer Jugendstil.* Stuttgart: Metzler, 1969.

Juhl, P. D. *Interpretation: An Essay in the Philosophy of Literary Criticism.* Princeton: Princeton UP, 1980.

Kaes, Anton, ed. *Weimarer Republik: Manifeste und Dokumente zur deutschen Literatur 1918–1933.* Stuttgart: Metzler, 1983.

Kahn-Reach, Hilde. "Thomas Mann: Mein 'Boss.' " *Neue Deutsche Hefte* 20 (1973): 51–64.

Kamenetsky, Christa. "Thomas Mann's Concept of the 'Bürger.' " *College Language Association Journal* 5 (1962): 184–94.

Kane, B. M. "Thomas Mann and Visconti." *Modern Languages* 53 (1972): 74–80.

Karst, Roman. *Thomas Mann: Der deutsche Zwiespalt.* München: Heyne, 1987.

Karsunke, Yaak. " '. . . Von der albernen Sucht, besonders zu sein': Thomas Manns *Der Tod in Venedig*—wiedergelesen." Arnold 85–93.

Kaufmann, Fritz. *Thomas Mann: The World as Will and Representation.* Boston: Beacon, 1957.

Keiser-Hayne, Helga. *"Beteiligt euch, es geht um eure Ende": Erika Mann und ihr politisches Kabarett die "Pfeffermühle" 1933–1937.* München: Spangenberg, 1990.

Keller, Ernst. *Der unpolitische Deutsche: Eine Studie zu den* Betrachtungen eines Unpolitischen *von Thomas Mann.* Bern: Francke, 1965.

Kelley, Alice van Buren. "Von Aschenbach's *Phaedrus*: Platonic Allusion in *Der Tod in Venedig.*" *Journal of English and Germanic Philology* 75 (1975): 228–40.

Kiell, Norman. *Freud without Hindsight: Reviews of His Work, 1893–1939.* Madison: International Univs., 1988.

Kirchberger, Lida. "*Death in Venice* and the Eighteenth Century." *Monatshefte* 58 (1966): 321–34.

————. "Popularity as a Technique: Notes on *Tonio Kröger.*" *Monatshefte* 63 (1971): 321–34.

————. Rev. of *Thomas Mann's Doctor Faustus*, by Gunilla Bergsten. *German Quarterly* 48 (1975): 525–28.

————. "Thomas Mann's *Tristan*." *Germanic Review* 36 (1961): 282–97.

Knüfermann, Volker. "Die Gefährdung des Narziss oder: Zur Begründung und Problematik der Form in Thomas Manns *Der Tod in Venedig* und Robert Musils *Die Verwirrungen des Zöglings Törless*." *Im Dialog mit der Moderne: Zur deutschsprachigen Literatur von der Gründerzeit bis zur Gegenwart.* Ed. Roland Jost and Hansgeorg Schmidt-Bergmann. Frankfurt: Athenäum, 1986. 84–95.

Koch, Hans-Albrecht, and Uta Koch. "Thomas Mann." *Internationale Germanistische Bibliographie 1980, 1981, 1982.* München: Saur, 1981– .

Koch-Emmery, E. "Thomas Mann in English Translation." *German Life and Letters* 6 (1953): 275–84.

Kohut, Heinz. "*Death in Venice* by Thomas Mann: A Story about the Disintegration of Artistic Sublimation." Ruitenbeek, *Psychoanalysis* 282–302.

Kolbe, Jürgen. *Heller Zauber: Thomas Mann in München 1894–1933.* Berlin: Siedler, 1987.

Koopmann, Helmut. *Die Entwicklung des "intellektualen Romans" bei Thomas Mann.* Bonn: Bouvier, 1980.

————. "Forschungsgeschichte." Koopmann, *Handbuch* 941–76.

————. "Gegen- und nicht naturalistische Tendenzen in der deutschen Literatur zwischen 1880 und 1900." *Jahrhundertende—Jahrhundertwende.* 1. Teil. Ed. Helmut Kreuzer. Wiesbaden: Athenaion, 1976. 199–224.

————. " 'German Culture Is Where I Am': Thomas Mann in Exile." *Studies in Twentieth Century Literature* 7 (1982): 5–20.

————. "Hanno Buddenbrook, Tonio Kröger und Tadzio: Anfang und Begründung des Mythos im Werk Thomas Manns." *Gedenkschrift für Thomas Mann: 1875–1975.* Ed. Rolf Wiecker. Copenhagen: Text und Kontext, 1975. 53–65.

————. *Der schwierige Deutsche: Studien zum Werk Thomas Manns.* Tübingen: Niemeyer, 1988.

————, ed. *Thomas-Mann-Handbuch.* Stuttgart: Kröner, 1990.

————. *Thomas Mann: Konstanten seines literarischen Werks.* Göttingen: Vandenhoeck, 1975.

————. "Thomas Manns Autobiographien." Ley et al. 198–213.

————. "Zur Thomas Mann Forschung 1961–1979." Koopmann, *Entwicklung* 171–93.

Koopmann, Helmut, and Clark Muenzer, eds. *Wegbereiter der Moderne: Festschrift für Klaus Jonas.* Tübingen: Niemeyer, 1990.

Koppen, Erwin. *Dekadenter Wagnerismus: Studien zur europäischen Literatur des Fin de siècle.* Berlin: Gruyter, 1973.

————. "Vom Décadent zum Proto-Hitler: Wagner-Bilder Thomas Manns." Kurzke, *Stationen* 228–46.

Kristiansen, Børge. Rev. of *Thomas Mann*, by Volkmar Hansen. *Text und Kontext* 13 (1985): 216–21.

————. "Thomas Mann und die Philosophie." Koopmann, *Handbuch* 259–83.

Kroll, Fredric, and Klaus Täubert. *Sammlung der Kräfte: Klaus-Mann-Biographie (1933–1934)*. Vol. 1. Wiesbaden: Blahak, 1992.

Krotkoff, Hertha. "Zur Symbolik in Thomas Manns *Tod in Venedig*." *MLN* 82 (1967): 445–53.

Krüll, Marianne. *Im Netz der Zauberer: Eine andere Geschichte der Familie Mann*. Zürich: Arche, 1991.

Kurzke, Hermann. *Auf der Suche nach der verlorenen Irrationalität: Thomas Mann und der Konservatismus*. Würzburg: Königshausen, 1980.

————. "Auswahlbibliographie 1976–1983." Kurzke, *Stationen* 296–304.

————. "Auswahlbibliographie zu Thomas Mann." Arnold 238–62.

————. "Das Elend der Frankfurter Thomas-Mann-Ausgabe." *Text und Kontext* 14 (1986): 140–47.

————. "Die politische Essayistik." Koopmann, *Handbuch* 696–706.

————. Rev. of *Aufsätze, Reden, Essays*, by Thomas Mann. Ed. Harry Matter. *Thomas Mann Jahrbuch* 2 (1989): 179–82.

————, ed. *Stationen der Thomas-Mann-Forschung: Aufsätze seit 1970*. Würzburg: Königshausen, 1985.

————. "Tendenzen der Forschung seit 1976." Kurzke, *Stationen* 7–14.

————. *Thomas Mann: Epoche, Werk, Wirkung*. 2nd ed. München: Beck, 1991.

————. *Thomas-Mann-Forschung 1969–1976: Ein kritischer Bericht*. Frankfurt: Fischer, 1977.

Kutzbach, Karl August, ed. *Die neuklassische Bewegung um 1905*. Emsdetten: Lechte, 1972.

Laage, Karl. "Thomas Manns Verhältnis zu Theodor Storm und Iwan Turgenjew (dargestellt an der Novelle *Tonio Kröger*)." *Blätter der Thomas Mann Gesellschaft* 20 (1983–84): 15–29.

La Capra, Dominick. "Mann's *Death in Venice*: An Allegory of Reading." *History, Politics, and the Novel*. Ithaca: Cornell UP, 1987. 111–28.

Lange, Victor. "Thomas Mann in Exile." Corngold, Lange, and Ziolkowski 39–45.

————. "Thomas Mann: Politics and Art." *Wert und Wort: Festschrift für Else M. Fleissner*. Ed. Marion Sonnenfeld et al. Aurora: Wells Coll., 1965. 69–75.

————. "Thomas Mann the Novelist." Corngold, Lange, and Ziolkowski 1–8.

Laqueur, Walter. "The Artist in Politics." Rev. of *Reflections of a Nonpolitical Man*, by Thomas Mann. Trans. Walter D. Morris. *New York Times Book Review* 15 May 1983: 11+.

————. *Weimar: A Cultural History 1918–1933*. New York: Putnam's, 1974.

Large, David C., and William Weber, eds. *Wagnerism in European Culture and Politics*. Ithaca: Cornell UP, 1984.

Lehmann, Herbert. "Sigmund Freud and Thomas Mann." Ruitenbeek, *Freud* 504–17.

Lehnert, Herbert. "Another Note on 'motus animi continuus' and the Clenched-Fist Image in *Der Tod in Venedig*." *German Quarterly* 40 (1967): 452–53.

————. "Fictional Orientations in Thomas Mann's Biography." *PMLA* 88 (1973): 1146–61.

————. "Hundert Jahre Thomas Mann: 1. Thomas Mann—ein Klassiker?—Neues zur Biographie." *Orbis Litterarum* 32 (1977): 97–115.

————. "Hundert Jahre Thomas Mann: 2. Neue Thomas Mann Literatur." *Orbis Litterarum* 32 (1977): 341–58.

————. "Neue Quellen für die Thomas Mann Forschung." *Orbis Litterarum* 44 (1989): 267–77.

————. "Notes on Mann's *Der Tod in Venedig* and *The Odyssey*." *PMLA* 80 (1965): 306–07.

————. Rev. of *The Brothers Mann*, by Nigel Hamilton. *German Quarterly* 53 (1980): 249–50.

————. *Thomas Mann: Fiktion, Mythos, Religion*. 2nd ed. Stuttgart: Kohlhammer, 1968.

————. *Thomas-Mann-Forschung: Ein Bericht*. Stuttgart: Metzler, 1969.

————. "Thomas Mann in Exile 1933–1938." *Germanic Review* 38 (1963): 277–94.

————. "Thomas Mann in Princeton." *Germanic Review* 39 (1964): 15–32.

————. "Thomas Mann's Early Interest in Myth and Erwin Rohde's *Psyche*." *PMLA* 79 (1964): 297–304.

————. "Thomas Mann's Interpretations of *Der Tod in Venedig* and Their Reliability." *Rice University Studies* 50 (1964): 41–60.

————. "Thomas Mann und Schiller." *Rice Institute Pamphlet: Studies in Modern Languages* 47 (1960): 99–118.

————. "Tonio Kröger and Georg Bendemann: Artistic Alienation from Bourgeois Society in Kafka's Writings." Ley et al. 222–37.

————. "*Tristan, Tonio Kröger* und *Der Tod in Venedig*: Ein Strukturvergleich." *Orbis Litterarum* 24 (1969): 271–304.

————. *Vom Jugendstil zum Expressionismus*. Vol. 5 of *Geschichte der deutschen Literatur*. Stuttgart: Reclam, 1978.

Lehnert, Herbert, and Peter C. Pfeiffer, eds. *Thomas Mann's* Doctor Faustus: *A Novel at the Margin of Modernism*. Columbia: Camden, 1991.

Leibrich, Louis. "Thomas Mann in Frankreich: Rezeption, persönliche Beziehungen, Wirkungsgeschichte." Bludau, Heftrich, and Koopmann 387–97.

Leppmann, Wolfgang. "Time and Place in *Der Tod in Venedig*." *German Quarterly* 48 (1975): 66–75.

Lesér, Esther H. *Thomas Mann's Short Fiction: An Intellectual Biography*. Rutherford: Fairleigh Dickinson UP, 1989.

Leupold-Löwenthal, Harald. "Vienna and the Birth of Psychoanalysis." *Vienna 1890–1920*. Ed. Robert Waissenberger. New York: Rizzoli, 1984. 99–108.

Lewisohn, Ludwig. *Goethe*. New York: Farrar, 1949.

Ley, Ralph, et al., eds. *Perspectives and Personalities: Studies in Modern German Literature Honoring Claude Hill*. Heidelberg: Winter, 1978.

Lichtheim, George. *Europe in the Twentieth Century*. New York: Praeger, 1972.

Lillyman, William J. "Analogies for Love: Goethe's *Die Wahlverwandtschaften* and Plato's *Symposium.*" *Goethe's Narrative Fiction: The Irvine Goethe Symposium.* Ed. Lillyman. Berlin: Gruyter, 1983. 128–44.

Lillyman, William, Hannelore Mundt, and Egon Schwarz, eds. *Horizonte: Festschrift für Herbert Lehnert zum 65. Geburtstag.* Tübingen: Niemeyer, 1990.

Lindtke, Gustav. *Die Stadt der* Buddenbrooks: *Lübecker Bürgerkultur im 19. Jahrhundert.* Lübeck: Schmidt-Rümhild, 1965.

Linn, Rolf N. *Heinrich Mann.* New York: Twayne, 1967.

Loewy, Ernst. *Thomas Mann: Ton- und Filmaufnahmen: Ein Verzeichnis.* Frankfurt: Fischer, 1974.

Lotze, Dieter P. "Balduin Bählamm und Tonio Kröger. Der in die Kunst verirrte Bürger bei Wilhelm Busch und Thomas Mann." *Wilhelm-Busch-Jahrbuch* 44 (1978): 36–42.

Lubich, Frederick A. "Die Entfaltung der Dialektik von Logos und Eros in Thomas Manns *Tod in Venedig.*" *Colloquia Germanica* 18 (1985): 140–59.

Lublinski, Samuel. *Der Ausgang der Moderne.* Ed. Gotthart Wunberg. Tübingen: Niemeyer, 1976.

———. *Die Bilanz der Moderne.* Ed. Gotthart Wunberg. Tübingen: Niemeyer, 1974.

Luhan, Mabel Dodge. *Intimate Memories.* Vol. 2 of *Movers and Shakers.* New York: Harcourt, 1936.

Lukács, Georg. *The Destruction of Reason.* Trans. Peter Palmer. London: Merlin, 1980.

———. "In Search of Bourgeois Man." Ezergailis, *Critical Essays* 24–47.

Lunding, Erik. "Thomas Mann und Hispano-Amerika." *Zeitschrift für deutsche Philologie* 99 (1980): 288–93.

Mádl, Antal, and Judit Györi. *Thomas Mann und Ungarn: Essays, Dokumente, Bibliographie.* Wien: Böhlau, 1977.

Madsen, S. Tschudi. *Art Nouveau.* Trans. R. I. Christopherson. New York: McGraw, 1967.

Mann, Erika. *Briefe und Antworten.* Vol. 1: 1922–1950. Vol. 2: 1951–1969. Ed. Anna Zanco Prestel. München: Deutscher Taschenbuch, 1988.

———. *The Last Year of Thomas Mann.* Trans. Richard Graves. Freeport: Books for Libraries, 1970.

———. "Letter to My Father." Neider 55–58.

Mann, Erika, and Klaus Mann. *Escape to Life.* Boston: Houghton, 1939.

———. "Portrait of Our Father." Neider 59–76.

Mann, Golo. *The History of Germany since 1789.* Trans. Marian Jackson. New York: Praeger, 1968.

———. "Memories of My Father." *Universitas* 11 (1969): 151–66.

———. *Reminiscences and Reflections: Growing Up in Germany.* Trans. Krishna Winston. Introd. Peter Demetz. New York: Norton, 1991.

Mann, Heinrich. "My Brother." Neider 83–90.

————— . *Ein Zeitalter wird besichtigt*. Stockholm: Neuer, 1945.

Mann, Julia. *Aus Dodos Kindheit: Erinnerungen*. Konstanz: Rosgarten, 1958.

————— . *"Ich spreche so gern mit meinen Kindern": Erinnerungen, Skizzen, Briefwechsel mit Heinrich Mann*. Ed. Rosemarie Eggert. Berlin: Aufbau, 1991.

Mann, Katia. *Unwritten Memories*. Ed. Elisabeth Plessen and Michael Mann. Trans. Hunter Hannum and Hildegarde Hannum. New York: Knopf, 1975.

Mann, Klaus. *Briefe und Antworten 1922–1949*. Ed. Martin Gregor-Dellin. München: Ellermann, 1987.

————— . *Tagebücher: 1931–1933, 1934–1935, 1936–1937, 1938–1939, 1940–1943, 1944–1949*. Ed. Joachim Heimannsberg et al. 6 vols. München: Ellermann, 1989–91.

————— . *The Turning Point: The Autobiography of Klaus Mann*. Introd. Shelley L. Frisch. New York: Wiener, 1984.

Mann, Michael. *Fragmente eines Lebens: Lebensbericht und Auswahl seiner Schriften*. Ed. Frederic C. Tubach and Sally P. Tubach. München: Ellermann, 1983.

————— . "Thomas Mann and the United States of America: A Twenty-Year Relationship." Ley et al. 274–81.

————— . "Truth and Poetry in Thomas Mann's Work." Schulte and Chapple 84–94.

Mann, Monika. *Past and Present*. Trans. Frances F. Reid and Ruth Hein. New York: St. Martin's, 1960.

Mann, Viktor. *Wir waren fünf: Bildnis der Familie Mann*. Konstanz: Südverlag, 1949.

Marcus, Judith. *Georg Lukács and Thomas Mann: A Study in the Sociology of Literature*. Amherst: U of Massachusetts P, 1987.

Margetts, John. "Die 'scheinbar herrenlose' Kamera: Thomas Manns *Tod in Venedig* und die Kunstphotographie Wilhelm von Gloedens." *Germanisch-Romanische Monatsschrift* 39 (1989): 326–37.

Margolis, Joseph. *Art and Philosophy: Conceptual Issues in Aesthetics*. Brighton: Harvester, 1980.

————— , ed. *Philosophy Looks at the Arts*. Philadelphia: Temple UP, 1987.

Marson, E. L. *The Ascetic Artist: Prefigurations in Thomas Mann's Der Tod in Venedig*. Bern: Lang, 1979.

Martin, Robert K. "Walt Whitman and Thomas Mann." *Walt Whitman Quarterly Review* 4 (1987): 1–6.

Martini, Fritz. "*Der Tod in Venedig*." *Das Wagnis der Sprache: Interpretation deutscher Prosa von Nietzsche bis Benn*. Stuttgart: Klett, 1964. 176–224.

Marx, Leonie. "Thomas Mann und die skandinavischen Literaturen." Koopmann, *Handbuch* 164–99.

Mater, Erich. "Möglichkeiten und Grenzen einer historisch-kritischen Edition der Werke Thomas Manns." Wenzel, *Betrachtungen* 382–417.

Mathes, Jürg, ed. *Prosa des Jugendstils*. Stuttgart: Reclam, 1982.

————— . *Theorie des literarischen Jugendstils*. Stuttgart: Reclam, 1984.

Matter, Harry. *Die Literatur über Thomas Mann: Eine Bibliographie, 1898–1969*. 2 vols. Berlin: Aufbau, 1972.

Matthias, Klaus. *Thomas Mann und Skandinavien.* Lübeck: Schmidt-Römhild, 1969.

Maurer, K. W. "Tonio Kröger and Hamlet." *Modern Language Review* 43 (1948): 520.

Mautner, Franz H. "Die griechischen Anklänge in Thomas Manns *Tod in Venedig.*" *Monatshefte* 44 (1952): 20–26.

May, Keith M. *Nietzsche and Modern Literature: Themes in Yeats, Rilke, Mann, and Lawrence.* New York: St. Martin's, 1988.

Mayer, Hans. "On the Political Development of an Unpolitical Man." Ezergailis, *Critical Essays* 191–206.

———. *Outsiders: A Study in Life and Letters.* Trans. D. Sweet. Cambridge: MIT P, 1982.

———. *Thomas Mann.* Frankfurt: Suhrkamp, 1984.

———. "*Der Tod in Venedig*: Ein Thema mit Variationen." *Literaturwissenschaft und Geistesgeschichte: Festschrift für Richard Brinkmann.* Ed. Jürgen Brummack et al. Tübingen: Niemeyer, 1981. 711–24.

Mazzella, Anthony. "*Death in Venice*: Fiction and Film." *College Literature* 5 (1978): 183–94.

McClain, William H. "Wagnerian Overtones in *Der Tod in Venedig.*" *MLN* 79 (1964): 481–95.

McNamara, Eugene. "*Death in Venice*: The Disguised Self." *College English* 24 (1962): 233–34.

McWilliams, James R. "Conflict and Compromise: Tonio Kröger's Paradox." *Revue des langues vivantes* 32 (1966): 376–83.

———. "The Failure of a Repression: Thomas Mann's *Tod in Venedig.*" *German Life and Letters* 20 (1967): 233–41.

Mendel, Siegfried. "Helen Tracy Lowe-Porter: Once a Translator, Always a Translator." *Denver Quarterly* 17 (1982): 29–39.

Mendelssohn, Peter de. "Bekenntnis und Autobiographie." Bludau, Heftrich, and Koopmann 606–27.

———. *Die Frankfurter Ausgabe der Gesammelten Werke. (Vortrag).* Frankfurt: Fischer, 1981.

———. "Grenzlinien mit Wegweisern: Biographie und Autobiographie." *Von deutscher Repräsentanz* 9–47.

———. "Das Jahr Dreiunddreissig." *Neue Rundschau* 86 (1975): 199–216.

———. "Lebensbeschreibung des Schriftstellers: Unterwegs zu Thomas Mann." *Von deutscher Repräsentanz* 48–94.

———. *Nachbemerkungen zu Thomas Mann.* 2 vols. Frankfurt: Fischer, 1982.

———. "Der Schriftsteller als politischer Bürger." *Thomas Mann: 1875–1975.* München: Moos, 1975. 5–32.

———. "Ein Schriftsteller in München." Bludau, Heftrich, and Koopmann 14–36.

———. *S. Fischer und sein Verlag.* Frankfurt: Fischer, 1970.

———. *Von deutscher Repräsentanz.* München: Prestel, 1972.

———. *Der Zauberer: Das Leben des deutschen Schriftstellers Thomas Mann.* Teil 1. 1875–1918. Frankfurt: Fischer, 1975.

——. *Der Zauberer: Das Leben des deutschen Schriftstellers Thomas Mann. Jahre der Schwebe: 1919 und 1933. Nachgelassene Kapitel. Gesamtregister.* Ed. Albert von Schirnding. Frankfurt: Fischer, 1992.

Mercanton, Jacques. "Thomas Mann in seinen Briefen." *Sinn und Form* (1965): 379–87.

Mertz, Wolfgang. *Thomas Mann: Wirkung und Gegenwart.* Frankfurt: Fischer, 1975.

Michael, Wolfgang F. Rev. of *Reflections*, by Thomas Mann. *German Quarterly* 58 (1985): 138–39.

——. "Stoff und Idee im *Tod in Venedig*." *Deutsche Vierteljahrsschrift für Literaturwissenschaft und Geistesgeschichte* 33 (1959): 13–19.

——. "Thomas Mann auf dem Wege zu Freud." *MLN* 65 (1950): 165–71.

Mitchell, Donald. "*Death in Venice*: The Dark Side of Perfection." Palmer, *Britten Companion* 238–49.

Moeller, Hans-Bernhard. "Thomas Manns venezianische Götterkunde, Plastik und Zeitlosigkeit." *Deutsche Vierteljahrsschrift für Literaturwissenschaft und Geistesgeschichte* 40 (1966): 184–205.

Morris, Marcia. "Sensuality and Art: Tolstoyan Echoes in *Tristan*." *Germano-Slavica* 5 (1987): 211–22.

Morse, J. Mitchell. "Joyce and the Early Thomas Mann." *Revue de littérature comparée* 36 (1962): 377–85.

Mosse, George L. *Nationalism and Sexuality: Respectability and Abnormal Sexuality in Modern Europe.* New York: Fertig, 1985.

Motschan, Georges. *Thomas Mann—von nahem erlebt.* Nettetal: Matussek, 1988.

Moulden, Ken, and Gero von Wilpert, eds. Buddenbrooks-*Handbuch.* Stuttgart: Kröner, 1988.

Murata, Tsunekazu. "Thomas Mann in Japan." Bludau, Heftrich, and Koopmann 434–46.

Nebehay, Christian M. *Ver Sacrum 1898–1903.* Wien: Tusch, 1975.

Neider, Charles, ed. *The Stature of Thomas Mann.* Freeport: Books for Libraries, 1968.

Neumann, Erich. "Fortsetzung und Nachtrag zu Hans Bürgins Bibliographie *Das Werk Thomas Manns*." Wenzel, *Betrachtungen* 491–510.

Neumeister, Erdmann. *Thomas Manns frühe Erzählungen: Der Jugendstil als Kunstform im frühen Werk.* 3rd ed. Bonn: Bouvier, 1977.

Newman, Ernest. *The Wagner Operas.* New York: Knopf, 1972.

Newton, Caroline. "Thomas Mann and Sigmund Freud." *Princeton University Library Chronicle* 24 (1963): 135–39.

Nicholls, Roger A. *Nietzsche in the Early Works of Thomas Mann.* Berkeley: U of California P, 1955.

Nicklas, Hans W. *Thomas Manns Novelle Der Tod in Venedig: Analyse des Motivzusammenhangs und der Erzählstruktur.* Marburg: Elwert, 1968.

Nietzsche, Friedrich. *The Birth of Tragedy. Basic Writings of Nietzsche.* Trans. Walter Kaufmann. New York: Modern Library, 1968. 1–144.

————. *Human, All Too Human.* Trans. R. J. Hollingdale. Cambridge: Cambridge UP, 1986.

————. *Nietzsche contra Wagner. Portable Nietzsche* 661–83.

————. *The Portable Nietzsche.* Trans. Walter Kaufmann. Harmondsworth, Eng.: Penguin, 1982.

————. *Thus Spoke Zarathustra. Portable Nietzsche* 103–439.

————. *Twilight of the Idols. Portable Nietzsche* 463–563.

Noble, C. A. M. "Erkenntnisekel und Erkenntnisfreude: Über Thomas Manns Verhältnis zu Sigmund Freud." *Revue des langues vivantes* 38 (1972): 154–63.

Nordau, Max. *Degeneration.* Introd. George Mosse. New York: Fertig, 1968.

Northcote-Bade, James. "Thomas Mann's Use of Wagner's 'Sehnsuchtsmotiv' in *Tristan.*" *Seminar* 8 (1972): 55–60.

Novalis [Friedrich von Hardenberg]. *Hymns to the Night.* Trans. Dick Higgins. New Paltz: McPherson, 1984.

Ohl, Hubert. "Das Meer und die Kunst: Über den Zusammenhang von Erzählstruktur und Symbolik in Thomas Manns Novelle *Tonio Kröger.*" *Literatur in Wissenschaft und Unterricht* 22 (1989): 99–116.

Olsen, Henry. "Der Patient Spinell." *Orbis Litterarum* 20 (1965): 217–21.

O'Neill, Patrick. "Dance and Counterdance: A Note on *Tonio Kröger.*" *German Life and Letters* 29 (1976): 291–95.

Otto, Regine. "Bemerkungen zu Thomas Manns Auseinandersetzung mit Goethes *Wahlverwandtschaften.*" *Werk und Wirkung Thomas Manns in unserer Epoche.* Ed. Helmut Brandt and Hans Kaufmann. Berlin: Aufbau, 1978. 287–301.

Palmer, Christopher, ed. *The Britten Companion.* Cambridge: Cambridge UP, 1984.

————. "Towards a Genealogy of *Death in Venice.*" *Britten* 250–67.

Papenfuss, Dietrich, and Jürgen Söring, eds. *Rezeption der deutschen Gegenwartsliteratur im Ausland: Internationale Forschungen zur neueren deutschen Literatur.* Stuttgart: Kohlhammer, 1976.

Parkes, Ford B. "The Image of the Tiger in Thomas Mann's *Tod in Venedig.*" *Studies in Twentieth Century Literature* 3 (1978): 73–83.

Pascal, Roy. *From Naturalism to Expressionism: German Literature and Society 1880–1918.* New York: Basic, 1973.

Pawel, Ernst. "Including Laundry Lists." Rev. of *Thomas Mann: Diaries 1918–1939,* ed. Hermann Kesten. *New York Times Book Review* 14 Nov. 1982: 13+.

Peacock, Ronald. "Much Is Comic in Thomas Mann." Ezergailis, *Critical Essays* 175–91.

Petersen, Jürgen. "Die Rolle des Erzählers und die epische Ironie im Frühwerk Thomas Manns: Ein Beitrag zur Untersuchung seiner dichterischen Verfahrensweise." Diss. U Köln, 1967.

Petriconi, H[ellmuth]. *Das Reich des Untergangs: Bemerkungen über ein mythologisches Thema.* Hamburg: Hoffmann, 1958.

Pfäfflin, Friedrich. *Hundert Jahre S. Fischer Verlag 1886–1986: Buchumschläge. Über Bücher und ihre äussere Gestalt.* Frankfurt: Fischer, 1986.

Phillipps, Kathy J. "Conversion to Text, Initiation to Symbolism, in Mann's *Der Tod in Venedig* and James' *The Ambassadors.*" *Canadian Review of Comparative Literature* 6 (1979): 376–88.

Pierrot, Jean. *The Decadent Imagination, 1880–1900.* Trans. D. Coltman. Chicago: U of Chicago P, 1981.

Pike, Burton. "Thomas Mann and the Problematic Self." *Publications of the English Goethe Society* 37 (1966–67): 120–41.

Plank, Robert. "*Death in Venice*: Tragedy or Mishap?" *Hartford Studies in Literature* 4 (1972): 95–103.

Platen, August von. *Sämtliche Werke.* Ed. Max Koch. 12 vols. Hildesheim: Olms, 1969.

Plato. *The Collected Dialogues.* Ed. Edith Hamilton and Huntington Cairns. New York: Pantheon, 1961.

Porter, Andrew. "The Last Opera: *Death in Venice.*" *The Operas of Benjamin Britten.* Ed. David Herbert. New York: Columbia UP, 1979. 59–62.

Potempa, Georg. *Thomas Mann: Beteiligung an politischen Aufrufen und anderen kollektiven Publikationen: Eine Bibliographie.* Morsum: Cicero, 1988.

Probst, Gerhard F. "Bemerkungen zu H. T. Lowe-Porters englischer Übersetzung von Thomas Manns *Tonio Kröger.*" *Germanic Notes* 7 (1976): 51–53.

Pütz, Peter. "Der Ausbruch aus der Negativität: Das Ethos im *Tod in Venedig.*" *Thomas Mann Jahrbuch* 1 (1988): 1–11.

———. *Kunst und Künstlerexistenz bei Nietzsche und Thomas Mann: Zum Problem des ästhetischen Perspektivismus in der Moderne.* 3rd ed. Bonn: Bouvier, 1987.

———. "Thomas Manns Wirkung auf die deutsche Literatur der Gegenwart." Bludau, Heftrich, and Koopmann 453–65.

———, ed. *Thomas Mann und die Tradition.* Frankfurt: Athenäum, 1971.

———. "Thomas Mann und Nietzsche." *Thomas Mann und die Tradition* 225–49.

Radcliff-Umstead, Douglas. "The Journey of Fatal Longing: Mann and Visconti." *Annali d'Italianistica* 6 (1988): 199–219.

Rasch, Wolfdietrich. "Jugendstil im Frühwerk Thomas Manns." *Deutsche Vierteljahrsschrift für Literaturwissenschaft und Geistesgeschichte* 40 (1966): 206–16.

———. "Thomas Manns Erzählung *Tristan.*" *Zur deutschen Literatur der Jahrhundertwende.* Stuttgart: Metzler, 1967. 146–85.

Reed, Philip. "Aschenbach Becomes Mahler: Thomas Mann as Film." *Benjamin Britten: Death in Venice.* Ed. Donald Mitchell. New York: Cambridge UP, 1987. 178–83.

Reed, T[erence] J[ames]. "Einfache Verulkung, Manier, Stil: Die Briefe an Otto Grautoff als Dokument der frühen Entwicklung Thomas Manns." Heftrich and Koopmann 48–65.

———. "Der Fall Wagner." Koopmann, *Handbuch* 122–24.

———. " 'Geist und Kunst': Thomas Mann's Abandoned Essay on Literature."
    Oxford German Studies 1 (1966): 53–101.

———. "Introduction." *Thomas Mann: Der Tod in Venedig*. Ed. Reed. Oxford:
    Oxford UP, 1971. 9–51.

———. Rev. of *Thomas Mann und die Tradition*, by Peter Pütz. *Modern Language Review* 68 (1973): 704–05.

———. "Text and History: *Tonio Kröger* and the Politics of Four Decades." *Publications of the English Goethe Society* 57 (1987): 39–54.

———. "Thomas Mann and Tradition: Some Clarifications." Ezergailis, *Critical Essays* 219–37.

———. *Thomas Mann, Der Tod in Venedig: Text, Materialien, Kommentar mit den bisher unveröffentlichten Arbeitsnotizen Thomas Manns*. München: Hanser, 1983.

———. "Thomas Mann, Heine, Schiller: The Mechanics of Self-Interpretation."
    Neophilologus 47 (1963): 41–50.

———. *Thomas Mann: The Uses of Tradition*. Oxford: Oxford UP, 1974.

———. "Thomas Mann: The Writer as Historian of His Time." *Modern Language Review* 71 (1976): 82–96.

Reichel, Jochen, ed. *Der Tod in Venedig: Ein Lesebuch zur literarischen Geschichte einer Stadt*. Berlin: Henssel, 1991.

Reich-Ranicki, Marcel. *Thomas Mann and His Family*. Trans. Ralph Manheim.
    London: Fontana, 1990.

Reinhardt, Kurt F. *Germany: Two Thousand Years*. Milwaukee: Bruce, 1950.

Renner, Rolf Günter. *Das Ich als ästhetische Konstruktion: Der Tod in Venedig und seine Beziehung zum Gesamtwerk Thomas Manns*. Freiburg: Rombach, 1987.

———. *Lebens-Werk: Zum inneren Zusammenhang der Texte von Thomas Mann*.
    München: Fink, 1985.

———. "Literarästhetische, kulturkritische und autobiographische Essayistik."
    Koopmann, *Handbuch* 629–77.

———. "Verfilmungen der Werke von Thomas Mann." Koopmann, *Handbuch*
    799–822.

Requadt, Paul. "Jugendstil im Frühwerk Thomas Manns." *Deutsche Vierteljahrsschrift für Literaturwissenschaft und Geistesgeschichte* 40 (1966): 206–16.

Rey, William H. "Tragic Aspects of the Artist in Thomas Mann's Work." *Modern Language Quarterly* 19 (1958): 195–203.

Ridley, Hugh. *Thomas Mann: Buddenbrooks*. Cambridge: Cambridge UP, 1987.

Rieckmann, Jens. "Brüderliche Möglichkeiten: Thomas Manns *Tonio Kröger* und Heinrich Manns *Abdankung*." *Wirkendes Wort* 34 (1984): 422–26.

———. Rev. of *Frage und Antwort: Interviews mit Thomas Mann 1909–1955*, ed.
    Volkmar Hansen and Gert Heine. *German Quarterly* 58 (1985): 137–38.

Rimbaud, Arthur. *Œuvres complètes*. Ed. Antoine Adam. Paris: Gallimard, 1972.

Robertson, J. G., Edna Purdie, et al. *A History of German Literature*. 5th ed.
    New York: British Book Centre, 1966.

Rockwood, Heidi M. "Mann's *Death in Venice.*" *Explicator* 39 (1981): 34.

Rockwood, Heidi M., and Robert J. R. Rockwood. "The Psychological Reality of Myth in *Der Tod in Venedig.*" *Germanic Review* 59 (1984): 137–41.

Root, Winthrop H. "Grillparzer's *Sappho* and Thomas Mann's *Tonio Kröger.*" *Monatshefte* 29 (1937): 59–64.

Rosenthal, Macha L. "The Corruption of Aschenbach." *University of Kansas City Review* 14 (1947): 49–56.

Rossbach, Bruno. "Der Anfang vom Ende: Narrative Analyse des 1. Kapitels der Novelle *Der Tod in Venedig* von Thomas Mann." *Sprache in Vergangenheit und Gegenwart: Beiträge aus dem Institut für Germanistische Sprachwissenschaft der Philipps-Universität Marburg.* Ed. Wolfgang Brandt, with Rudolf Freudenberg. Marburg: Hitzeroth, 1988. 237–49.

———. *Spiegelungen eines Bewusstseins: Der Erzähler in Thomas Manns* Tristan. Marburg: Hitzeroth, 1989.

Rotkin, Charlotte. "Form and Function: The Art and Architecture of *Death in Venice.*" *Midwest Quarterly* 29 (1988): 497–505.

———. "Oceanic Animals: Allegory in *Death in Venice.*" *Papers on Language and Literature* 23 (1987): 84–88.

Rubin, William, ed. *"Primitivism" in Twentieth Century Art.* 2 vols. New York: Museum of Modern Art, 1984.

Ruitenbeek, Hendrik M., ed. *Freud As We Knew Him.* Detroit: Wayne State UP, 1973.

———, ed. *Psychoanalysis and Literature.* New York: Dutton, 1964.

Sachs, Hanns. "Das Thema *Tod.*" *Imago* 3 (1914): 456–61.

Sandberg, Hans-Joachim. " 'Der fremde Gott' und die Cholera: Nachlese zum *Tod in Venedig.*" Heftrich and Koopmann 66–110.

———. *Thomas Manns Schiller-Studien.* Oslo: Universitetsforlaget, 1964.

Saslow, James. *Ganymede in the Renaissance: Homosexuality in Art and Society.* New Haven: Yale UP, 1986.

Scher, Steven Paul. "Kreativität als Selbstüberwindung: Thomas Manns permanente 'Wagner-Krise.' " Papenfuss and Söring 263–74.

———. *Verbal Music in German Literature.* New York: Yale UP, 1968.

Scherrer, Paul, and Hans Wysling, eds. *Quellenkritische Studien zum Werk Thomas Manns.* Bern: Francke, 1967.

Schick, Alfred. "The Vienna of Sigmund Freud." *Psychoanalytic Review* 55 (1968–69): 529–51.

Schiffer, Eva. "In Memoriam [Richard and Clara Winston]." *German Quarterly* 57 (1984): 518–20.

———. *Zwischen den Zeilen: Manuskriptänderungen bei Thomas Mann—Transkriptionen und Deutungsversuche.* Berlin: Schmidt, 1982.

Schiller, Friedrich von. *Don Carlos. Sämtliche Werke* 7–219.

———. "Dritter Brief über *Don Carlos.*" *Sämtliche Werke* 230–40.

———. *Sämtliche Werke.* 4th ed. Vol. 2. München: Hanser, 1965.

Schmidt, Ernst A. "Künstler und Knabenliebe: Eine vergleichende Skizze zu Thomas Manns *Tod in Venedig* und Vergils zweiter Ekloge." *Euphorion* 68 (1974): 437–46.

———. " 'Platonismus' und 'Heidentum' in Thomas Manns *Tod in Venedig.*" *Antike und Abendland* 20 (1974): 151–78.

Schmitz, Walter. "*Der Tod in Venedig*: Eine Erzählung aus Thomas Manns Münchner Jahren." *Blätter für den Deutschlehrer* 1 (1985): 2–20.

Schnitman, Sophia. "Musical Motives in Thomas Mann's *Tristan.*" *MLN* 86 (1971): 399–414.

Schoeller, Wilfried F. *Heinrich Mann: Bilder und Dokumente.* München: Spangenberg, 1991.

Schopenhauer, Arthur. *The World as Will and Representation.* Trans. E. F. J. Payne. 2 vols. New York: Dover, 1969.

Schrader, Bärbel, and Jürgen Schebera. *The "Golden" Twenties: Art and Literature in the Weimar Republic.* New Haven: Yale UP, 1988.

Schröter, Klaus. *Heinrich Mann in Selbstzeugnissen und Bilddokumenten.* Reinbek: Rowohlt, 1967.

———. "Literatur zu Thomas Mann um 1975." *Monatshefte* 69 (1977): 66–75.

———. *Thomas Mann im Urteil seiner Zeit: Dokumente 1891 bis 1955.* Hamburg: Wegner, 1969.

———. *Thomas Mann in Selbstzeugnissen und Bilddokumenten.* Reinbek: Rowohlt, 1975.

Schulte, Hans H. "Ist Thomas Mann noch lebendig? Verständigungsschwierigkeiten zwischen einem deutschen Klassiker und seinem Publikum." Schulte and Chapple 95–126.

Schulte, Hans H., and Gerald Chapple, eds. *Thomas Mann: Ein Kolloquium.* Bonn: Bouvier, 1978.

Schultz, H. Stefan. "Thomas Mann und Goethe." Pütz, *Thomas Mann und die Tradition* 151–79.

Schutte, Jürgen, and Peter Sprengel, eds. *Die Berliner Moderne 1885–1914.* Stuttgart: Reclam, 1987.

Schwartz, Murray M., and David Willbern. "Literature and Psychology." *Interrelations of Literature.* Ed. Jean-Pierre Barricelli and Joseph Gibaldi. New York: MLA, 1982. 205–24.

Seidlin, Oskar. "Stiluntersuchung an einem Thomas Mann Satz." *Von Goethe zu Thomas Mann.* Göttingen: Vandenhoeck, 1963. 148–61.

Seitz, Gabriele. *Film als Rezeptionsform von Literatur: Zum Problem der Verfilmung von Thomas Manns Erzählungen* Tonio Kröger, Wälsungenblut, *und* Der Tod in Venedig. 2nd ed. München: Tuduv, 1981.

Selz, Peter. *German Expressionist Painting.* Berkeley: U of California P, 1957.

Selz, Peter, and Mildred Constantine, eds. *Art Nouveau: Art and Design at the Turn of the Century.* New York: Museum of Modern Art, 1959.

Seyppel, Joachim. "Adel des Geistes: Thomas Mann und August von Platen." *Deutsche Vierteljahrsschrift für Literaturwissenschaft und Geistesgeschichte* 33 (1959): 565–73.

Shaw, Leroy R. "Biographie als Literaturwissenschaft." Papenfuss and Söring 247–54.

Sheppard, Richard. "*Tonio Kröger* and *Der Tod in Venedig*: From Bourgeois Realism to Visionary Modernism." *Oxford German Studies* 18–19 (1989–90): 92–108.

Siefken, Hinrich. Rev. of *August Graf von Platen—Thomas Mann*, by Frank Busch. *Modern Language Review* 86 (1991): 250–51.

———. Rev. of *Music, Love, Death, and Mann's* Doctor Faustus, by John F. Fetzer. *Modern Language Review* 86 (1991): 1052–53.

———. *Thomas Mann: Goethe—"Ideal der Deutschheit." Wiederholte Spiegelungen 1893–1949*. München: Fink, 1981.

———. "Thomas Mann's Essay 'Bruder Hitler.'" *German Life and Letters* 35 (1981–82): 165–81.

Simpson, William. *Hitler and Germany*. Cambridge: Cambridge UP, 1991.

Singer, Irving. "*Death in Venice*: Visconti and Mann." *MLN* 91 (1976): 1348–59.

Slochower, Harry. "Thomas Mann's *Death in Venice*." *American Imago* 26 (1969): 91–122.

Soergel, Albert, and Curt Hohoff. *Dichtung und Dichter der Zeit*. 2 vols. Düsseldorf: Bagel, 1964.

Sokel, Walter H. "Demaskierung und Untergang wilhelminischer Repräsentanz: Zum Parallelismus der Inhaltsstruktur von *Professor Unrat* und *Tod in Venedig*." *Herkommen und Erneuerung: Essays für Oskar Seidlin*. Ed. Gerald Gillespie and Edgar Lothner. Tübingen: Niemeyer, 1976. 387–412.

Sommerhage, Claus. *Eros und Poesis: Über das Erotische im Werk Thomas Manns*. Bonn: Bouvier, 1983.

Sonnenfeld, Albert. "*Tristan* for Pianoforte: Thomas Mann and Marcel Proust." *Southern Review* 5 (1969): 1004–18.

Sonner, Franz Maria. *Ethik und Körperbeherrschung: Die Verflechtung von Thomas Manns Novelle* Der Tod in Venedig *mit dem zeitgenössischen intellektuellen Kräftefeld*. Opladen: Westdeutscher, 1984.

Sontheimer, Kurt. "Thomas Mann als politischer Schriftsteller." Koopmann, *Handbuch* 165–226.

Spackman, Barbara. *Decadent Genealogies*. Ithaca: Cornell UP, 1989.

Spalek, John, and Joseph Strelka, eds. *Deutsche Exilliteratur seit 1933*. Vol. 1. Bern: Francke, 1976.

Spangenberg, Eberhard. *Karriere eines Romans: Mephisto, Klaus Mann und Gustof Gründgens*. 2nd ed. München: Ellermann, 1984.

Spann, Meno. "A New Translation." Rev. of Tonio Kröger *and Other Stories by Thomas Mann*. Trans. David Luke. *Modern Fiction Studies* 17 (1971): 109–11.

Speirs, R[onald] C. "Aus dem Leben eines Taugenichts: Zu den Tagebüchern Thomas Manns." Arnold 148–63.

Spengler, Oswald. *The Decline of the West*. 1918. Ed. A. Helps. Trans. C. Atkinson. New York: Knopf, 1962.

Stammen, Theo. "Thomas Mann und die politische Welt." Koopmann, *Handbuch* 18–53.

Stanzel, Franz K. *A Theory of Narrative.* Cambridge: Cambridge UP, 1984.

Stavenhagen, Lee. "The Name *Tadzio* in *Der Tod in Venedig.*" *German Quarterly* 35 (1961): 20–23.

Steakley, James D. *The Homosexual Emancipation Movement in Germany.* New York: Arno, 1975.

Steffensen, Steffen. "Thomas Mann und Dänemark." *Gedenkschrift für Thomas Mann: 1875–1975.* Ed. Rolf Wiecker. Copenhagen: Text und Kontext, 1975. 223–82.

Steinecke, Hartmut. "Brief-Regesten: Theorie und Praxis einer neuen Editionsform." *Zeitschrift für deutsche Philologie* 101 (1982): 199–210.

———. Rev. of *Band 13: Gesammelte Werke,* by Thomas Mann. *Zeitschrift für deutsche Philologie* 95 (1976): 595–97.

Steiner, George. Rev. of *The Brothers Mann,* by Nigel Hamilton. *New Yorker* 9 July 1979: 98 + .

Stelzmann, Rainulf A. "Thomas Mann's *Death in Venice:* Res et Imago." *Xavier University Studies* 3 (1964): 160–67.

Stendhal. *Red and Black.* Ed. and trans. Robert M. Adams. New York: Norton, 1969.

Stern, Fritz. *The Politics of Cultural Despair.* Berkeley: U of California P, 1974.

Stewart, Walter K. "*Der Tod in Venedig:* The Path to Insight." *Germanic Review* 53 (1978): 50–55.

Stresau, Hermann. *Thomas Mann und sein Werk.* Frankfurt: Fischer, 1963.

Sultan, Stanley. "Mann and Joyce: Affinities of Two Masters." K. Hughes 67–94.

Swales, Martin. Buddenbrooks: *Family Life as the Mirror of Social Change.* Boston: Hall, 1991.

———. "In Defence of Weimar: Thomas Mann and the Politics of Republicanism." Bance, *Weimar Germany* 1–13.

———. "Punctuation and the Narrative Mode: Some Remarks on *Tonio Kröger.*" *Forum for Modern Language Studies* 6 (1970): 235–42.

———. *Thomas Mann: A Study.* London: Heinemann, 1980.

Tarbox, Raymond. "*Death in Venice:* The Aesthetic Object as Dream Guide." *American Imago* 26 (1969): 123–44.

Thalmann, Marianne. "Thomas Mann: *Tod in Venedig* (Eine Aufbaustudie)." *Germanisch-Romanische Monatsschrift* 15 (1927): 374–78.

Thirlwall, John C. *In Another Language: A Record of the Thirty-Year Relationship between Thomas Mann and His American Translator, Helen Tracy Lowe-Porter.* New York: Knopf, 1966.

Thomalla, Ariane. *Die "femme fragile."* Düsseldorf: Bertelsmann, 1972.

Thomas, R. Hinton. *Thomas Mann: The Mediation of Art.* Oxford: Clarendon–Oxford UP, 1963.

———. "*Die Wahlverwandtschaften* and Mann's *Der Tod in Venedig:* A Comparative Study." *Publications of the English Goethe Society* 24 (1955): 101–30.

Thunich, Martin. *Thomas Mann:* Tonio Kröger. Hollfeld: Bange, 1984.

Traschen, Isadore. "The Uses of Myth in *Death in Venice.*" *Modern Fiction Studies* 11 (1965): 165–79.

Trilling, Lionel. "Art and Neurosis." *Liberal Imagination* 155–75.

———. "Freud and Literature." *Liberal Imagination* 32–54.

———. *The Liberal Imagination: Essays on Literature and Society.* Garden City: Anchor, 1953.

Tschechne, Wolfgang. *Thomas Manns Lübeck.* Hamburg: Ellert, 1991.

Urban, Bernd, ed. *Thomas Mann, Freud und die Psychoanalyse: Reden, Briefe, Notizen, Betrachtungen.* Frankfurt: Fischer, 1991.

Urdang, Constance. "Faust in Venice: The Artist and the Legend in *Death in Venice.*" *Accent* 18 (1958): 253–67.

Vaget, Hans Rudolf. "Die Erzählungen." Koopmann, *Handbuch* 534–618.

———. "Film and Literature: The Case of *Death in Venice*: Luchino Visconti and Thomas Mann." *German Quarterly* 53 (1980): 159–75.

———. " 'Goethe oder Wagner': Studien zu Thomas Manns Goethe-Rezeption 1905–1912." Vaget and Barnouw 3–81.

———. Rev. of Death in Venice *and Other Stories by Thomas Mann,* trans. David Luke. *Monatshefte* 83 (1991): 464–66.

———. Rev. of *Die Thomas-Mann-Literatur,* by Klaus Jonas. *Monatshefte* 75 (1983): 230–31.

———. Rev. of *Faust as Musician,* by Patrick Carnegy. *German Quarterly* 48 (1975): 524–25.

———. Rev. of From The Magic Mountain, by Henry Hatfield. *German Quarterly* 53 (1980): 246–48.

———. Rev. of *Nachträge,* by Thomas Mann. Ed. Hans Bürgin and Peter de Mendelssohn. *German Quarterly* 48 (1975): 528–30.

———. *Thomas Mann: Kommentar zu sämtlichen Erzählungen.* München: Winkler, 1984.

———. "Thomas Mann und die Neuklassik: *Der Tod in Venedig* und Samuel Lublinskis Literaturauffassung." *Jahrbuch der Deutschen Schiller-Gesellschaft* 17 (1973): 432–54.

———. "Thomas Mann und kein Ende: 1. Thomas-Mann-Literatur zur Zentenarfeier." *Zeitschrift für deutsche Philologie* 90 (1980): 276–88.

———. "Thomas Mann und Wagner: Zur Funktion des Leitmotivs in *Der Ring des Nibelungen* und *Buddenbrooks.*" *Literatur und Musik: Ein Handbuch zur Theorie und Praxis eines komparatistischen Grenzgebietes.* Ed. Steven Paul Scher. Berlin: Schmidt, 1984. 326–47.

———. *"Der Tod in Venedig* und *Die Wahlverwandtschaften."* Vaget and Barnouw 35–40.

Vaget, Hans Rudolf, and Dagmar Barnouw, eds. *Thomas Mann: Studien zu Fragen der Rezeption.* Bern: Lang, 1975.

Vordtriede, Werner. "Richard Wagners *Tod in Venedig.*" *Euphorion* 52 (1958): 378–96.

Wagner, Richard. *Tristan und Isolde*. Trans. Stewart Robb. New York: Dutton, 1965.

Wanner, Hans. *Individualität, Identität und Rolle: Das frühe Werk Heinrich Manns und Thomas Manns Erzählungen* Gladius Dei *und* Der Tod in Venedig. 2nd ed. München: Tuduv, 1977.

Wapnewski, Peter. "Der Magier und der Zauberer: Thomas Mann und Richard Wagner." *Thomas Mann und München*. Frankfurt: Fischer, 1989. 78–103.

Ward, Mark G. "More Than 'Stammesverwandtschaft'? On Tonio Kröger's Reading of *Immensee*." *German Life and Letters* 36 (1983): 301–16.

Warren, Patricia Nell. *The Front Runner*. New York: Morrow, 1974.

Watts, Cedric. "The Protean Dionysus in Euripides' *The Bacchae* and Mann's *Death in Venice*." *Studi dell'Istituto Linguistico* 3 (1980): 151–63.

Wegner, Matthias. *Exil und Literatur: Deutsche Schriftsteller im Ausland 1933–1945*. Frankfurt: Athenäum, 1967.

Wehler, Hans-Ulrich. *Das deutsche Kaiserreich, 1871–1918*. 5th ed. Göttingen: Vandenhoeck, 1983.

Weigand, Hermann J. *The Magic Mountain: A Study of Thomas Mann's Novel* Der Zauberberg. 1933. Chapel Hill: U of North Carolina P, 1965.

Weigand, Paul. "Thomas Mann's *Tonio Kröger* and Kleist's *Ueber das Marionettentheater*." *Symposium* 12 (1958): 133–48.

Weiner, Marc A. "Silence, Sound, and Song in *Der Tod in Venedig*: A Study in Psycho-social Repression." *Seminar* 23 (1987): 137–55.

Weiss, Walter. *Thomas Manns Kunst der sprachlichen und thematischen Integration*. Düsseldorf: Schwann, 1964.

Wellek, René. "The Poet as Critic, the Critic as Poet, the Poet-Critic." *The Poet as Critic*. Ed. Frederick P. W. McDowell. Evanston: Northwestern UP, 1967. 92–107.

Wellek, René, and Austin Warren. *Theory of Literature*. New York: Harcourt, 1977.

Wenzel, Georg, ed. *Betrachtungen und Überblicke: Zum Werk Thomas Manns*. Berlin: Aufbau, 1966.

———. *Thomas Manns Briefwerk: Bibliographie gedruckter Briefe aus den Jahren 1889–1955*. Berlin: Akademie, 1969.

Wetzel, Heinz. "Erkenntnisekel: Motivkorrespondenzen zwischen Heines 'Götterdämmerung' und Thomas Manns *Tonio Kröger*." *Heine Jahrbuch* 20 (1981): 163–69.

———. "The Seer in the Spring: On *Tonio Kröger* and *The Waste Land*." *Revue de littérature comparée* 44 (1970): 322–32.

White, Andrew. *Thomas Mann*. New York: Grove, 1965.

White, James F. *The Yale* Zauberberg-*Manuscript: Rejected Sheets Once Part of Thomas Mann's Novel*. Pref. Joseph Warner Angell. Bern: Francke, 1980.

Wich, Joachim. "Thomas Manns frühe Erzählungen und der Jugendstil: Ein Forschungsbericht." *Literaturwissenschaftliches Jahrbuch im Auftrage der Görres-Gesellschaft* 16 (1975): 257–75.

———. "Thomas Manns *Gladius Dei* als Parodie." *Germanisch-Romanische Monatsschrift* 22 (1972): 389–400.

Wiehe, Roger E. "Of Art and Death: Film and Fiction Versions of *Death in Venice.*" *Literature and Film Quarterly* 16 (1988): 210–15.

Wiese, Benno von. "*Der Tod in Venedig.*" *Die deutsche Novelle von Goethe bis Kafka: Interpretationen.* Vol. 1. Düsseldorf: Bagel, 1967. 304–24.

Wiesner, Herbert. "Thomas Mann und seine Zeit: Ein synchronoptischer Überblick und eine Lesehilfe zu dessen politischem Verständnis." *Thomas Mann: 1875–1975.* München: Moos, 1975. 33–52.

Wilde, Oscar. *The Picture of Dorian Gray.* Ed. Donald Lawler. New York: Norton, 1988.

Wilkinson, Elizabeth M. "*Tonio Kröger*: An Interpretation." Hatfield, *Mann: A Collection* 22–34.

Willey, Thomas E. "Thomas Mann's Munich." *The Turn of the Century: German Literature and Art, 1890–1915.* Ed. Gerald Chapple and Hans H. Schulte. Bonn: Bouvier, 1981. 477–91.

Williams, W. D. "August von Platen." *German Men of Letters.* Ed. Alex Natan. Vol. 5. London: Wolff, 1969. 131–52.

Wilson, Kenneth G. "The Dance as Symbol and Leitmotiv in Thomas Mann's *Tonio Kröger.*" *Germanic Review* 29 (1954): 282–87.

Windisch-Laube, Walter. "Thomas Mann und die Musik." Koopmann, *Handbuch* 327–42.

Winkler, Michael. "Tadzio-Anastasios: A Note on *Der Tod in Venedig.*" *MLN* 92 (1977): 607–09.

Winston, Richard. "Being Brothers: Thomas and Heinrich Mann." Ley et al. 349–61.

———. *Thomas Mann: The Making of an Artist 1875–1911.* London: Constable, 1982.

Wisskirchen, Hans. "Die Thomas-Mann-Gesamtausgaben." Koopmann, *Handbuch* 773–98.

———. *Zeitgeschichte im Roman: Zu Thomas Manns* Zauberberg *und* Doktor Faustus. Bern: Francke, 1986.

Withon [=Whiton], John. "H. T. Lowe-Porters *Death in Venice.*" *Mannheimer Berichte* 27 (1985): 3–11.

Witte, Karsten. " 'Das ist echt! Eine Burleske!' Zur *Tristan*-Novelle von Thomas Mann." *German Quarterly* 41 (1968): 660–72.

Witthoft, Brucia. "*Tonio Kröger* and Muybridge's 'Animals in Motion.' " *Modern Language Review* 62 (1967): 459–61.

Wöhrmann, Andreas. *Das Programm der Neuklassik: Die Konzeption einer modernen Tragödie bei Paul Ernst, Wilhelm von Scholz und Samuel Lublinski.* Frankfurt: Lang, 1979.

Wolf, Ernest M. "A Case of Slightly Mistaken Identity: Gustav Mahler and Gustav Aschenbach in Visconti's Film *Death in Venice.*" *Magnum Opus: Studies in the Narrative Fiction of Thomas Mann.* Bern: Lang, 1989. 209–23.

Wolff, Rudolf, ed. *Thomas Mann: Erzählungen und Novellen.* Bonn: Bouvier, 1984.

Woodward, Anthony. "The Figure of the Artist in Thomas Mann's *Tonio Kröger* and *Death in Venice.*" *English Studies in Africa* 9 (1966): 158–67.

Woodward, Kathleen. "Youthfulness as a Masquerade." *Discourse* 11 (1988–89): 119–42.

Wyatt, Frederick. "The Choice of the Topic in Fiction: Risks and Rewards: A Comparison of André Gide's *The Immoralist* and Thomas Mann's *Death in Venice*." *Janus: Essays in Ancient and Modern Studies*. Ed. L. L. Orlin. Ann Arbor: U of Michigan P, 1975. 213–41.

Wysling, Hans. "Aschenbachs Werke: Archivalische Untersuchungen an einem Thomas Mann Satz." *Euphorion* 59 (1965): 272–314.

——— , ed. *Dokumente und Untersuchungen: Beiträge zur Thomas-Mann-Forschung*. Bern: Francke, 1974.

———. "Dokumente zur Entstehung des *Tonio Kröger*." Scherrer and Wysling 48–63.

———. " 'Ein Elender': Zu einem Novellenplan Thomas Manns." Scherrer and Wysling 106–22.

———. "Fünfundzwanzig Jahre Arbeit im Thomas-Mann-Archiv: Rückblick und Ausblick." Bernini et al. 370–80.

———. " 'Geist und Kunst': Thomas Manns Notizen zu einem 'Literatur-Essay.' " Scherrer and Wysling 123–33.

———. " 'Mythus und Psychologie' bei Thomas Mann." *Dokumente und Untersuchungen* 167–80.

———. *Narzissmus und illusionäre Existenzform: Zu den Bekenntnissen des Hochstaplers Felix Krull*. Bern: Francke, 1982.

———. "Schopenhauer-Leser Thomas Mann." *Schopenhauer-Jahrbuch* 64 (1983): 61–79.

———. "Schwierigkeiten mit Thomas Mann." *Thomas Mann heute* 94–111.

———. "Thomas Mann als Tagebuchschreiber." Bernini et al. 139–55.

———. "Thomas Mann—Der Unpolitische in der Politik." *Neue Rundschau* 91 (1980): 36–57.

———. *Thomas Mann heute: Sieben Vorträge*. Bern: Francke, 1976.

———. "Thomas Manns Deskriptionstechnik." *Thomas Mann heute* 64–84.

———. "Thomas Manns Goethe-Nachfolge." *Jahrbuch des Freien Deutschen Hochstifts* (1978): 498–551.

———. "Thomas Manns Rezeption der Psychoanalyse." *Probleme der Moderne: Studien zur deutschen Literatur von Nietzsche bis Brecht: Festschrift für Walter Sokel*. Ed. Benjamin Bennett et al. Tübingen: Niemeyer, 1983. 201–22.

———. "Thomas Manns unveröffentlichte Notizbücher." *Thomas Mann Jahrbuch* 4 (1991): 119–35.

———. "Zu Thomas Manns Briefwerk." *Thomas Mann heute* 85–93.

Wysling, Hans, and Cornelia Bernini, eds. *Jahre des Unmuts: Thomas Manns Briefwechsel mit René Schickele 1930–40*. Bern: Francke, 1992.

Wysling, Hans, and Yvonne Schmidlin. *Bild und Text bei Thomas Mann: Eine Dokumentation*. 1975. Bern: Francke, 1989.

Young, Frank W. *Montage and Motif in Thomas Mann's* Tristan. Bonn: Bouvier, 1975.

Zeller, Bernhard. *S. Fischer, Verlag: Von der Gründung bis zur Rückkehr aus dem Exil.* Marbach: Deutsche Schillergesellschaft, 1985.

Ziolkowski, Theodore. "Thomas Mann and the Emigré Intellectuals." Corngold, Lange, and Ziolkowski 24–38.

———. "Thomas Mann as a Critic of Germany." Corngold, Lange, and Ziolkowski 17–23.

Žmegač, Viktor. "Zu einem Thema Goethes und Thomas Manns: Wege der Erotik in der modernen Gesellschaft." *Goethe-Jahrbuch* 103 (1986): 152–67.

Zola, Emile. *Nana.* Trans. George Holden. New York: Penguin, 1972.

Zuckerman, Elliott. *The First Hundred Years of Wagner's Tristan.* New York: Columbia UP, 1964.

Zweig, Stefan. *Briefwechsel mit Hermann Bahr, Sigmund Freud, Rainer Maria Rilke und Arthur Schnitzler.* Ed. Jeffrey B. Berlin, Hans-Ulrich Lindken, and Donald A. Prater. Frankfurt: Fischer, 1987.

———. *The World of Yesterday.* Lincoln: U of Nebraska P, 1964.

Audiovisual Aids

Britten, Benjamin. *Death in Venice: Piano Score.* London: Faber Music, 1973.

Jarman, Derek, dir. *Caravaggio.* Kino International, 1986.

Mann, Thomas. Bekenntnisse des Hochstaplers Felix Krull: *Gespräch zwischen Krull und Professor Kuckuck.* Read by Thomas Mann. Hamburg: Deutsche Grammophon, 3321127, 1957.

———. Buddenbrooks. *"Die Revolution" (chs. 2–4).* Read by Günther Lüders. Hamburg: Deutsche Grammophon, 3321116, 1975.

———. *Deutsche Hörer: Radiosendungen aus dem Exil 1940–45.* Read by Thomas Mann. Ed. Walter Andreas Schwarz. Wermatswil and Zürich: Leuberg Edition, 1988.

———. *Dichtung und Wahrheit: Thomas Mann*—Tod in Venedig. Available from Inter Nationes, Kennedy Allee 91–103, D-5300 Bonn, Germany.

———. *Das Eisenbahnunglück–Das Wunderkind.* Read by Thomas Mann. Hamburg: Deutsche Grammophon, 43 063 LMPS, 1965.

———. *"Fülle des Wohllauts": Ein Kapitel aus dem Roman* Der Zauberberg. Read by Martin Benrath. Hamburg: Deutsche Grammophon, 423464-4, 1987.

———. *Herr und Hund: Ein Idyll.* Read by Will Quadflieg. Hamburg: Deutsche Grammophon, 413992-4, 1984.

———. *Thomas Mann Reading in German:* Tonio Kröger, ch. 1; "Lob der Vergänglichkeit"; "Die Busse" from Der Erwählte. New York: Caedmon, 51004, 1952.

———. *Der Tod in Venedig.* Read by Will Quadflieg. Hamburg: Deutsche Grammophon, 415734-4, 415735-4, 1985.

———. *Tonio Kröger*. Adaptation for the screen by Erika Mann and Ennio Flaiano. With Jean-Claude Briarly, Nadja Tiller, and Gert Frobe. Sandy Hook: Video Yesteryear, 1983.

———. *Unordnung und frühes Leid*. New York: West Glen Films, 1976.

———. *Versuch über Schiller: Ansprache im Schiller-Jahr gehalten am 8. Mai 1955*. Read by Thomas Mann. Hamburg: Deutsche Grammophon, 43005.

Mendelssohn, Peter de. *Thomas Mann and the Germans*. Production: Wolf H. Habermehl. Inter Nationes Film 3174. [Available from German Information Center, 950 Third Avenue, New York, NY 10022.]

Piper, Myfanwy. Death in Venice: *An Opera in Two Acts*. Libretto. Based on the short novel by Thomas Mann. Set to music by Benjamin Britten. Opus 88. London: Faber Music, 1973.

Szabó, István, dir. *Colonel Redl*. Facets Multimedia, 1984.

Visconti, Luchino, dir. *Death in Venice*. With Dirk Bogarde. Burbank: Warner Home Video, 1984.

INDEX

Modern Language Association of America
Approaches to Teaching World Literature
Joseph Gibaldi, series editor

Achebe's Things Fall Apart. Ed. Bernth Lindfors. 1991.
Arthurian Tradition. Ed. Maureen Fries and Jeanie Watson. 1992.
Atwood's The Handmaid's Tale *and Other Works*. Ed. Sharon R. Wilson,
    Thomas B. Friedman, and Shannon Hengen. 1996.
Austen's Pride and Prejudice. Ed. Marcia McClintock Folsom. 1993.
Balzac's Old Goriot. Ed. Michal Peled Ginsburg. 2000.
Baudelaire's Flowers of Evil. Ed. Laurence M. Porter. 2000.
Beckett's Waiting for Godot. Ed. June Schlueter and Enoch Brater. 1991.
Beowulf. Ed. Jess B. Bessinger, Jr., and Robert F. Yeager. 1984.
Blake's Songs of Innocence and of Experience. Ed. Robert F. Gleckner and
    Mark L. Greenberg. 1989.
Boccaccio's Decameron. Ed. James H. McGregor. 2000.
British Women Poets of the Romantic Period. Ed. Stephen C. Behrendt and
    Harriet Kramer Linkin. 1997.
Brontë's Jane Eyre. Ed. Diane Long Hoeveler and Beth Lau. 1993.
Byron's Poetry. Ed. Frederick W. Shilstone. 1991.
Camus's The Plague. Ed. Steven G. Kellman. 1985.
Cather's My Ántonia. Ed. Susan J. Rosowski. 1989.
Cervantes' Don Quixote. Ed. Richard Bjornson. 1984.
Chaucer's Canterbury Tales. Ed. Joseph Gibaldi. 1980.
Chopin's The Awakening. Ed. Bernard Koloski. 1988.
Coleridge's Poetry and Prose. Ed. Richard E. Matlak. 1991.
Dante's Divine Comedy. Ed. Carole Slade. 1982.
Dickens' David Copperfield. Ed. Richard J. Dunn. 1984.
Dickinson's Poetry. Ed. Robin Riley Fast and Christine Mack Gordon. 1989.
Narrative of the Life of Frederick Douglass. Ed. James C. Hall. 1999.
Eliot's Middlemarch. Ed. Kathleen Blake. 1990.
Eliot's Poetry and Plays. Ed. Jewel Spears Brooker. 1988.
Ellison's Invisible Man. Ed. Susan Resneck Parr and Pancho Savery. 1989.
Faulkner's The Sound and the Fury. Ed. Stephen Hahn and Arthur F. Kinney. 1996.
Flaubert's Madame Bovary. Ed. Laurence M. Porter and Eugene F. Gray. 1995.
García Márquez's One Hundred Years of Solitude. Ed. María Elena de Valdés and
    Mario J. Valdés. 1990.
Goethe's Faust. Ed. Douglas J. McMillan. 1987.
Hebrew Bible as Literature in Translation. Ed. Barry N. Olshen and
    Yael S. Feldman. 1989.
Homer's Iliad *and* Odyssey. Ed. Kostas Myrsiades. 1987.
Ibsen's A Doll House. Ed. Yvonne Shafer. 1985.
Works of Samuel Johnson. Ed. David R. Anderson and Gwin J. Kolb. 1993.
Joyce's Ulysses. Ed. Kathleen McCormick and Erwin R. Steinberg. 1993.
Kafka's Short Fiction. Ed. Richard T. Gray. 1995.

Keats's Poetry. Ed. Walter H. Evert and Jack W. Rhodes. 1991.

Kingston's The Woman Warrior. Ed. Shirley Geok-lin Lim. 1991.

Lafayette's The Princess of Clèves. Ed. Faith E. Beasley and Katharine Ann Jensen. 1998.

Works of D. H. Lawrence. Ed. M. Elizabeth Sargent and Garry Watson. 2001.

Lessing's The Golden Notebook. Ed. Carey Kaplan and Ellen Cronan Rose. 1989.

Mann's Death in Venice *and Other Short Fiction*. Ed. Jeffrey B. Berlin. 1992.

Medieval English Drama. Ed. Richard K. Emmerson. 1990.

Melville's Moby-Dick. Ed. Martin Bickman. 1985.

Metaphysical Poets. Ed. Sidney Gottlieb. 1990.

Miller's Death of a Salesman. Ed. Matthew C. Roudané. 1995.

Milton's Paradise Lost. Ed. Galbraith M. Crump. 1986.

Molière's Tartuffe *and Other Plays*. Ed. James F. Gaines and Michael S. Koppisch. 1995.

Momaday's The Way to Rainy Mountain. Ed. Kenneth M. Roemer. 1988.

Montaigne's Essays. Ed. Patrick Henry. 1994.

Novels of Toni Morrison. Ed. Nellie Y. McKay and Kathryn Earle. 1997.

Murasaki Shikibu's The Tale of Genji. Ed. Edward Kamens. 1993.

Pope's Poetry. Ed. Wallace Jackson and R. Paul Yoder. 1993.

Shakespeare's King Lear. Ed. Robert H. Ray. 1986.

Shakespeare's Romeo and Juliet. Ed. Maurice Hunt. 2000.

Shakespeare's The Tempest *and Other Late Romances*. Ed. Maurice Hunt. 1992.

Shelley's Frankenstein. Ed. Stephen C. Behrendt. 1990.

Shelley's Poetry. Ed. Spencer Hall. 1990.

Shorter Elizabethan Poetry. Ed. Patrick Cheney and Anne Lake Prescott. 2000.

Sir Gawain and the Green Knight. Ed. Miriam Youngerman Miller and Jane Chance. 1986.

Spenser's Faerie Queene. Ed. David Lee Miller and Alexander Dunlop. 1994.

Stendhal's The Red and the Black. Ed. Dean de la Motte and Stirling Haig. 1999.

Sterne's Tristram Shandy. Ed. Melvyn New. 1989.

Stowe's Uncle Tom's Cabin. Ed. Elizabeth Ammons and Susan Belasco. 2000.

Swift's Gulliver's Travels. Ed. Edward J. Rielly. 1988.

Thoreau's Walden *and Other Works*. Ed. Richard J. Schneider. 1996.

Voltaire's Candide. Ed. Renée Waldinger. 1987.

Whitman's Leaves of Grass. Ed. Donald D. Kummings. 1990.

Woolf's To the Lighthouse. Ed. Beth Rigel Daugherty and Mary Beth Pringle. 2001.

Wordsworth's Poetry. Ed. Spencer Hall, with Jonathan Ramsey. 1986.

Wright's Native Son. Ed. James A. Miller. 1997.